Praise for *Pause. Breathe. Choose.*

"This book helps us take back our power at a time in history when we have been conditioned to place achievement and success over all else. The pressure to succeed and achieve in our society is immense, and with the global pandemic it has intensified to an unbearable degree. Well-being and health are truly our greatest wealth, and Naz Beheshti provides a roadmap back to our authentic selves, our greatest potential, true success, and vibrant well-being. *Pause. Breathe. Choose.* is a gift to anyone who feels stuck, overwhelmed, powerless, or defeated in career or life in general. As empowering as it is enlightening, this book will help set in motion a new generation of thrivers."

— **Kelly Noonan Gores**, writer/director of the *HEAL* documentary

"Naz Beheshti's insights into overcoming the challenges and obstacles that get in the way of achieving our goals, pursuing our dreams, and experiencing fulfillment provide both a starting point and a roadmap for taking control of one's life, career, and well-being. Through her experience working for the iconic Steve Jobs, serving in roles at several Fortune 500 companies, and embarking upon a more-than-two-decades-long wellness journey, Naz has established herself as not only a wellness thought leader but as the CEO of her own successful company. As someone who has worked with Naz and her company professionally, I can attest that this book provides access to the wealth of knowledge, practices, and tools that can help companies, as well as individuals, bring well-being and mindfulness into their lives and the lives of their employees and clients. I highly recommend *Pause. Breathe. Choose.* to anyone who is either in a leadership position or aspires to be in one, and to anyone seeking a guide to help them achieve both personal and professional well-being."

— **Paul Scialla**, founder and CEO of
Delos and founder of International WELL Building Institute

"A clear and inspiring guide to living, working, and choosing a path of profound well-being."

— **Marc Lesser**, former CEO of the
Search Inside Yourself Leadership Institute

"Taking responsibility and being accountable for our actions and our choices are cornerstones that I believe will set you on a path toward your optimum well-being. In her book, *Pause. Breathe. Choose.*, Naz Beheshti brings together years of passionate service to others, a quest to shine a brighter light on purposeful leadership, and lessons learned from working closely with one of the greatest innovators and minds of our time. Through this lens we get a rare snapshot and blueprint of how each and every one of us can apply for the job and succeed at being the CEO of our well-being."

— **Joe Cross**, filmmaker, *Fat, Sick & Nearly Dead*

"Many business leaders forget one important aspect of leading others, and that is to lead with both the head and the heart. Naz Beheshti has studied the techniques of the best leaders and combined that knowledge with her unique style and innovation to present an effective method to integrate every aspect of your best self into your career and life. Read this book and you'll gain confidence in leadership, and your well-being will skyrocket!"

— **Sari Feinberg**,
senior media and entertainment marketing executive

"Naz Beheshti's book, *Pause. Breathe. Choose.*, provides practical tools to unlock your highest potential for total well-being."

— **Deepak Chopra**, author of *Total Meditation*

"*Pause. Breathe. Choose.* is a go-to guide for anyone who wants to take charge of their life and reach their true potential. You'll be delighted by the beautiful prose and the helpful structure of each chapter. I urge you to let this wonderful book be a game changer for you."

— **BJ Fogg, PhD**, *New York Times* bestselling author of
Tiny Habits and behavior scientist, Stanford University

"When I was the chief medical officer of Johnson & Johnson, we operated with the belief that well-being is mission critical. Driving and promoting well-being is about helping each person bring out their best, front and center. Everyone can be their best self regardless of how they look, where they are, or what their profession is. I've had the honor of working with Naz Beheshti on several well-being projects, and after reading her new book, *Pause. Breathe. Choose.*, I believe it brings tremendous value to leaders in the industry who recognize that good health is good business. Naz has eloquently articulated a roadmap to living well and being well, as well as demonstrating the 'how' for leaders to apply well-being principles and create a strong culture of health within their organizations. I highly recommend you read and implement this book!"

— **Fikry Isaac, MD, MPH**, former chief medical officer and
head of global health services, Johnson & Johnson

"*Pause. Breathe. Choose.* The title itself conveys everything we need to know to become more thoughtful and fulfilled in work and life. Naz Beheshti's new book reminds us that the pursuit of *doing well* need not get in the way of *well-being.* Anyone seeking more fulfillment in their life will find something in this book to help."

— **Amy C. Edmondson**, professor, Harvard Business School,
and author of *The Fearless Organization: Creating Psychological Safety
in the Workplace for Learning, Innovation, and Growth*

"*Pause. Breathe. Choose.* is an engaging read, with relevant stories and practical tools. It helped me pause and think about what's most important to me. Naz Beheshti shares a roadmap of small steps that can bring positive energy to every aspect of our lives — challenges and opportunities; work and personal life; physical, mental, and emotional well-being."

— **Avid Modjtabai**, former senior executive vice president, Wells Fargo

"This book offers valuable tools to help you deal with all the craziness. Too often we just keep running on the treadmill without thinking about what is really going on. Pausing and becoming more aware is the key — the key to everything. If you want to embody the phrase 'the journey is the reward,' you really ought to read this book!"

— **Mike Slade**, partner and cofounder,
Second Avenue Partners, and former strategic advisor to Steve Jobs

"Naz Beheshti's book, *Pause. Breathe. Choose.*, is a must-read for executives, leaders, and everyone who wants to thrive professionally and personally. The actionable, practical suggestions in the book are gems!"

— **Behnam Tabrizi**,
Stanford University's world-renowned expert in transformation

PAUSE.
BREATHE.
CHOOSE.

PAUSE.
BREATHE.
CHOOSE.

Become the CEO
of Your Well-Being

NAZ BEHESHTI

New World Library
Novato, California

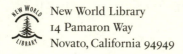

New World Library
14 Pamaron Way
Novato, California 94949

Text design by Tona Pearce Myers

Library of Congress Cataloging-in-Publication Data

Names: Beheshti, Naz, author.
Title: Pause, breathe, choose : become the CEO of your well-being / Naz Beheshti.
Description: Novato, California : New World Library, [2021] | Includes bibliographical
    references and index.
Identifiers: LCCN 2020043313 (print) | LCCN 2020043314 (ebook) |
    ISBN 9781608687237 (hardback) | ISBN 9781608687244 (epub)
Subjects: LCSH: Job stress. | Mindfulness (Psychology) | Well-being. | Self-realization.
Classification: LCC HF5548.85 .B4295 2021 (print) | LCC HF5548.85 (ebook)
   | DDC 158.7/2--dc23
LC record available at https://lccn.loc.gov/2020043313
LC ebook record available at https://lccn.loc.gov/2020043314

First printing, February 2021
ISBN 978-1-60868-723-7
Ebook ISBN 978-1-60868-724-4
Printed in the USA on 30% postconsumer-waste recycled paper

New World Library is proud to be a Gold Certified Environmentally Responsible Publisher. Publisher certification awarded by Green Press Initiative.

10   9   8   7   6   5   4   3   2   1

For Steve Jobs, for inspiring me to lead with my heart and intuition.
For my clients, who inspire me and remind me of my life's purpose.
For all leaders choosing to lead a happier, healthier,
and more purposeful life.

You can't connect the dots looking forward; you can only
connect them looking backward. So you have to trust that
the dots will somehow connect in your future. You have to trust
in something — your gut, destiny, life, karma, whatever.
This approach has never let me down, and it has made
all the difference in my life.
— Steve Jobs

CONTENTS

PART III: Promote Your Self to the CEO of Your Well-Being: The Three P's 181

PREFACE

The ultimate wealth is well-being. It is *everything*!

Growing up in the heart of Silicon Valley, in Palo Alto, I was surrounded by tech entrepreneurs who shared the *anything is possible, we are going to be gazillionaires* mindset. Unfortunately, such a mindset often comes with a cost: chronic stress and burnout. No matter who you are or how much money you have, if you do not take care of your Self* and adopt a healthy lifestyle, you will court premature death. No amount of money or status can change that.

Just as everyone needs to take care of themselves, companies need to take care of their employees. "Happy, healthy people are the greatest product we have," a CEO client recently remarked to me. He realized that happy and healthy employees are more productive and motivated to actualize their professional and personal goals, which in turn helps build a company's success.

Steve Jobs was highly aware that happiness and well-being were intricately connected with his success. He was the first person who showed me, up close and personally, what it meant to be *the CEO of your well-being* as well as the chief executive of a company. He truly embodied both. I was years away from thinking in those terms, much less writing a book on the topic. In retrospect, I understand that this was when the seed was planted. I was able to witness, and work alongside, someone who boldly and without compromise took control of his destiny. This, I knew, was an example I wanted to emulate.

---

* Throughout the book, "Self" is capitalized to refer to our core essence and higher Self.

People often ask me what it was like to work closely with Steve, assuming he was not the easiest person to work with. I know Steve was a controversial figure, but the Steve Jobs I knew was an extraordinary man who allowed me to see firsthand that you can have it all.

He had a successful business he was passionate about, a loving family, strong relationships, and a healthy lifestyle — all essential driving forces for his continued success. He found a balance between living in his nonstop, logical, working mind and being, at the same time, truly self-aware and leading with his heart.

I could never have imagined, as Steve Jobs was interviewing me in his boardroom at 1 Infinite Loop, that I would be forever changed as a result of our meeting. Steve soon became my greatest mentor. He was the catalyst in my journey toward living with drive, purpose, passion, awareness, and flowing prana (or vital energy, which is a focus of this book and my business). He showed me how to focus on the path that was best for me and to never stop exploring.

One of the many crucial lessons Steve taught me was this: *Never settle for less, no matter what obstacles you face.*

These very words have defined my character. They are the driving force that has enabled me to turn my passion into my profession. Now, every day, I have the good fortune and opportunity to pay it forward, by working with inspiring leaders and organizations with the mission of changing lives and helping companies excel.

I have written this book to provide you with a window into a better present and a more fulfilling future, just as Steve Jobs did for me. My vision is that you, too, will seek to live with greater authenticity, purpose, passion, and prana.

There is no one-size-fits-all approach to becoming the CEO of your well-being. I hope this book will be a catalyst, providing needed insights that will help you make your own active choices to improve your life.

We can all strive for more focus, awareness, clarity, vitality, and purpose, where we perform at the top of our game and lead by example. This book takes a holistic approach. Think of it as a guiding map that will lead you through better choices, ones that start from within and move outward. If you start down this path toward a more conscious and meaningful future, you will have the confidence and vitality to help make the world a smaller, smarter, and better place to live.

I am confident that you will thrive at work and across *all* aspects of life.

A Dream

I would never have written this book if Steve Jobs had not appeared to me in a vivid dream on the night of February 14, 2014, more than two years after he passed. Simply and clearly, the way Steve always spoke to me in life, in my dream he told me that I should write a book about how my first job, and working for him, impacted the rest of my life and career.

I have had countless lucid dreams that I was able to recall afterward. However, I have seen people's faces in my dreams only three times. Each time, it was the face of someone dear to me who had recently passed away. First, my beloved grandfather, whom I called Daddy. Next, my mother's dearest friend, Hita joon. Then, my mentor, Steve Jobs.

I took Steve's prophetic words seriously, and I soon began to write. Over the past few years, I have been able to uncover the deeper meaning that underlies this project. This book represents the first time that I have been able to truly connect the dots of my experiences to my passion for well-being.

The lessons that Steve taught me in life (through words and by example) have now rolled into one big idea. This book is not about Steve. It is not about me, either. It is about *you* and about *fulfilling your highest business, personal, and social potential.*

Start by focusing on what is right for *you.*

Focus on what gives you energy to fully engage in life and at work.

Show up, engaged and energized, wherever you are. This is key to a life well-lived.

Most of us live either in our hearts or in our minds. Steve Jobs lived in both and inspired me to do the same.

I invite you, too, to connect your head with your heart.

INTRODUCTION

You *can* live your best life. But how?

Our lives are marked by a singular focus on achievement. We are surrounded by a culture that puts unrelenting pressure on us, which can lead to chronic stress and even premature death. Due to the demands of this high-pressure environment, people often climb the career ladder through visible sacrifice:

- We measure how long we can go without sleep.
- We neglect our family and friends.
- We give up and devalue the crucial parts of our lives that make life worth living.

We prioritize *doing well* over *being well*.

But the truth is, we can have both — success *and* well-being! And in my experience, success and well-being are synonymous.

Many of us are in constant pursuit of happiness and fulfillment. We are students of life seeking ways to better our Self, our careers, our relationships, and our lives. However, when we search outside our Self to attain happiness (in people, places, or things), we end up chasing a perpetually moving and elusive target.

True happiness emerges from our authentic Self. The real challenge lies, however, in accessing our true Self, which often is buried deep beneath our stresses, distractions, and spinning wheels.

We must stop sacrificing our self-care and our connections with loved ones. There is no need to live for the weekends when we can thrive the entire week. Real success is about achieving the goals that fulfill our passion, bring us joy, and help the world. It is about having deep and meaningful connections. Success is not about working to death, the amount of money we make, or the title we hold.

Regardless of your professional level, you can become the *CEO of your well-being.* Consider your well-being like a company you run. Well-being at its core is being happy, energized, healthy, and prosperous. It means promoting good mental, emotional, physical, social, financial, professional, and environmental health. It means managing stress and building resilience. In other words, well-being is being well in *all* areas of your life.

As CEO of your well-being, you have chief decision-making authority. You are responsible for the company's overall operations and performance. So ask yourself how your company is doing. Are you performing at the top of your game and feeling happy, socially connected, and purposeful? Are all of the different departments in your company — your career, relationships, social and family life, self-care and health, personal and professional growth, finances, sense of purpose and life satisfaction — running smoothly? What are your short-term and long-term goals? What is the mission and vision of your well-being? What is the organizational culture of your well-being — your attitudes, mindsets, values, and beliefs? Are you investing in yourself? As the CEO, you want your company to thrive. You have the power to lead your well-being company to success and be the best CEO you can be.

For over a decade, I worked at startups and Fortune 500 companies, including my first job after college alongside Steve Jobs at Apple. I was on the verge of burnout and lived on autopilot. I can tell you, with conviction, that the first step to beating burnout and living a meaningful life is through *mindfulness* (awareness of your present state).

My clients, who are successful executives and leaders, face challenges with burnout and emotional intelligence, among other things. I work with them to make better choices for a better life through upgraded mindsets and behaviors. My mission in my work, in my life, and in this book is leadership well-being: helping people be well and do well in both their professional and personal lives. The *Pause. Breathe. Choose.* Method offers a way to foster authentic self-discovery, better choices, and purposeful growth. It explores well-being in the fullest sense: the well-being of mind, body, and prana (vital life force or energy).

We are all leaders if we choose to be, in every aspect of our lives. This book will teach you how to live up to your highest potential and be the best version of your authentic Self. Reaching for that potential is an active, mindful choice. It is the path of someone taking charge of their destiny.

Now more than ever, when stress and burnout are ubiquitous, we must access our authentic Self by closing the gap between leading with our head and our heart. When we integrate every aspect of our life and fuel that ecosystem as a whole, we can both *be well* and *do well*. This holistic approach connects the dots of our past and future into a coherent narrative and actionable roadmap to more energy, clarity, creativity, confidence, and success.

The key to thriving in today's culture is to cultivate deep self-awareness and strong emotional intelligence. This creates a solid ground from which to make aligned choices that transform our life. One conscious choice begets another.

When we make conscious choices, we avoid unnecessary, dangerous stress and tap into the productive energy of good stress (yes, there is such a thing). We adopt healthy habits and routines to generate higher energy and focus throughout our days. Some of the most important habits are in our heads: habits of mind. Much of our ability to manage stress and explore our full potential comes down to mindset. This book offers a variety of tools and strategies for upgrading your mindset.

Mindful choices also enable us to embrace pain as a teacher and to emerge from difficult challenges stronger than before. We can do more than survive life's storms; we can thrive amid them. We can also attain and sustain an in-the-zone feeling I call the *prana flow state*. In both your professional and personal life, accessing your vital life force or energy enables you to flourish and become the best version of yourself.

Finally, mindful choices are the building blocks for creating a purposeful life. Finding your purpose, and designing a life that feeds that purpose, is a process. If you live each day and each moment with intention and presence, you will discover the purpose of igniting a fully engaged and fulfilling life.

Are you someone who:

- wants a more fulfilling and purposeful life and needs a playbook to navigate change and growth with confidence?

- is a CEO, entrepreneur, or leader who would like guidance, tools, and strategies to be at the top of your game in *all* areas of your life?
- finds yourself slipping at work and not being as successful as you used to be or hope to be?
- is in need of greater clarity and focus?
- is at a stage in your career where you want to be next in line for a promotion?
- wants or needs to practice mindfulness, manage stress, and build resilience to be more effective, healthy, and successful?
- is enduring trying times or a life transition and wants to pick yourself back up?
- needs more energy to be able to do all the things you love and more?
- is feeling disconnected and isolated and wants to feel more connected with yourself, others, and the world around you?
- wants to make a change — no matter how big or small — to move forward and is unsure how to take the first step?

Everyone, regardless of age, title, success, and status, encounters challenges, uncertainties, fears, and insecurities. We collect baggage. At times, we feel at a tipping point or breaking point, as if we are standing close to or right at the edge of a cliff. Sometimes, we feel as if we have already fallen and hit rock bottom. Sometimes, we simply know we need to improve and better ourselves to reach our goals. Whatever your particular situation and needs, you can benefit from reading this book.

In *Pause. Breathe. Choose.: Become the CEO of Your Well-Being*, I weave together stories about my work at Apple and other Fortune 500 companies, my clients, my Iranian American upbringing, and my battle with my well-being. I also offer straightforward, actionable strategies for organizations and individuals to take well-being into their own hands. I share valuable insights about total well-being that I have uncovered in my work coaching leaders, consulting startups, and leading global organizations. This book focuses on practicing mindful leadership and taking empowered and aligned action as a personal and professional strategy. I encourage you to make active, healthier lifestyle choices to fulfill your highest potential in all areas of your life — which contributes to making our world a better place.

A few key concepts underlie the book:

- The *Pause. Breathe. Choose.* Method is a practice that enables you to take a pause (from mind wandering or any situation), to pay attention and become present, to hit the reset button, and to gain a fresh perspective. A simple pause followed by conscious breathing better equips you to make a mindful choice and take aligned action.
- *Prana* is a Sanskrit word for breath, life force, or life energy. This vital energy moves through everything and everyone, promoting healing. Prana represents your breath and being. It defines your life and well-being and is the very essence that keeps you alive and thriving.
- *Mindfulness* is a state of active awareness in the present. It represents a practice of observing thoughts and feelings without judgment. Being mindful is often the catalyst of conscious and thoughtful choices for our highest good and well-being. In this framework, taking a conscious breath (prana) is an act of being mindful.
- *Being the CEO of your well-being* is occupying an active state that empowers you to be in charge of your life so that you can live your best life. When you use *Pause. Breathe. Choose.* to evaluate what is in your best interest and make executive decisions that optimize your overall well-being, you experience how being the CEO of your well-being significantly improves all areas of your life.
- *Being a Mindful MAP Maker* is when you employ your personal compass (intuition) to navigate change and growth, taking empowered and aligned action to create the experiences and outcomes you desire. You choose who you want to be and where you want to go as the driver, not the passenger, of your journey. The MAP Method is an acronym for my holistic approach and for this book's three guiding principles: M stands for *master mindfulness*; A is for *apply the Seven A's to manage stress and build resilience* (the Seven A's); and P stands for *promote your Self to the CEO of your well-being* (the Three P's). As a metaphor of an actual map, MAP helps you create and shape your path according to your life experiences and

the meanings you attach to them. The MAP Method is akin to a business plan.

In addition, at the end of each chapter, I provide two sections with exercises and actions you can implement immediately — called Business Hacks (which are geared mostly toward high-level decision makers, including C-suite and HR) and Action Steps (which are for everyone) — along with the chapter's Key Takeaways. *Pause. Breathe. Choose.* is a holistic guide to making better choices for a better life.

In part I, "Master Mindfulness: The Big M," you will learn how to discover your authentic Self. I explore a simple and powerful method for practicing mindfulness as well as the value of choosing to be mindful both in stillness and in action.

In part II, "Apply Better Choices to Manage Stress and Build Resilience: The Seven A's," I describe the Seven A's. These are as follows:

- Adopt a healthy lifestyle
- Allocate play and recovery time
- Avoid unnecessary stress
- Alter the situation
- Adapt to the stressor
- Accept what you cannot change
- Attend to connection with Self, others, world, and universe

These seven strategies help you make better choices daily and offer actionable ways to upgrade your mindset and behaviors, inevitably improving inner peace and leading you toward a healthier and happier lifestyle.

In part III, "Promote Your Self to the CEO of Your Well-Being: The Three P's," I explain the Three P's: pain, prana, and purpose. I explore how to make pain your greatest teacher for growth, how you can use prana to become fully engaged at work and in life, and how to be driven by your passion and purpose.

In *Pause. Breathe. Choose.* I guide you through this journey of well-being and help you navigate your mindful MAP of self-discovery, better choices, and purposeful growth. Ultimately, you choose who you want to be and where you want to go. With a well-drawn map, you can locate where you are in the overall scheme of your life and pinpoint your dream destination. Becoming a Mindful MAP Maker is the subject of the book's final chapter, where we connect all the dots.

The choice of how to live your best life is yours. I encourage you to use this book to take explorative action and map out a path to a mindful, purposeful, healthy, and fulfilled life. The principles and exercises within these pages will empower you to elevate your energy, clarity, creativity, confidence, and success, just as they have for my clients and me. As a result, I am confident that you will feel a stronger connection with your Self, others, the world, and the universe.

PART I

Master Mindfulness

THE BIG M

We see light because we have seen darkness. We know our strengths because we know our weaknesses. We feel love when fear is absent. We feel peace because we know what distress feels like. In other words, we understand something by knowing its opposite. Similarly, to truly know and understand mindfulness, one must have experienced its opposite. In order to consciously and intentionally pursue a connected life, we must understand the disconnected life.

Mindfulness (the Big M) is the foundation of authentic self-discovery and a life well-lived, and it is the focus of part I. Mindfulness provides many practical benefits that improve our lives on every level. One of the most important is addressing the wellness gap. This arises when we neglect our well-being, or when we believe that success means sacrificing our self-care. Mindfulness helps us recognize stress, and it increases our awareness in the moment, both of ourselves and others, and these things improve our energy, effectiveness, decision-making, and leadership.

When we are not present, we are often thinking about either the past or the future. When we pause, we stop our mind from wandering. When we take a conscious breath, we engage in the present moment, which in turn, equips us to make a better choice. The *Pause. Breathe. Choose.* Method aligns our head and heart and awakens us to infinite potential.

CHAPTER ONE

START WITH MINDFULNESS

The Origins of the
Pause. Breathe. Choose. Method

Some of us awaken with energy and excitement. Others opt to stay in bed and routinely hit the snooze button. I have experienced both scenarios, which is why I have a profound appreciation for the power of mindfulness. Mindfulness unites action and awareness, which in turn energizes us. For a while, I was living the opposite of a mindful life. I was sleepwalking on autopilot. Later I found my way back to purpose, engagement, vitality, and eventually to this book. That journey and the lessons I learned along the way are what I wish to share with you. Mindful leaders, organizations, and culture are fundamental to our lives. Today, more than ever, we need mindful mindsets and practices for breaking the cycles that drive a wedge between doing and being, action and awareness.

I was thirty-one years old. On the surface, my career was smooth sailing. I had landed a job as a sales rep for AstraZeneca, a Fortune 500 pharmaceutical company. At first, it was fun and challenging. Unlike my previous sales role at Yahoo! (the Google of its time), I was working in outside sales in an entirely different industry and landscape. I have always enjoyed testing and pushing myself, and I embraced the change as an opportunity to pick up new skills and capabilities. The job paid well, had great benefits, and gave me a lot of autonomy. I was on course.

It did not take long before the novelty wore off and a staleness crept in. I had mastered my new skill set, and what had been a fresh challenge lapsed into a routine that deadened rather than enlivened me. Each morning I found myself hitting the snooze button, opting for fifteen minutes of extra time in bed, even if that meant skipping breakfast. Why was I not able to meet the day with energy and excitement? I longed to be the kind of person who did not need an alarm clock.

I knew I needed to make some changes. I started meditating. Meditation led me back to my abandoned yoga practice and back to school for holistic health, long an interest of mine. I put my new knowledge into practice, and my energy improved. Still, something was missing. I was healthier but uninspired. I was off track and on a treadmill. Where had I gone wrong?

Dropping the "i"

Ten years earlier, my career (and, in a sense, my adult life) had begun at Apple, where I served as executive assistant to Steve Jobs. It was an exciting experience for a young woman just out of college. Before I graduated, my roommate, Samantha, saw me working on my résumé and offered to pass it on to a friend who was a corporate recruiter. At most, I was hoping for some feedback on the résumé — not a job, much less one working for perhaps the greatest visionary of our time.

Initially, nothing came of it. I did not hear from Sam's friend, and the whole thing almost slipped my mind. I was due to travel overseas for a couple of months after graduation: first to the Greek isles for a family reunion, then to my birthplace, Iran. Shortly after I returned, I received a call from a woman named Andrea, Steve's senior executive assistant. I was puzzled. I had not sent my résumé to Apple — though I later learned Sam's friend was a recruiter for Apple and had passed it to Andrea. I agreed to an interview, never seriously thinking I had a chance at the job. Plus, my heart was set on working and living in San Francisco, not Cupertino, where Apple is located. I approached the entire process with zero expectations, feeling no pressure, just a desire to gain valuable experience in the art of interviewing.

Andrea and I connected instantly. She was classy, calm, grounded, and smart. It immediately occurred to me that I could learn a lot from her. We talked for almost an hour, after which she invited me back for follow-up interviews. When I returned to Apple's headquarters at 1 Infinite Loop, instead of naturally feeling nervous before an interview, I felt more like a curious student. I was ushered into a glass conference room on the executive floor — a private suite of offices. One by one, each executive assistant from Steve's direct reports sat with me and asked many of the same questions as Andrea. Finally, after three hours, I was led back to Andrea's office. She checked to see if Steve was available to meet with me.

Before I knew it, I found myself in a smaller conference room, across the table from Steve Jobs. He was dressed in his signature Levi's, black Issey Miyake mock turtleneck, and gray New Balance sneakers. He leaned back, crossed his right leg over his left, and steepled his fingers together. "Why Apple?" he asked. I told him how much I admired its brand and innovation. "Why UCSC?" I talked about its beautiful campus in the Santa Cruz Mountains, its great psychology department, how it was close to San Francisco and my family. He asked a lot of questions, all while holding me with his intense piercing eyes. I confidently returned his gaze, still more curious than nervous. Our connection felt strong and natural. As I would learn in the months to come, Steve trusted his gut. He stood, shook my hand, and said, "Great, you're hired!" I doubt this would have been possible without my parents' continual advice to be my Self — or true to my higher Self — which instilled confidence in me.

That job helped shape who I am today. Steve was my first and most influential mentor. He passed on life lessons I continue to absorb to this day. This was also a pivotal period for Apple. After twelve years away from the company he had founded, Steve Jobs returned to Apple in 1997 as interim CEO to help the struggling company restructure and reboot. Two years later, on the day I was hired, he dropped the "i" for "interim" and officially became the CEO again (until he resigned in August of 2011 due to health reasons).

As formative and enriching as my time at Apple was, I lost something as well. Only in retrospect was I able to see that I dropped and lost my own "i" — myself. Caught up in Steve's otherworldly charisma and in the excitement of working for him in a high-stress, fast-paced environment, my own needs and life faded from view. Steve was extremely mindful of his well-being, and one of my responsibilities was to see he was taken care of and performing at the top of his game. Day after day, I made sure he had the strict vegetarian meals that were essential to his daily routine. While attending faithfully to Steve's well-being, I ignored my own. I snacked on chocolate and remained wired and stressed long after the workday was over. One day I surprised Steve by including an oatmeal cookie with his meal, thinking it was a healthy choice for dessert. Clearing up later, I found the cookie in his trash can. My healthy was Steve's garbage.

Ten years later, I would look back on that moment as a warning sign I did not pay enough attention to. Outwardly, I was successful and thriving. Inwardly, I had drifted and lost touch with my authentic Self. I was paying the price for not making mindful choices grounded in a clear and holistic understanding of well-being.

I see this pattern play out with my clients, in the companies they run, and in society at large. We prioritize doing well over being well. We get caught up in a rat race that urges us to forge ahead and stay on top, regardless of the cost. A vicious cycle sets in, encouraging us to make unhealthy and mindless choices that undermine and threaten our well-being. On an individual and an organizational level, all too often, we act as if success and well-being are competing virtues.

The Wellness Gap

I was experiencing what I would later discover as a wellness gap: a disconnect between my aspiration to lead a thriving and engaged life and the daily practices and habits that fuel and energize such a life. Today, this gap has become ingrained in our culture. Chasing wealth, status, and achievement, we feel pressure to wring productivity from every waking minute. More and more of us are burning out. In fact, the Japanese have a word for working oneself to death: *karoshi*.

Although I started on the path to burnout at Apple, only a decade later did I fully come to grips with the problem and begin to make some real changes. My time in pharmaceutical sales introduced me to a societal wellness gap as well. I traveled from medical office to medical office, hospital to hospital, meeting with about eight doctors each day. When I would check in and catch a glimpse of a jam-packed patient list, it struck me how little time the doctors had for each patient. Patients were getting temporary fixes at best. Root causes like stress and lifestyle were left un-addressed. A wellness gap is built into our healthcare system. Even the now-ubiquitous corporate wellness programs fall short, primarily focusing on preventing disease rather than promoting well-being. As leaders, we must face this wellness gap head-on — in our lives and in our organizations.

It took me a while to make a clean break with my old ways and put myself on a new path. I remained in pharmaceutical sales for four years. Only after a mind-clearing trip to Antarctica, a painful breakup, and a life-changing journey to India was I ready to declare independence.

The day after I returned from India, I quit my sales job and began laying the groundwork for my own business. I was leaping into the unknown. My decision shocked many of those close to me. Deep in my heart, I had no doubts. I was not yet thinking in these terms, but that day, I chose to become the CEO of my company and my well-being.

My mission is to build, restore, and strengthen what I call *leadership well-being*. Many of my clients are CEOs, founders, and business leaders who have not been living their best lives and need guidance to get back on track. They aspire to a purposeful and joyful life, but their mindset and habits are at odds with this plan. They are burned out or stuck on autopilot or both. They need a jump start, a jolt, a reset. Often, their company's culture needs rejuvenation as well.

My vision of leadership, and of leadership well-being, goes beyond CEOs and the C-suite. Leadership is about taking ownership to become the CEO of your well-being. It is about taking control of your destiny — about intentionally, deliberately, and mindfully shaping your life, as opposed to letting life happen to you. You can make executive decisions that boldly and unapologetically set the course of your life, regardless of your professional title or status. This book is about the tools and strategies that can empower you to take aligned action and ownership over your life.

At the heart of leadership well-being is bridging the gap between being well and doing well — and refusing to accept the false dichotomy between the two. Doing and being must work hand-in-glove, just as with the mind and body. We cannot afford to compartmentalize action and awareness. When we strive for productivity and performance without awareness, we open the door for the wellness gap — which runs rampant in the business world and society at large. At the individual level, that wellness gap leads to burnout and a disconnected life. At the organizational level, it can infect a business, leading to high turnover and low employee engagement and satisfaction.

Whatever our professional roles, we must draw the line. We have to say no to disconnection, to distraction, to burnout, to living on autopilot. Instead, we have to say yes to a life driven by purpose and defined by deep connections with our Self, others, and the world. We have the power to restore energy and engagement in our personal lives, our professional lives, our organizations, and even our society. The journey that mindfulness takes us on is transformative.

That journey starts with a pause.

Before We Can Press Reset, We Have to Press Pause

During my trip to India, and in the months that followed, I began formulating a method not just for attaining mindfulness but for acting on it. Finding a state of clarity and awareness in a setting designed to encourage mindfulness — a yoga studio, a meditation session, whatever works for you — is a good start. Bringing that clarity and awareness with you into the rest of your life, especially to your most challenging moments, is the powerful, ultimate goal.

When mindfulness becomes part of our very being, it becomes portable. We can take it with us anywhere. When mindfulness informs our life choices, small and large, it becomes mindfulness in action. Once we get in the habit of making strong choices, the ripple effects travel far and wide. One mindful choice begets another. In business, active choices produce sounder strategy and a stronger vision and culture.

First, however, we have to break the cycle of disconnection and distraction. We have to step away from the noise of the world, from the noise of our minds. When we find ourselves slipping into stress, into self-sabotage, into sleepwalking mode — anything that disconnects us from our authentic Self — we must pause. Organizations often need to pause as well. Under the pressure of competition and high turnover, we can find ourselves defaulting into crisis-management mode, putting out individual fires and losing sight of the big picture.

Sometimes that pause is literally just a pause: taking a moment to gather ourselves before a crucial meeting or presentation. Sometimes that pause is a walk in the park, a weekend retreat, a sabbatical. My six-week trip to India was an extended pause. I needed to step back, reassess, and renew. The small steps I had taken to be happier and healthier were a start, but not enough. My life needed a deliberate jolt for me to achieve the liberation I craved. I was struggling with heartache and feeling complacent and trapped in my corporate career. I longed to deepen my mindfulness practice, connect with my higher Self, and start a new life. My trip was both a pause and a catalyst — a conscious effort to shake up my life. It was a much-needed reset.

However long or short, the pause sets the stage for the next step. It carves out space and time for us to breathe. A conscious breath is the best way to become present and aware. Try it now. Take a deep, steady breath and then slowly exhale it all out. How does that feel?

Taking a mindful breath is like hitting the reset button. It calms us both physically and mentally and gives us a moment to reason and gain perspective. It is about a physical breath, yes — but so much more. We also allow our thoughts and feelings to breathe, our heart and mind to reconnect. We become aware of our bodies and of how our thoughts and emotions manifest physically.

We are now ready to make a mindful choice. The path to a conscious choice is straightforward but rarely easy. That hard truth was brought home to me on my very first night in India.

My destination was Rishikesh, a small town in the Himalayan foothills known as the "Yoga Capital of the World." First, I had to fly into New Delhi, the capital of India, a teeming city often cloaked in heavy smog. I arrived at three in the morning, exhausted from the long flight. After waiting in vain for the hired car service, I headed to a van at the front of a line of taxis. The driver was hunched over the wheel. I tapped on the window and startled him out of his slumber. He frantically rolled down the window, looking disheveled and disoriented. My gut told me not to get into the car, but I was desperate to get to my hotel.

I quickly regretted my decision. The driver seemed to literally be asleep behind the wheel. He weaved in and out of traffic and brushed up against the median of the poorly lit street. My heart racing, I dug my nails into the upholstery, sure this night was going to be my last. I have experienced harrowing taxi rides in New York City and in the Middle East, where it is typical to drive on the sidewalks. They paled in comparison.

When the driver finally pulled into what appeared to be an abandoned alley, my stomach lurched. I imagined the worst and braced to make a run for it or to defend myself. Thankfully, two people were walking in our direction, so I hurriedly rolled down the window and asked if they knew where my hotel was, the map shaking in my hands. We were just around the corner from the hotel. The driver had turned one street too soon. Trembling, I gathered my luggage, made it to the hotel, and collapsed on the bed of my dingy room.

As I struggled to regroup, my mind ran in circles, which happens to all of us in stressful or fearful moments. I was tempted to chastise myself for climbing into the taxi against my better judgment; to chastise myself for being paranoid and distrustful; to tell myself that this was a bad sign; to convince myself that I should be grateful for my job and not yearn for something more. In the end, I resisted the urge to fall into the rabbit hole. I was here for a reason. I realized my only task was to return to the moment at hand.

I paused. I observed what was happening in the room, in my mind, and in my heart, without judgment: *I'm sitting on a bedcover with stains on it. The room smells like mildew. I'm halfway around the world from home. I'm exhausted, alone, and afraid. I wasn't harmed. I'm closer to Rishikesh and will be there soon. I will be okay.*

That pause is a small, essential first step. It seems so simple but can be so difficult. The gravity of the rabbit hole can be hard to resist. As our thoughts spin and accelerate, we feel ourselves pulled in. The pause creates space for us to breathe, to return to the moment, to return to ourselves and our intention.

Mindfulness is sometimes conflated with bliss. We see someone effortlessly striking a cross-legged lotus pose, eyes closed, face beaming with contentment. Sometimes, that is the image of mindfulness. Yet we really need mindfulness when the journey gets messy and the path ahead is unclear. Sometimes the picture of mindfulness is a dingy hotel room in New Delhi after a terrifying taxi ride. Or a pristine boardroom during a heated debate. Mindfulness is too valuable a tool to be left in the meditation room or on the yoga mat. As leaders, we must incorporate mindful principles into both our individual practice and our organizational practice.

How often do you find yourself unable to pause? Unable to break the cycle?

Say you notice that your performance at work has hit a wall. You are no longer on your game in the way you would like to be. This is not a time to scold yourself, but rather to pause, to reassess, to reset. You might find yourself irritable and prone to losing your patience. This is a sign you have depleted your reserves, that you have not devoted sufficient time to keep the well of your resilience full. This is a time to pause, to reset, to restore.

Or perhaps, as I did, you might notice yourself sliding into autopilot. You sleepwalk through your day, relying on quick fixes to boost your energy. This is a time to pause, to step back, to remember your purpose and return to your intention.

Companies sometimes need a moment to pause and reconnect with purpose and intention as well. When facing an unexpected challenge, such as a disappointing earnings report or a disruption in the market, entire organizations can tense up. Smart leaders will give their teams a chance to take a collective breath to ensure they are moving forward with calmness and clarity.

Resetting starts with a pause, even if that first step can sometimes feel like a stumble.

Meditating in a Cave with a Silent Monk

The method I call *Pause. Breathe. Choose.* crystallized during my time at the ashram in Rishikesh. For ten days, I followed a strict regimen of meditation, yoga, and introspection. The day began with a two-hour seated meditation. I experienced the power of a daily practice that allows us to step away from noise and distraction and into deep presence and awareness. We do not all have the luxury of traveling to India. Starting our day with a two-hour meditation is not typically feasible. The point is our intention: to create a necessary pause in whatever way works in the moment.

Meditation was followed by yoga, working our way through a series of poses or asanas. Yoga, for me, is a kind of moving meditation. At the ashram, my yoga practice felt like a seamless continuation of the seated meditation. Literally, it was mindfulness embodied, mindfulness in motion. Both practices gave me the space to pause and connect with myself, which allowed me to gain clarity about what I wanted to do with my life.

Long before the trip to India, I knew I had to leave my job in pharmaceutical sales. I wanted to chart a new course, using my life experiences and the knowledge I had gained from my psychology training and the holistic health program I was in at the time. Yet I was holding back, waiting for the right time, not ready to take the leap.

India changed all of that. Everything became clear, the lens was no longer foggy. I knew I could not go another day living a life that was not true to my authentic Self. The process of personal change and transformation also became clear. I saw how a pause gives birth to breath, and breath to a mindful choice: *Pause. Breathe. Choose.* Mindfulness in motion. I was ready.

One of the most powerful experiences in my life, one that has buoyed me in the years after, was with a silent monk in India.* According to a swami at the ashram, he had not spoken in nineteen years. I was hiking in the foothills of the Himalayan mountains with a few people from the ashram when we crossed paths with a gaunt and mysterious man. Clothed in only a discolored white loincloth, he had a calming, friendly demeanor. He motioned us to follow him.

We crouched down and made our way to a small cave on the cliff edge of the Ganga River. This cave, his home, was adorned only by a modest shrine of his gurus, a lit candle, and a worn yoga mat that appeared to double as his bed. We followed him in, and he motioned for me to sit beside him. We all sat cross-legged on the bare earth, closed our eyes, and began to meditate.

I found myself surrendering to the moment and meditating more deeply than ever. I could feel and hear nothing but the monk's energy and breath beside me. When I finally opened my eyes, I could not ascertain how much time had passed. Once I peered outside of the small entrance of the cave, the only clue was the golden sun descending behind the Himalayan peaks.

We needed to hike down the mountain before dark, so we quickly rose and, accompanied by the silent monk, made our way back to the trail. Before we parted, the silent monk kneeled at my feet, took hold of my hand between his, and placed it firmly upon his dreadlocked head.

---

* Since he had been in silence for nineteen years, I was not able to ascertain whether the ascetic I met in India was a monk, yogi, or swami. For the purposes of this book, I refer to him as a monk.

I looked around at my companions, wondering what was happening. *What should I do?* I shrugged off my hesitation and focused on my interaction with the monk. I knew I needed to be entirely present to this moment.

I felt an intense heat radiating from his head. It traveled through my hand, up to my arm, down my spine, and throughout my entire body. I was flush with heat and energy, while chills simultaneously rippled over me. In a profound, visceral way, as if my DNA were changing, something shifted within me in that moment. I have not been the same since.

I would later learn that the monk's gesture was a recognized form of blessing. Indeed, that was how I received it. That nonverbal encounter became more profound and meaningful to me than any conversation I have ever had or any book I have ever read. Being an analytical thinker, I had lived primarily in my mind and defaulted to it whenever my heart was not making sense. Yet over the years, meditation and yoga had been awakening my heart. I could not have had this profound experience, this stillness, if I had remained in my head. The silent monk deepened that awakening and allowed me to glimpse the possibilities of fully aligning my head with my heart. I was ready to move onward and upward, not only in India, but in my life back home. I knew I would carry this experience for the rest of my life.

A photo a companion snapped of me with the monk in front of his cave sits on my desk, where I can see it every day. When I look at it, I am reminded that I can drop from my mind to my heart and create silence amid chaos. I do not need to be in a cave in the middle of the jungle to experience this. You, too, can learn to create powerful experiences around which to build a mindfulness practice. It is not about the distance we travel physically, but about how far and deep we travel in our heart and head.

Although mindfulness is sometimes conflated with inner peace, often the true test of mindfulness in action is how it empowers and emboldens us to go beyond our comfort zone. I returned from India ready to take what I call *explorative action*: choices without certainty, without guarantees, that allow us to test our limits and set a new standard for ourselves.

Explorative action also enables us (as it did in my case) to realign with the intentions of our authentic Self. When we pause, breathe, and make a strong, mindful choice, we are choosing not to let circumstances derail us. We may choose to return to our intention and recommit to a path we have drifted from. Or we may realize that our intention has evolved and changed and that we need to alter our path.

This ability to self-direct or self-correct is more critical now than ever. Most of us will not remain in the same career our entire working lives. Circumstances may force us to reinvent ourselves. Or we may choose to do so proactively. To stay nimble in today's business world, companies must also learn to pivot and, at times, reinvent themselves. These are life's large resets — and being able to navigate change successfully starts with mindfulness. We must also become skilled at life's smaller resets, at overcoming the daily challenges that threaten to push us off course. Leaders who cultivate agility and adaptability stay ahead of the curve and serve as inspiring role models.

Change is inevitable. *Pause. Breathe. Choose.* is a tool for navigating change and growth.

We Stray, We Return: Moshing with Monks

Even after we find something — our intention for the day, or clarity about our life's purpose — it is just as easy to lose it, if only for a moment. That pattern of stray and return is built into the flow and flux of life. It is built into the practice of mindfulness.

A common anxiety for those embarking on a meditation practice is fear of failure. We think: *I know I'm supposed to sit quietly and focus on my breath without any thoughts. What if my attention wanders?*

That what-if is part of the premise of meditation. It would not be a practice if our attention did not wander. (Also, we would either be dead or enlightened if we did not have any thoughts.) There is no failure. It is expected that we will stray. What Buddhists call our *monkey mind* will assert itself as our thoughts leap from one branch to another. What matters is that we take note of our wandering — merely observing it as a fact of life, without anxiety or judgment — and then return to our breath, to the here and now.

Every time we return to our breath, to our intention and purpose, to mindfulness, we exercise our attentional muscle. We strengthen our ability to self-correct. Stray and return. This is how we build mindfulness and the ability to make better choices. Organizations that learn to self-correct improve their agility and increase their resilience.

I received a humbling lesson on this score during my final days in India. I had come face to face with my authentic Self during my time at the ashram. My encounter with the silent monk had aligned my head and heart as never before. But did that mean I was no longer vulnerable to straying and stumbling? Hardly.

At the end of my trip, I met a close friend in Dharamshala, where the Dalai Lama led a three-day teaching for Russian Buddhist monks at his residence. The event was open to the public, and we arrived early to get our tickets and a Walkman-like translation device. Behind us, buses full of maroon-robed monks began arriving.

Before long, the entrance to the Dalai Lama's temple was a sea of maroon as more and more monks converged on the scene. My friend left to get coffee while I attempted to hold our place in the chaos that passed for a line. I wondered if she would ever find my five-foot-three frame amid thousands of giant monks, almost entirely men. I began to feel claustrophobic. I could feel one monk's breath on my neck, and I was only a nose's length from the next man's robe. I could barely see anything but the color maroon.

After almost an hour, my friend still not returned, the monks suddenly started pushing and shoving me forward. They moved as one huge mass, thrusting me even though there was nowhere to go. I was being crushed. The sea of monks beat me forward like unrelenting waves on a cliffside.

The pressure on my ribs was painful. I managed to call out, "Stop! Please, stop!" There was no room to turn my head to see what was going on. Towering Russian men surrounded me, their eyes fixed on the doors, oblivious to my pain. Barely able to breathe, I looked up at the sky, tears running down my face, calling out, *"Nonviolence! Nonviolence, people. Help!"* I felt invisible. I no longer cared about making it into the temple. I just wanted to get out of there alive.

This went on for what seemed like an eternity until we heard the sound of a violent thump up ahead. The maroon sea shifted momentarily, and I was able to squeeze my way out to the edge of the crowd. A heavy-set monk had fallen from the ramp leading to the open doors, landing hard on the concrete below. Nervous that the man had severely injured himself in his fall, I caught a glimpse of him down below. Amazingly, he picked himself up and shoved his way back into the throng.

I somehow made it up to the ramp and into the compound and eventually the temple. I could finally breathe again and tried to collect myself. Even still, my mind clouded with anger; my *monkey mind* (a term the Dalai Lama taught us that day) jumped in every direction. *These monks are impostors*, I thought. Here I was, in a sea of supposedly devout monks, waiting to hear the wise words of the Dalai Lama (who above all teaches nonviolence), while fearing for my life. This mosh pit of monks had nothing to do with mindfulness or compassion. *This is not what His Holiness is about. This is not what I am about*, my monkey mind exclaimed.

Just then, I heard the Dalai Lama laugh. The sweet sound of his giggle cut through the tension and brought me back to the present moment. My anger, confusion, and judgment left me like air from a punctured balloon. I remembered my intention and what had brought me there.

It was a valuable lesson. Even after my transformative experience in the cave, mindfulness and an open heart were no guarantee. I was only human. I would stray from my intention and then have to return to it. The monks were only human as well. Like drunk teens moshing at a Metallica concert, these maroon-robed fan-monks were just swept up by their excitement to see the Dalai Lama. They were not impostors. We were all in this moment together.

The Dalai Lama's sweet laugh prompted me to pause and step back from all of the noise — in and of my head. I was able to breathe. I chose to be present to the moment with openness and curiosity. I let go of my judgment and relaxed a bit. Shortly after, my friend found me and we spent the rest of the day engrossed with the Dalai Lama.

As I did in that hotel room in New Delhi, I learned that mindfulness is most critical at times when fear and emotion threaten to take over. For the rest of that day, and every day after that, I vowed to reflect upon and reframe my experiences to focus on the positive. I made a conscious decision to frame moments like that in curiosity rather than negativity, and in mindfulness rather than judgment.

Pause. Breathe. Choose. Again, it is so simple, but it is not always easy in the moment. I have thought back often to what now seems a humorous paradox of nearly being killed by moshing monks. It reminds me never to take myself too seriously and that there will be times when it seems like I just cannot come up for air. I might be in an overcrowded subway on a hot summer day. Or feeling suffocated by a to-do list that just keeps growing longer and longer. I think of the Dalai Lama's laugh and make a conscious choice to replace judgment with curiosity. I connect with the reality around me, however messy and chaotic it might be. I connect with myself. I reset.

We all have times when it feels like life and circumstance are suffocating us. We have to make a conscious decision to pause, to break the cycle, to nip panic and fear and stress in the bud. Even as life crowds in on us, we have to carve out space enough to breathe. Our breath is our lifeline in such situations. We can follow our breath back to ourselves, to the moment, and to a healthy mindful choice.

The cost of not being mindful is steep. When we are not attuned to ourselves and our surroundings, we are apt to ignore the early warning signs of stress, within ourselves and in others. When our decision-making is not mindful, it is all too easy to lapse into bad choices and quick fixes. A lack of mindfulness opens the door for our monkey mind to take over, jumping from thought to thought, unable to sustain deep focus. Most important, when we are not mindful, we are vulnerable to losing our way, as individuals and as organizations. We miss out on the opportunity to be our best.

Catalysts for Mindful Change

As this rhythm of stray and return plays out in our lives, we often need a prompt to remind us to self-correct and get back on course. Sometimes a gentle reminder is all we need. At other times we require a stronger jolt, a real shock to the system. Life can deliver these jolts on its own, like when a health scare or the death of a loved one suddenly awakens us from our slumber. Or we can deliberately inject a catalyst into our lives. This was the case for me when I traveled to India.

A big part of the *Pause. Breathe. Choose.* Method is to consciously introduce catalysts and cues for mindful change into your life. Call it a planned reset. Perhaps you have a continuous nagging feeling or thought that can be your prompt for a planned reset. This is the time to change things up. If something is important to you, you will prioritize and allocate time for it. I tell my clients this all the time when it comes to prioritizing self-care. Just as you would schedule an important business meeting, you should also schedule things in your calendar that are essential to your health and well-being.

This deliberate approach to change is backed up by the growing science of habit formation. Leadership coach Marshall Goldsmith calls these cues *triggers*. Behavioral economists like Cass Sunstein research what they call *nudges*. Triggers, nudges, and cues exist in our lives (and in our world) whether we create them or not. The point is to be intentional about them.

One of the most useful tools I teach my clients is a regular *mindful self-check-in* (see chapter 5). Especially in a fast-paced, high-pressure professional environment, it is easy to ignore the early warning signs of stress or imbalance. We are almost conditioned to neglect these symptoms, to deny and tough it out rather than pause and assess. Periodically checking in with ourselves is an essential mindfulness practice — an intentional pause in our day that allows us to step back, breathe, take inventory of our thoughts and emotions, and then choose to self-correct or adjust as needed.

Those who practice mindful self-check-ins make a positive habit of taking stock of themselves, which cultivates *emotional intelligence*. This is the ability to monitor one's own thoughts and emotions and those of others and to make sound choices accordingly. Studies show there is no more critical leadership skill in today's world — where interpersonal skills, collaboration, and organizational culture are all key drivers of performance and of happiness.

Emotional intelligence thus translates directly into leadership well-being. When we regularly take stock of ourselves and our situation, we are better positioned to make sound choices in both our personal and professional lives. This is practical, applied mindfulness. This is how *Pause. Breathe. Choose.* can become a method for taking ownership of your well-being.

Again, sometimes life creates a catalyst for us, and we have to recognize and seize the opportunity. Sometimes we receive a gift, like the laugh of the Dalai Lama, gently reminding us to reset. More often than not, however, positive change happens when we proactively build catalysts and cues into our lives.

Think of this as mindfulness by design. Leadership well-being involves creating space — space in our days, in our hearts and minds, and in our organizations — to step back and take stock, to assess and reassess. In doing so, we create a cycle of growth and renewal in our lives. We mindfully activate a growth mindset.

Mindfulness begins with small steps but leads to big changes.

Tame the Monkey Mind

Monkey mind refers to an overactive mind. In such a state, your mind jumps from one thought to the next, as a monkey jumps from one branch to another, making it challenging to stay focused and effective.

When your monkey mind is taking over before an important meeting or after a conflict with your boss, tame any negativity, anxiety, and uncertainty you are experiencing through a simple meditation practice.

This is a moment to pause and breathe.

As your monkey mind tries to get your attention and disrupt the pattern of your breath or mantra, acknowledge the thought without any judgment.

Imagine a balloon in the sky. Put the thought into the balloon and allow it to float away. Let it go and return to your breath or mantra.

An alternative is to think of an anchor — this can be any stimulus that is associated with a learning experience — that can ground you and bring you back to the moment, reminding you of what is important. One of my anchors is the Dalai Lama's laughter coming through the crowd of monks.

Another option is to speak with the monkey. First, associate the monkey with a funny voice — Scooby-Doo, Mickey Mouse, Donald Duck, or Pepé Le Pew, perhaps — to take away its power, and then listen to it.

Ask questions such as: What is the source of this unrest? Is this your mind's way of ignoring your to-do list? Or are you experiencing stress about something to come? Is your monkey mind sending you thoughts of regret or shame for something in the past?

If you answer yes to these questions, recognize that these may be signs to create a plan to mitigate these thoughts. Take a moment to address the concerns of your funny-voiced monkey and take action. Reassure your monkey mind that everything will be fine. Sometimes, all that is needed for your monkey mind to settle down is for it to be heard and acknowledged.

Pause and Breathe Before You Hit Send

Practice mindfulness and refrain from responding to emails when emotions are running high. Sending emails and communicating when you are angry, upset, stressed, or overwhelmed does more harm than good, both to you and the recipient, especially when the recipient is the source of your negative feelings.

Before writing or sending anything, pause. Take a deep breath and reflect on what is behind your anger. Take a moment for yourself. You do not need to reply immediately. Get it all out of your system so you can let yourself wind back down before responding. Open a blank document and blow off steam in a message you will never actually send. Take a break. Breathe, and then make the best available choice.

If it is not a time-sensitive matter, sleep on it and return rested and with a fresh perspective. After taking the time to pinpoint the source of anger or frustration, figure out what remedial actions can be made, then you can respond calmly. Avoid outright reactive or judgmental statements like, "It's ridiculous that you said…" Instead, claim your reaction and offer mitigation or a solution: "I'm surprised by what you said, and I'd prefer to do this…" When in doubt, less is more. Take another moment to breathe and edit what you have written.

Remember that once you hit send, your response is out of your hands and impossible to take back. Give the correspondences a final read to make sure you are okay with everything you have written, no matter who might view it.

ACTION STEPS

Meditate Daily

If you are a beginner to meditation, start small. Try sitting comfortably and still for two minutes. Gradually increase the time to ten and then twenty minutes over your first month, or whatever feels right for you. On the other hand, if you have tried meditation and find that you are not completely hooked on it yet, explore different types of meditation by researching online or taking an introductory class. Here are a few popular types to get you started:

- Concentration or focused meditation typically involves focusing on an object like a flower or candle, or a sensation like your breath, or sounds in your environment, and then zeroing in on all the details.
- Open monitoring meditation, such as mindfulness meditation, is the practice of observing your present thoughts and emotions without judgment or engagement as they come and go like clouds in a windy sky.
- Self-transcending meditation, such as Transcendental Meditation, is the practice of internally repeating the same mantra specific to each practitioner.

Transcendental Meditation is a personal preference of mine (see "Self: Morning Ritual," pages 161–62). This simple, highly researched type of meditation has countless evidence-based health benefits.

Only practicing once or twice will not be enough to reap the full benefits. Consistency is key to deepen your practice. Afterward, adopt your meditative state of presence in your daily life. The ultimate goal is to be present throughout your day, not just in your meditation practice. This is the art of being truly mindful.

Incorporate Daily Mindful Habits

Start by committing to short periods of mindfulness throughout your day. Dedicate five to ten minutes when you actively pay attention to the present moment in a gentle, accepting way. It can be while you are walking, sitting, brushing your teeth, washing your hands, taking a shower, or any other activity. During these moments, pay close attention to the sensations in your body. Do not just go through the motions. Take time to notice what thoughts and emotions come and go. As your mind wanders, acknowledge the thoughts without judgment and return to the present moment. Tap into your other senses: What are you feeling, seeing, smelling, touching, and tasting?

When you wash your hands, *feel* the temperature of the water on your hands.

Smell the fragrance of the soap.

Think about how you lather your hands by rubbing them together with soap.

Listen to the way the water splashes off your hands and hits the sink bowl.

Sense the soft cloth of the towel as you dry your hands.

See the door handle as you turn it to open the door.

Be mindful.

Be present in every moment and in every little aspect of your day. Let that be your intention.

- A *wellness gap* is a disconnect between the aspiration to lead a thriving and engaged life and the daily practices and habits that would fuel and energize such a life. At the individual level, that wellness gap leads to burnout and a disconnected life. At the organizational level, it can infect a business, leading to high turnover and low employee engagement and satisfaction.

- *Leadership well-being* bridges the gap between *being well* and *doing well* — and refusing to accept the false dichotomy between the two. Leadership is about taking ownership to be the CEO of your well-being. It is about taking control of your destiny — about intentionally, deliberately, and mindfully shaping your life, as opposed to letting life happen to you. Make executive decisions that boldly and unapologetically set the course of your life, regardless of your professional title or status.

- *Pause. Breathe. Choose.* is a powerful method for translating mindfulness into action and taking ownership of your well-being — enabling you to become present and make better choices. To pause is to stop and take a step back instead of spiraling downward. To take a conscious breath is a way to become present and gain perspective. To choose is an opportunity to self-direct or self-correct and choose wisely. Once we get in the habit of making strong choices, the ripple effects travel far and wide. One mindful choice begets another.

- *Explorative action* refers to active choices we make without certainty, without guarantees. It enables us to test our limits and to set a new standard for ourselves, as well as to realign with the intentions of our authentic Self.

CHAPTER TWO

─────────────── ● ───────────────

MINDFULNESS
IN ACTION

─────────────── ● ───────────────

Mindfulness can be elusive in today's world when we do not create space for it. We so easily become lulled into a state of complacency, numbness, stress, and distraction. Once the cycle begins, it can be hard to break. Taking the time to pause and then to breathe is a small but powerful step. That small step opens the door for mindfulness to enter the room and for mindful awareness to become mindful action.

My Magic Mat

It is easier to return when we have a strong home base — a foundation for mindful awareness. Like the soil in which a plant sets its roots, this foundation grounds us and frees us to grow taller and stronger.

For me, that foundation has always been yoga, and my magic mat is my home base. For you, it may be something entirely different. It may be a seated meditation practice, cycling, or running. You must find a practice that works best for you, and when you do, cultivate it, feed it, and protect it.

My mother took me to my first yoga class at the age of eighteen. At that time in my life, I viewed yoga as purely an exploration of the physical realm. I enjoyed the challenge of mastering the various poses, or asanas. My mat was just that, a mat, a location on which to pursue this physical practice. It was very much a surface practice for me at the beginning.

It was also my mother who, at various points in my life, urged me to practice seated meditation. I resisted. Years later, caught up in the hamster wheel of my pharmaceutical sales job, I was not able to see my parents as much as I (or they) would have liked. Whenever my mother saw me, my stress and exhaustion were evident. She encouraged me to take up meditation as a way to mitigate my stress. She had been practicing herself for over two decades. "Meditation makes you more productive and will give you more energy," she assured me. In my mind, however, it sounded like losing forty minutes of productive time.

I was not yet ready for meditation, but yoga had planted the seed for mindfulness. When I first practiced yoga, it was from the Bikram school: a regimented series of twenty-six asanas in a heated room. It was mainly a way to exercise and to be strong and flexible. Later, I discovered Vinyasa yoga, where there is more dynamic flow from posture to posture, with a strong emphasis on synchronizing the breath with each movement. I fell in love with Vinyasa yoga as it became more than just exercise. It was my moving meditation. Meditation is a powerful tool for cultivating mindfulness and for unblocking your vital energy or prana. For me, yoga was my introduction to both.

Instead of focusing solely on the physical, I learned to withdraw deep within my Self, focusing on each conscious breath while quieting my overactive mind. I learned that the answers I seek can be found internally, rather than externally. I discovered a wiser, stronger, more peaceful version of myself. Yoga became a powerful way for me to strengthen my heart and mind and the connection between them.

My yoga practice made me realize that mindfulness is the presence of the heart.

In time this daily practice became my home and my compass. Yoga also finally opened me to pursuing Transcendental Meditation. Both bring me internal clarity and peace. After years of consistent practice, I can carry this clarity — and usually peace — with me throughout the day, even when I am not on my magic mat. This simple yoga mat (an otherwise unremarkable rectangle of sticky plastic) has become a constant in my life. It has carried me through devastation, heartbreak, and stress for more than twenty years.

Paradoxically, the stronger this home base is, and the more deeply we plant our foundation, the easier it is to take with us. Our mindfulness practice may start on the yoga mat or a meditation cushion, but it does not stay there. We bring that same wisdom, strength, and peace with us into all aspects of our lives, especially our most challenging moments.

Mindfulness and Energy

Once we learn to carry mindfulness over into the fabric of our daily lives, it creates powerful ripple effects. It transforms our choices, our being, our energy. Mindful choices energize us — not just by improving our health and well-being, but by aligning our hearts and minds and aligning us with our purpose.

When I began studying holistic health and taking better care of myself, my energy improved incrementally. When I returned from India and quit my job and took full control of my destiny, my energy went through the roof.

Energy might seem like a nebulous concept, maybe even a New Age-ish one. It is not. Business leaders are increasingly putting a lot of thought into energy. A *Harvard Business Review* article argues rightly that we should focus on managing our energy, not our time. One of the co-authors, Tony Schwartz, founded the Energy Project to take a different approach to employee engagement — one focused on improving the overall employee experience. What is employee engagement but another way to describe energy? The engagement of employees — their motivation, their sense of purpose — is the vital life force of any organization.

One limitation of many corporate wellness programs is a misguided emphasis on the so-called work-life balance. The term suggests that life and work are two separate things — and that we should expect our personal lives to somehow mitigate or balance out the stresses of our professional lives.

Work and life are not at opposite ends of some imaginary scale, and neither are work and play. I watched Steve Jobs use play as an essential part of his work. The objective should be to infuse the whole of our lives with meaning and purpose, which is what I call *work-life engagement*. We should be engaged and energized in all facets of our lives, and those multiple facets should complement and feed one another. Engagement is energy.

Living in an Age of Distraction and Overload

Across different cultures and eras, mindfulness has long been a concern of humanity. Although we associate meditation with Eastern religious and spiritual traditions, the practice has a history in Christianity, Islam, and Judaism. "Know thyself" was a central tenet in the philosophy of Socrates — really just another way of describing the aim of mindfulness and emotional intelligence.

Never before, however, has mindfulness been so sorely needed. It is almost as if modern life has been deliberately programmed to undermine mindfulness. We live in an age of information overload, distraction, and disconnection. Americans take in five times as much information as we did fifty years ago. We allow our digital devices to constantly interrupt us, preventing deep and sustained focus. We convince ourselves that multitasking is productive, even when evidence demonstrates this is not the case. Social media promises to connect us but seems to make it harder for people to truly be present with one another.

In such a state of perpetual overload and distraction, how are we to make the kind of mindful choices that lead to personal and professional fulfillment? How are we to quiet our minds, become more present, and stop our monkey mind from taking over?

Mindfulness is not a magic bullet. But just as our breath is a lifeline that can lead us back to ourselves, mindfulness leads us back to the present moment. It grounds us in self-awareness and situational awareness. Being mindful creates a solid foundation for making better choices. It also helps us align ourselves with a higher life purpose. Research shows that mindfulness is significantly linked to resilience: the ability to bounce back from difficulties. Mindfulness enables us to mitigate bad stress and tap into the upside of stress by adopting a growth mindset.

Mindfulness may begin with a formal practice like meditation or yoga. In this chapter's Action Steps, I present options for attaining and deepening mindfulness. Like multiple hiking trails to the top of a mountain, the paths are different, but the ultimate objective is the same. You have to find the practice that works best for you — that serves as your foundation, your home base. The goal is to attain an informal and unforced state of awareness that you can carry with you all day. That state of awareness enables you to attune to and tap into your prana, an energy that can fuel focus, peak performance, and fulfillment in all areas of your life. When mindfulness becomes a way of life, it translates into all of your choices. It becomes part of your wiring: both an active state of mind and a way of being.

The practice of mindfulness awakens your mind and your heart from autopilot and enables you to experience life unfolding in the present moment. It unlocks your ability to tap into your intuition and creativity so that you can receive new information, and develop new perspectives, with a beginner's mind.

Putting Mindfulness to Work

Formal research into mindfulness has come a long way in recent decades. Although we tend to think of mindfulness in terms of its psychological benefits, its health benefits are actually more exhaustively documented. The term itself is misleading in this sense. Mindfulness is not just about the mind but the body, the heart, and the connection between them.

Numerous studies show that a mindfulness practice can reduce blood pressure. For high-stress individuals, it can also improve breathing rate, heart rhythm, and boost the immune system. Another study found the practice lowers levels of C-reactive proteins associated with inflammation and heart disease. Other reviews document reduced symptoms in a range of health conditions — including chronic pain, arthritis, multiple sclerosis, fibromyalgia, psoriasis, and HIV. New research suggests that mindfulness might be able to reverse the effects of chronic stress at the genetic level.

The benefits for mind and body are deeply interconnected. A significant part of the toll stress takes on our health stems from our perception of stress and of potentially stressful events. Those who perceive themselves to be under a great deal of stress and who believe stress adversely affects their health are 43 percent more likely to experience premature death. Conversely, if we teach ourselves to view challenging situations as opportunities rather than threats (what I call a *mindset upgrade*), we can tap into the upside of stress.

Being mindful changes how we perceive stress and anxiety and how we experience these and other forms of psychological distress. A mindfulness practice has been shown to decrease anxiety, mood swings, and symptoms of depression. Several studies suggest mindfulness intervention may be more effective than medication at reducing long-term depression and other forms of mental illness.

New technology allows us to see how these changes manifest in the brain itself. A study led by Massachusetts General Hospital was the first to document meditation-produced changes in the brain's gray matter. Researchers studied the brains of participants who took part in an eight-week meditation program. Even after such a relatively short program of study, participants showed increased gray-matter density in the hippocampus, a center of learning and memory, and in areas associated with self-awareness. The same participants showed decreased density in the amygdala, which plays a role in anxiety and stress. Mindfulness can literally reshape and rewire the brain, a process called neuroplasticity, in which new habits reorganize or rewire neural connections.

We know that mindfulness can improve performance in a variety of settings. Programs in the workplace have been demonstrated to help employees improve emotional regulation, significantly reducing measures of emotional exhaustion and enhancing job satisfaction. A paper published in the journal *Progress in Brain Research* reported that US Army soldiers who went through a month of mindfulness training exhibited better decision-making and improved working memory under chaotic conditions. Major General Piatt joked about his soldiers calling him General Moonbeam: "There's a stereotype this makes you soft. No, it brings you on point."

Research shows that meditation builds resilience, boosts emotional intelligence, enhances creativity, improves our relationships, and helps us focus. It brings us into alignment with our inner compass, thus helping us to obtain greater awareness and to connect with our inner guide (our Mindful MAP Maker; see chapter 13). When this connection is established with our Self, we are not easily swayed by outer influences. In turn, this results in a deeper focus on our purpose and intentions.

Given all this evidence, it is not surprising that some of the most innovative Fortune 500 companies offer regular meditation classes in the workplace. Benefits for employees include improved focus, creativity, and well-being and the ability to cope better with stress and coworkers. Mindfulness programs also increase individual and team engagement, which are measures of vital energy or prana in the workplace. Successful CEOs such as Rupert Murdoch, Bill Ford, Marc Benioff, Oprah Winfrey, Jeff Weiner, Ray Dalio, and Steve Jobs attribute their success and well-being to their meditation practice.

What has not been studied extensively is exactly how mindfulness training plays out in the workplace. As two significant reviews of the literature point out, mindfulness has been studied primarily at the level of individual psychology — and not in terms of occupational or organizational psychology. Moreover, the most popular and most studied form of workplace mindfulness training is adapted from Mindfulness-Based Stress Reduction (MBSR), the technique Jon Kabat-Zinn developed at the UMass Memorial Center for Mindfulness. There remain many unanswered questions about how best to bring mindfulness into the workplace.

What does this mean for me, you, and this book? We are only beginning to scratch the surface of how mindfulness can transform the workplace, other organizations and institutions, and by extension, society itself. This is uncharted and exciting territory. In the years to come, we will better be able to translate the power of mindfulness into a new vision of leadership well-being that can transform lives at both the professional and personal level.

We cannot afford to treat mindfulness as a perk or a luxury. If we leave mindfulness on the yoga mat or in the meditation room, we are passing up a wealth of potential. It is like allowing our money to sit idle in a zero-interest bank account. We must put that resource to work for us.

How will you commit to a daily mindfulness practice? Challenge yourself to put mindfulness to work and reap the benefits.

Fulfilling Our Potential

In retrospect, I realize that I succeeded in my interview with Steve Jobs because I was able to calmly and naturally be my authentic Self. Being present prevented me from worrying about future outcomes, which diffused the anxiety I might otherwise have felt. I freed myself to simply be open and curious, showing up as my best Self.

What I lacked, however, was a deliberate mindfulness practice that would allow me to consistently stay in touch with my authentic Self. I dropped my "i" and stopped taking ownership of my health and well-being. It took a decade of slipping into burnout and autopilot for me to realize what I had lost and then to find my way back.

In the years since I founded my corporate wellness company, Prananaz, I have finally found myself in a position to put some of Steve's lessons into practice. I often think about those lessons: Raise the bar and never settle. We are here to put a dent in the universe. Follow your heart and intuition. Create your own reality. Think outside the box. "Think different."

Steve, too, traveled to India to explore mindfulness and Buddhism. I returned from India determined to embark on a new journey. I no longer needed certainty. Fear and anxiety about the future are products of the monkey mind. With my heart and mind aligned in a new way, I was free to take explorative action: choices outside of my comfort zone, without guarantees.

Part of that explorative action involves not just moving forward in shaping our future but looking back and connecting the dots of our past in new ways and through new eyes. When we practice *Pause. Breathe. Choose.* and reconnect with our purpose, we are able to view the arc of our own personal narrative through a different lens. Our mindfulness practice becomes a compass for navigating the future and for reinterpreting the past. We see with clarity where we have been and where we want to go — as the driver and not the passenger of our lives. This deliberate, mindful mapmaking is the ultimate objective of *Pause. Breathe. Choose.*

I have shared my journey and my insights into mindfulness to encourage you to step up and take ownership of your destiny — to become the CEO of your well-being.

In our lives, we are going to have cave days, and we are going to have taxi days. One of my low moments was in the taxi with the somnolent driver. Only a few days later, one of my highest moments was in a cave with the silent monk. Both can play a meaningful role in our lives when we pause, breathe, and make mindful choices.

We all experience awakenings, breakthroughs, epiphanies, aha moments, crises, and times when we hit rock bottom. These moments allow us to wake up and see where we have been and to realize that, as one thing ends, something else begins. Just as I will remember the terrible taxi day, my profound cave day will forever be a part of me. Both experiences led to the same transformative internal dialogue:

Wake up! Snap out of it!
Awaken your mind!
Awaken your heart!
What are you doing?
What are you feeling?
What's the upside?
What mindful choice can you make now?

Ask yourself these questions. Connect your mind with your heart. Let go of your fear and replace it with love.

Practicing mindfulness empowers you in any situation. *Pause. Breathe. Choose.* is a powerful method for translating mindfulness into action. In moments small and large, it is a way to reset and position yourself to make better choices.

As I did in India, I hope you, too, are ready to make this leap — to overcome whatever holds you back from living your best life, to listen to your heart and not the fears of the monkey mind. We all face challenges and struggles. We also have unknown depths of untapped potential. We have the power of choice, the power to transform our lives. And we can best gain access to that power through mindfulness.

BUSINESS HACKS

Sit Still in Silence

Bringing mindfulness into your meetings enables everyone to become grounded and focused. It also provides an opportunity for each person to set an intention for the meeting and to be open to possibility. The practice is simple: At the beginning of a meeting, after everyone has settled into their chairs, ring a bell or tap a glass with a pen, and sit silently for one to two minutes.

This practice may be uncomfortable for some people in the beginning, as time may seem to slow down, and people might fidget in their seats. Yet with consistent practice, everyone will reap the benefits, and your meetings will have more effective outcomes.

If your team is not open to this practice, this can also be done on an individual basis. In this case, sit still in silence before going into your meeting; you will find that both you and your team will still benefit.

Encourage Visible Thoughts

Imagine that your brain is transparent, making all of your thoughts visible to everyone. This will help you refrain from thinking negatively about other people. Instead, practice compassion by imagining yourself in another person's shoes, thinking through their mind, and feeling through their heart. This is a useful way to better understand another person's perspective.

When you are upset about something or disappointed, ask your Self, *Is this a tragedy or an inconvenience?* Most of the time, it tends to be the latter.

Mindfulness helps you realize that there are no positive or negative outcomes. Think instead of outcomes as A, B, C, or D, each with its own challenges and opportunities.

ACTION STEPS

Explore the RPM Method

Start your day with a mindfulness practice. I use a straightforward method: RPM or "rise, pee, meditate" (see "Self: Morning Ritual," pages 161–62). I meditate every morning for twenty minutes, but if you prefer a different type of mindfulness practice, you can incorporate breathwork (see "Breathwork: Ujjayi Pranayama," pages 219–21), a gratitude practice (see "Pause. Breathe. Choose Gratitude." page 139), mindful movement, or visualizations of your best Self. Decide what works best for you. Take explorative action by creating a ritual that fits your lifestyle, and then make a commitment to practicing it for thirty days. When your mindfulness practice becomes a habit, it will change your life!

Practice Intentional Yoga

If you would like to incorporate yoga as part of your mindfulness practice, set an intention before your session or as soon as you get on the mat. Dedicate your practice to someone, to yourself, or to something meaningful. Focus on your breath as you synchronize it with each movement. Pay close attention to its quality. I use my breath as a stress barometer both on and off the mat. Notice how, if you are in a challenging pose, your breath may pause or become shallow. Whereas if you are flowing with ease, your breath is deeper and longer. Continue to breathe deeply and rhythmically.

Implement a Tech-Free Fun Day

Choose a day that works best for you and your family to commit to completely disconnecting from all electronic devices. This digital detox will minimize distractions and support more eye-to-eye and heart-to-heart connections. The quality of your relationships will improve and grow more meaningful, which will impact the quality of your life.

- *Work-life engagement* infuses the whole of your life with meaning and purpose. When you are engaged and energized in all facets of your life, each facet complements and feeds one another. Engagement is energy.

- The cost of not being mindful is steep. When we are not attuned to ourselves and our surroundings, we are apt to ignore the early warning signs of stress, within ourselves and in others. When our decision-making is not mindful, it is all too easy to lapse into bad choices and quick fixes. A lack of mindfulness opens the door for our monkey mind to take over, jumping from thought to thought, unable to sustain deep focus. We are also vulnerable to losing our way, as individuals and as organizations.

- Mindfulness may begin with a formal practice like meditation or yoga. The goal is to attain an informal and unforced state of awareness that you can carry with you all day. That state of awareness enables you to attune to and tap into your prana, an energy that can fuel focus, peak performance, and fulfillment in all areas of your life. When mindfulness becomes a way of life, it translates into all of your choices. It becomes part of your wiring: both an active state of mind and a way of being.

- The practice of mindfulness awakens your mind and your heart from autopilot and enables you to experience life unfolding in the present moment. It unlocks your ability to tap into your intuition and creativity so that you can receive new information and develop new perspectives with a beginner's mind.

- Research on the health benefits of mindfulness is vast. Many Fortune 500 companies offer regular meditation classes, and many successful CEOs attribute their success and well-being to their meditation practice.

PART II

Apply Better Choices
to Manage Stress
and Build Resilience

THE SEVEN A's

• THE SEVEN A's •

ADOPT a healthy lifestyle
Achieve your highest potential to perform at the top of your game

ALLOCATE play and recovery time
Reboot your mind, body, and creativity

AVOID unnecessary stress
Take preventative measures to avoid chronic stress

ALTER the situation
Make a change to attain a better outcome

ADAPT to the stressor
Understand the bigger picture to gain perspective

ACCEPT what you cannot change
Gain greater peace of mind

ATTEND to connection with Self, others, world, and universe
Cultivate meaningful relationships and limitless possibilities

Being mindful is the heart of the Seven A's and the Three P's, and it is the foundation for making mindful choices, which is the subject of part II.

The Seven A's are a set of interconnected strategies you can use to upgrade your mindset and habits to make better choices to live a healthy, engaged, and connected life. This necessarily begins with the first two of the Seven A's: You must first adopt a healthy lifestyle and allocate time for play and recovery in order to effectively practice the other five strategies and achieve sustainable success.

The concept of the Seven A's evolved in fits and starts when I was in my corporate jobs experiencing stress and burnout, and they are designed to help you make better choices, manage stress, and build resilience beyond just bouncing back and surviving, but rather bouncing forward and thriving amid challenging situations.

The quality of your life depends on the quality of your choices.

Unfortunately, we are not born with the ability to make good decisions. We must learn the critical skill of decision-making, often the hard way. The choices you make throughout your life determine whether or not you will promote your Self to the CEO of your well-being.

If practiced consistently and with awareness, these seven strategies can rewire your brain. Our current patterns of thought and behavior are not permanent, which has been shown by a wealth of research on the science of habit formation.

If we do not make a conscious effort to live a healthier lifestyle, we are willingly accepting premature death. If we do not fully connect with ourselves, with our work, with others, and with the world around us, we will find ourselves living on autopilot. We will settle for something less than our best Self.

What can we do? We can be mindful. We can pause and breathe before making a choice. We can shift our mindset to avoid living on autopilot.

We can choose to engage the world with self-awareness, to notice and address stress, to make adjustments when necessary, and to align our actions with our goals.

Practicing mindfulness and the Seven A's is about adopting a happier and healthier life. You have the choice, so why not choose happiness?

CHAPTER THREE

·

ADOPT
A HEALTHY LIFESTYLE

·

THE SEVEN A's

ADOPT

Allocate

Avoid

Alter

Adapt

Accept

Attend

Are you willing to accept premature death?

I am not writing about skydiving, bungee jumping, or any other kind of adrenaline-pumping activity you might indulge in. These are calculated risks that are perhaps worth the thrill. My question concerns if you are willing to accept premature death every day if you are overworked and carry excess stress. Let that sink in for a moment. Jumping out of a plane or day-to-day stress? Which is more likely to kill you?

Every single day that we live on autopilot, doing without being, over-stressing, overworking, sacrificing sleep, and neglecting our self-care, we invite disease and choose to accept premature death. No one can force us to change or act on our behalf.

Thus, the first of the Seven A's is to *adopt a healthy lifestyle*, which is a matter of life and death.

Only *you* can choose to make a change and create better lifestyle habits in order to achieve your highest potential and perform at the top of your game. Ultimately, this is how you promote your Self to the CEO of your well-being.

Karoshi: A Legitimate Killer

In the late sixties in Japan, a twenty-nine-year-old healthy man died from karoshi, which quite literally means "death by overwork." More specifically, the excessive hours that he was working led to a cardiovascular attack that killed him. This young man suffered a stroke after pulling grueling shifts in the shipping department of the nation's largest newspaper. Karoshi remains such an epidemic that antikaroshi movements in Japan regularly lead to strikes.

This man's case may sound extreme. Unfortunately, it is not an outlier. The Japanese labor ministry has estimated that as many as 2,310 Japanese workers may die of karoshi annually, but this may only be the tip of the iceberg. The National Defense Council for Victims of Karoshi says the actual figure may be as high as 10,000 per year, roughly the same number of deaths as from traffic accidents.

According to a recent Japanese government report on karoshi, nearly a quarter of companies surveyed said some employees were working more than eighty hours of overtime every month. The title of a 2017 *New York Times* article summed up another extreme case: "Young Worker Clocked 159 Hours of Overtime in a Month. Then She Died."

Alarmingly, such excessive work habits are not exclusive to Japan. Americans work an average of nine weeks longer annually than other nations, with fewer paid vacation days. Many Americans forgo using all of the vacation days available to them, and 30 percent do a significant amount of work when they are on vacation.

Every year, forty million people die prematurely from noncommunicable disease, which means chronic conditions that do not result from an acute infectious process and are not communicable. That makes up 70 percent of global deaths. Over 90 percent of these premature deaths could have been prevented. They are attributed to lifestyle choices such as an unhealthy diet, smoking, physical inactivity, and alcohol.

Dr. Ralph L. Keeney of Duke University writes, "The leading cause of death is personal decision-making. Making better personal decisions could potentially prevent millions of premature deaths per decade."

In Austin, Texas, Jonas Koffler was an ambitious recent college graduate who quickly rose up the corporate ladder, putting in seventy or more hours per week in the office. However, before long, lack of sleep and overwork caused him to have a stroke while giving a presentation. He was twenty-six years old.

After he woke up in his hospital bed, Koffler was asked if he understood what had happened to him. That is when he finally realized he needed to make a change. Luckily, he survived.

In 2013, twenty-one-year-old Moritz Erhardt was found dead in his shower. An intern for Bank of America Merrill Lynch in London, he died from epilepsy triggered by working seventy-two hours straight. Afterward, the bank instituted a cap on interns' working hours — to only seventeen hours per day.

Karoshi happens everywhere and far more often than we may think. But outside of Japan, we have traditionally not had a medical term for death by overwork. This is part of the problem.

Our bigger issue is that overworking is often embraced as a badge of honor. Arriving early and staying late, skipping meals while downing copious amounts of caffeine: These are accepted as a necessary part of paying our dues. Working ourselves to death is a kind of status symbol.

Here are a few more shocking statistics:

- The most likely day of the week to commit suicide is Wednesday, due to increased workplace pressures and stress.
- Every major system in the body is influenced by chronic stress, mainly by suppressing the immune system, manifesting as a severe illness.
- Seventy-five to 90 percent of all doctor's office visits are for stress-related ailments and complaints.
- Chronic stress is a major contributing factor to the six leading causes of death: cancer, heart disease, lung ailments, accidents, cirrhosis of the liver, and suicide.

Karoshi has entered my own circle of corporate clients. One of the executives I coach reached out to me after the death of one of his employees, a man in his early thirties with no existing health issues. These tragic stories happen every day. This young professional is not a rare case. He could be you.

We have all felt despair. We have at times felt hopeless in the face of the future, feeling perhaps that there is no way out. This might be chronic stress or depression. How do we break this epidemic, change our habits, and transform our lives?

The Productivity Trap

How can we choose to avoid falling into a productivity trap, a constant chasing of productivity through more hours and more-efficient time management? Working harder is not the answer. Working smarter is. In fact, a growing body of evidence shows that we would be better off paying attention to the quality of our work, not the quantity of hours we put in, and to managing our energy and not our time.

Time is a limited resource, but your energy is renewable. Sustainable energy and focus, or what I call *free-flowing prana*, begins with mindfully pursuing a healthy lifestyle. A healthy lifestyle enables you to get out of bed with energy, motivation, and inspiration. Your prana will be fluid; you will not be exhausted and stressed, enabling you to perform better and more joyfully.

Build a bridge between the demands of work and life, and the demands of you as a CEO. When we choose anything less, we are likely to fall into a productivity trap and widen our wellness gap. If we choose anything less, we are inviting karoshi.

A recent Harvard Medical School study of senior leaders found that 96 percent reported experiencing some degree of burnout. One-third described their condition as "extreme." At what point does obsession with productivity become destructive? This destruction is not only harmful to our health but to our work, and it becomes counterproductive as we battle exhaustion and self-chosen overwhelming demands.

Let us look at this problem from a corporate point of view. No company can be successful without paying attention to the well-being of its people. People cannot be successful without feeling good every day. Therefore, healthy employees equate to better business outcomes.

Here is the bottom line:

- Healthy people are engaged and happy.
- Healthy people work smarter, not harder, to achieve their goals.
- Healthy people help others and are more efficient.
- Unhealthy people are generally disengaged, tired, unhappy, and unable to perform at a high level.

I have experienced both sides of the wellness gap, having fallen into the productivity trap in my professional and personal life. Getting on the right track begins with mindfulness, which enables us to attune to our needs and to make mindful choices about a healthy lifestyle.

Productivity without awareness creates a wellness gap. Without mindfulness, rising productivity will mask early signs of burnout. Then, as the wellness gap widens, it spreads like a cancerous growth unless it is addressed through improved company culture. If you single-mindedly chase productivity, you can literally run yourself and your employees into the ground.

Instead, approach productivity from a quality paradigm instead of a quantity paradigm. This means the priority is not working hard. The priorities are the quality, engagement, and efficiency of work.

The bottom line is that individual well-being translates into collective profitability. Focusing on a quality paradigm is mutually beneficial for employees and employers. See this chapter's Business Hacks for tips about creating a workplace culture of wellness.

Three PM Autopilot Junkie

I am thankful that my own story is not about karoshi. Indeed, how would I have written this book from the grave? However, I once found myself on the same autopilot that sacrifices personal health for productivity and leads, eventually, to atrophy.

When I started at Yahoo!, I was excited about the opportunity to delve into my new role in sales. I arrived at work with a spring in my step.

Before long, however, I found myself hitting the snooze button and waking up with brain fog due to a residual sugar hangover.

Day after day, I sat in an open desk "sales pit" with many driven, productive people; we were on and off the phone constantly. The sound of a Coke can being cracked open every other minute, and the smell of Doritos and Cheetos wafting through the air, were a given part of the work environment.

Upon arrival each day, I looked forward to my next break to feed my sugar addiction. I obsessed over the clock by watching the minutes tick away. First midmorning break, then lunch, and then at 3 PM, my afternoon slump, postlunch coma triggered my junkie habit. The minute the clock hit three, I automatically stopped what I was doing and walked like a zombie to the vending machine to get myself a cookie, a bag of Cheetos, or a Twix bar. Mindlessly eating junk food did not sustain me for long. I soon hit a wall, and my energy level plummeted.

Somewhat aware of my habit, I upgraded from a cheap sugar-junkie to a gourmet sugar-junkie. Instead of eating vending machine snacks, I graduated to gourmet baked goods from a place called Specialty's. I quickly became addicted to their warm, fat, freshly baked, gooey chocolate chip cookies. I thought I was making a significant improvement in my health. Looking back as a wellness coach, I now see that a healthy lifestyle was the last thing on my mind. Only my career mattered. At the time, I simply did not see it. For years, I remained on autopilot. Although the junk food was convenient, and an easy break from work, it was a bad habit I had to stop.

Then one day, *I became sick and tired of being sick and tired.*

When you live like this, at some point, two things happen: Either the consequences of your bad choices become intolerable, or a jolt in your world awakens you from your zombielike frenzy and makes you realize the need for dire change. Sometimes, both happen at once.

One day, I could no longer take waking up feeling lethargic, unmotivated, and with brain fog. I could not face my reflection in the mirror: my puffy lifeless eyes, swollen face, and ghostly pallor. I took action and chose to make essential changes in my life. Once a week, during my lunch break, I went to the gym. Gradually, I worked my way up to two and then three times a week. At the same time, I cut back on my trips to the vending machine. I also did the "Master Cleanse" diet — which is a modified juice fast, also known as the lemonade diet — to eliminate the toxins that had been building up for years within my body. Initially, people thought I was crazy. However, when they noticed my renewed energy and glowing skin, some soon followed suit.

The realization that I needed to make better choices initially led me down the path to a healthier lifestyle, but it definitely did not happen overnight. I instinctively knew to start with one area of my life and continue to build better habits from there. Changing habits is typically not sustainable if you try to change everything all at once.

What truly yanked me out of autopilot, though, was a family tragedy. My beloved grandfather was killed in a car accident. I was very close to him, and his death shocked my system. My heartbreak helped me commit to changing my unhealthy routines. In my grandfather's honor, I gave up my cookie addiction, and I have not had a cookie since he passed away in 2006. Instead, on special occasions, I take pleasure in eating ice cream, knowing it was my grandfather's favorite treat.

Have you had a wake-up call?

A doctor's visit? A heart attack? A car accident? Like me, did you suddenly realize one day that you were sick and tired of being sick and tired? If not, what will it take to break any bad habits and replace them with good ones? If you find yourself on autopilot, how will you turn it off, so that this does not lead to karoshi? What will you do to promote your Self to CEO of your well-being?

Choose to adopt a healthy lifestyle. Affirm that your life is more important than your career; but you can have both. Once you make this choice, you can truly live your best life. You will be able to build fulfilling relationships and feel good, both in body and mind. You will be able to perform at the top of your game at work and at home. You will walk with a spring in your step. You will not wear out your snooze button. The choice to adopt a healthy lifestyle not only serves you; it makes you better able to serve others.

"What's New and Good?"

We are often unaware of how profoundly exhausted or stressed we have become or of how deeply we have fallen into bad habits. Sometimes it takes an unexpected tragedy, yet a mindfulness practice can also be the wake-up call.

Something positive can motivate us to break bad habits and adopt new ones. In my case, my love for my grandfather helped motivate me to kick my cookie habit. An aspirational goal can be critical in adopting new, healthier habits. More important than what we are leaving behind is what positive things we look forward to creating.

Conversely, a preoccupation with the negative can be a sign that we are on the wrong track. I once had a client named Mark who was initially challenged by my question, "What's new and good?" Later in our session, he described a success at work, and I asked him why he had not mentioned that earlier. Mark always glossed over a deal he had just closed or a fun dinner with an old friend because he was unable to realize the good. He was on autopilot, focusing only on the bad. If this sounds like you, do not worry; this is a habit many of us have, often without realizing it.

I gave Mark a new action step: Write down what was *new and good* every day. I asked him to do it after he brushed his teeth, and over time, he grew more mindful of the positive developments in his life and looked forward to sharing them.

For Mark, the repetition and focus on both his intentions and his actions, combined with ongoing external acknowledgment, successfully rewired his brain. He adopted a new mental habit of acknowledging the positive, and this made a positive impact in his day-to-day life and, eventually, in his business's bottom line.

Build a Healthy Lifestyle, Habit by Habit

No matter where you are or where you want to be on the spectrum of mindfulness, the first step in choosing to adopt a healthy lifestyle is to identify what you want to improve. Decide what you want to change and take small steps toward doing so. Make small changes, be mindful, and acknowledge your successes, no matter how big or small.

Making those small changes stick is a matter of habit, not willpower. Think of habits as building blocks for creating a healthy lifestyle. I recommend using the Fogg Method, which was developed by BJ Fogg, a behavioral psychologist at Stanford University. His systematic approach involves three steps:

1. **Get specific:** What behavior do you want? Translate target outcomes and goals into specific behaviors.
2. **Make it easy:** How can you make the behavior easy to do? Simplicity changes behavior.
3. **Trigger the behavior:** What will prompt the behavior? Some triggers are natural, and others you must design. No behavior happens without a trigger.

For example, my client Mark created a new habit of acknowledging the good in his life by first determining that he wanted to be mindful of the new and good on a daily basis. We made this easy by highlighting only one new and good thing per day. The daily trigger behavior for him was brushing his teeth. Every day after he brushed his teeth, he wrote down something new and good.

Of course, some habits are more powerful than others. In his book *The Power of Habit*, Charles Duhigg writes about what he calls "keystone habits." Such habits spark "chain reactions that help other good habits take hold."

All areas of life are interconnected. Choosing one keystone habit and improving one area in your life can create a ripple effect and generate positive outcomes in other areas. When another client changed his sleep habits, for example, this increased his energy to the point where he felt motivated enough to start going to the gym, which in turn improved his engagement and outlook at work and at home. He became happier and more patient with his colleagues and his wife.

Lastly, avoid an all-or-nothing mindset when you reach a new hurdle. Do not get stuck in the "failure" frame of mind. Instead, pause, hit the reset button, breathe, and choose to focus on progress, not perfection.

Another client, Jessica, worked for a global Fortune 500 company, and she had difficulty sticking to an exercise routine due to her demanding travel schedule. Even when she made time to go to the gym, she fell into the all-or-nothing mindset. If she felt too tired to put in a full workout, she would skip the gym altogether. I encouraged her to self-authorize to exercise for a minimum of fifteen minutes, which was better than skipping the gym entirely. The smaller commitment felt more attainable to her, and allowing herself to compromise helped get her to the gym in the first place, which was the hardest part and a victory in itself. Once there, her fifteen minutes usually turned into forty-five minutes.

Taking the minimum approach helped her achieve more and upgraded her mindset.

Like a snowball rolling down a hill, a new habit may start small. Over time it gathers force and momentum and helps to transform an unhealthy lifestyle into a healthy one. I have seen this snowball effect countless times, both in my own life and in the lives of my clients.

When you are on your deathbed, the last thing you will regret is adopting a healthy lifestyle and making a choice to be happy.

It is your responsibility. No one can force you or beg you to adopt a healthy lifestyle.

Pause. This is a big move in and of itself because you must be aware of the need to step back. Here you plant the seed for everything that follows. Stop. Step back. Reassess.

Breathe. Deepen what you started by pausing. Commit fully to the current moment, the here and now. Be present. Focus on your intention.

Choose.

Choose mindfulness.

Choose happiness.

Choose life.

BUSINESS HACKS

Promote a Healthy Lifestyle and Lead by Example

In the corporate world, many employees follow their boss's lead when it comes to striving for career success. It is common to feel the need to arrive before the boss and stay until after they leave.

As a leader, be aware of the messages you are sending, whether intentional or not. If you come in early and stay late, miss dinner with family, or eat lunch at your desk while working, you may unintentionally be a prominent source of stress for employees and colleagues who feel obligated to follow suit.

Recognize both the productivity trap and the wellness gap among your peers and employees. Then make a conscious choice to lead by example, promoting mindfulness and a healthy lifestyle.

- Take breaks.
- Engage often with your colleagues and employees.
- Refrain from eating at your desk.
- Avoid working excessive hours.
- Be involved with your company's wellness program.

Leaders are responsible for modeling a healthy workplace culture. When you commit to one or all of the above, you will notice a positive ripple in other areas in your life and in the lives of your employees.

Encourage Employees to Be Active During the Workday

As a leader in your workplace, communicate and demonstrate to employees that it is acceptable to take a midday break to hit the gym, even if it is over lunch. When employees understand they will not be scrutinized for leaving their workspaces, they will be more likely to find time for a workout.

A burst of physical activity in the middle of the day helps people return to work energized, happier, and more engaged. This is a win-win, beneficial for the well-being of both employees and the business.

A growing body of evidence finds that "sitting is the new smoking." James Levine, an endocrinologist at the Mayo Clinic, stresses that excessive sitting is not something you can correct later with a workout. Too much time in the chair actually shuts down parts of our metabolism. The key is to keep moving during the workday. Standing or treadmill desks are ideal, but even standing up during a phone call or walking down the hall to see a colleague will keep that metabolic switch from shutting down.

Nourish Mindfully

As appropriate for your role, do what you can to foster healthier food in your workplace, which provides everyone with the fuel to be more effective and productive.

- Keep break rooms and kitchens stocked with healthy snacks, such as fruit, vegetables, yogurt, and nuts (instead of soda, candy, donuts, and cupcakes).
- Replace junk-food vending machines with wholesome options.
- Provide healthy choices for company meetings, parties, and events.

Restrict After-Hours Communication

Some companies restrict emails or work calls between 7 PM and 7 AM as an opportunity to disconnect from work. This is a cherished time (or what some male clients call their "man-cave time"). We need these twelve hours to effectively decompress, recover, relax, and not think about work.

A new French law bans work emails after hours to prevent burnout. Workers and employers agree that this practice has long-term benefits. Companies such as Volkswagen, BMW, and Puma have also enacted policies and procedures to safeguard employees' time off. Harvard Business School professor Leslie A. Perlow has extensively studied the benefits of what she calls "predictable time off." Companies that commit to allowing employees to "turn off" report higher job satisfaction and retention rates. The conversations required to make that time off a reality, moreover, foster greater team communication and cohesiveness.

New company policies can be implemented in a number of ways, including shutting down email servers between certain hours and ceasing the forwarding of emails to employees' phones after their workday has ended. Exceptions can be permitted under exceptional circumstances. For global companies doing business in different time zones, allowing flexible hours is another option.

Implement Stress Management and Resilience-Building Workshops

Stress is a natural and inevitable part of life. It has also been called the health epidemic of the twenty-first century, linked to the six leading causes of death. The dire consequences of stress are what lead to karoshi.

We all experience different levels of stress and at varying frequencies. If we are not resilient, this can take a toll on our health, as well as on our effectiveness as a leader, colleague, friend, partner, or parent. We are not the only ones who are affected by our own stress.

This is why stress management is imperative. Using stress-management tools, or attending resilience-building workshops, we can bolster our total well-being, quality of life, and longevity. Learning how to be resilient and deal effectively with stress helps us, and others, become more productive, happy, healthy, mindful, engaged, and in control.

ACTION STEPS

Take Small Steps for Sustainable Change

Any significant change you want to make in your life starts with the smallest efforts. Take a moment to come up with a manageable plan of small first steps.

1. Identify and specify what you want to improve. Convert your goal into a behavior.
2. Start making a small change that you can easily achieve.
3. Determine what reminder or behavior will trigger your new habit every day.
4. Be mindful of your successes, no matter how small or big.
5. Be mindful of hurdles, and refrain from adopting a "failure" mindset or an all-or-nothing mindset.
6. When you hit a hurdle, revise your approach (starting with a small step), so you can get back on track.

Eat "Real" Food

Michael Pollan, author of *The Omnivore's Dilemma*, and a former professor of mine, summarizes the easiest way to remember to eat healthily in seven words: "Eat food, not too much, mostly plants."

- Eat when you are hungry and stop when you are not (approximately 70 to 80 percent full).
- Drink plenty of water.
- Shop the perimeter of your grocery store where all the fresh food is located. Eat mostly short shelf-life foods instead of long shelf-life foods.
- Avoid food products containing ingredients you would not keep in your pantry or that a child cannot pronounce.
- Treat treats as treats or follow the "No S" diet: No snacks. No sweets. No seconds. Except on days that start with S — Saturdays, Sundays, and special days.
- Eat mindfully by savoring each bite, trying to identify every ingredient, and chewing properly (thirty chews per bite).

- Pay attention to which foods give you energy and make you feel light and good versus those that deplete your energy and make you feel heavy and lethargic.
- Eat slowly and enjoy meals at a table with other people as often as possible.

Pause. Breathe. Move.

Regular physical activity helps you live longer (lowering the risk of premature death by up to 30 percent) and prevents many chronic illnesses. It helps reduce stress, anxiety, and depression, and it can significantly improve your mood, energy, creativity, memory, learning ability, sleep quality, and so much more.

Choose to incorporate physical activity into your everyday routine. In addition to working out at the gym, taking fitness classes, or playing your favorite sport, there are informal ways to add mindful movement throughout the day.

- Take the stairs instead of using the escalator or elevator. Start small if the distance is far and use the stairs for part of the way.
- Park farther away or get off the subway a stop early and enjoy the short walk to your destination.
- Walk over to your colleague's desk instead of sending them an email.
- Stand and flex. When standing or waiting in line, flex your abs for ten seconds, release, and repeat. Do calf raises while brushing your teeth.
- Use two reusable bags to carry your groceries instead of a shopping cart.

Schedule Your Workouts

Mark your calendar and set up reminders to avoid sacrificing self-care. Every Sunday night, I go through my fitness club's app schedule and add all of my favorite classes for the week into my calendar.

Refrain from thinking you do not have enough time, which is a limiting belief. We all have the same number of hours in the day, yet for some people working out is a must and for others it is a should. Change your shoulds to musts. There is always time if you shift your belief and prioritize exercise. Allocate this time with the same importance as a business meeting or any other high-priority obligation.

Use the Upgrade Method

Make mindful choices. Upgrade something, your mindset or your behavior, or both. Raise yourself to a higher standard.

For example, if you want to cut back or stop eating ice cream, upgrade to a healthier option, such as Greek yogurt with fruit and honey. This behavioral upgrade is a step toward a healthier lifestyle.

An example of an upgraded mindset would be to choose to focus on the positives of a situation instead of the negatives.

It is often more effective to find a healthier upgrade for something rather than to cut it out completely.

Promote Clarity of Thinking with Humming Meditation

I learned humming meditation while in India. It is said to promote brain circulation, energy, and clarity. Studies show that humming can help protect against sinus infections. Here are the steps to the practice:

1. Close your eyes, straighten your neck and spine, drop your shoulders, and relax. (Optional: Block your ears with your thumbs while covering your eyes with your fingers.) Lightly touch your lips together, so your hum travels easily into your head, face, and neck muscles.
2. Take in a deep, slow breath, and then create an "mmm" sound upon your exhale, keeping your lips closed. Continue to hum while you exhale. You can make it musical if you like. Traditionally, however, it is more about the tone than the tune. Be aware of the vibration and how you feel.
3. Renew your breath, then continue. Start with one minute of this exercise and increase over time to fifteen minutes.
4. Yogic and Tibetan wisdom puts weight on the importance of sitting still for a few minutes after your humming meditation.

The benefits of practicing humming meditation include the following:

- Dissolves unproductive thinking
- Decreases negative thoughts
- Promotes clarity
- Helps protect against sinus infections

Notice the shift in your thinking and the refreshing feeling in your mind as you feel the vibration of the hum, as if it is physically clearing obstacles, allowing your prana to flow. This meditation also has a soothing effect on your neck, face, and shoulder muscles, relieving you of tension and stress.

- Adopting a healthy lifestyle is a matter of life and death. Living on autopilot is an invitation to disease and premature death. We can choose to prevent premature death by making better lifestyle choices.

- Dying from complications arising from working excessive hours is so common that the Japanese have coined a word for it. However, karoshi ("death by overwork") happens not just in Japan, but all over the world. In a culture where putting in more hours than necessary is used to gauge productivity, working hard (not smart) is deemed necessary. This is counterproductive, both for the business and for its people.

- Overwork may seem at first like the path to productivity and success, but a more efficient and healthier path is through mindfulness. Modeling good health makes us more valuable and better leaders. Employers should also demonstrate a level of responsibility in taking care of their people. There is a mutual benefit because individual well-being translates into collective profitability.

- Productivity without awareness creates a wellness gap that will spread, infecting the business like a cancerous growth. This can be treated by shifting from a quantity paradigm to a quality paradigm.

- We all have our own version of a 3 PM autopilot junkie story. Awareness of our toxic behavior is the first step toward taking action to self-correct.

- Healthy habits are the building blocks of a healthy lifestyle. Start small and stay consistent, and the effects of those new habits will snowball over time.

CHAPTER FOUR

ALLOCATE PLAY AND RECOVERY TIME

THE SEVEN A's

Adopt

ALLOCATE

Avoid

Alter

Adapt

Accept

Attend

Are you waiting for the happiness fairy to appear? Do not hold your breath.

It is up to us to make the lifestyle choices that lead to joy and creativity as part of our self-care. In our work lives, we often face an overload of decisions to make and fires to extinguish every day. Such heavy mental work taxes our reserves. In order to be a visionary CEO, we must reboot daily to function optimally.

We reboot through a combination of play and recovery, which constitutes the second of the Seven A's. These two overlapping, fundamental, and interrelated activities give our brains a break, a chance to recharge and reset.

Play is its own kind of recovery. It is an opportunity for our brain to switch from a highly focused, goal-oriented, and often pressurized mode to one that revels in the moment, free of pressure and expectations.

Recovery is, first and foremost, rest. Sleep is the most intensive form of recovery, but recovery goes beyond rest and sleep. It encompasses downtime, inactivity, and what may appear to be mere idleness but is in fact so much more.

Sacrificing play and recovery hinders optimal functioning. Performing at less than our best has a cumulative effect. At some point, our vision of our most productive and fulfilled Self begins to fade from view.

Many people already know that they should allocate play and recovery time for the sake of their well-being and happiness. However, most people do not practice what they know.

Allocating time for play and recovery within your daily routine, both at work and outside of work, will bring clarity, release your creativity, and allow you to live your life free and unencumbered.

We were born to play. It is in our nature, and we see it in children every day. Play is how our creativity and joy come forward, and it is how we learn.

Why do we stop playing when we are older?

As children, before computer tablets and video games take over, what do we do? We scrape our knees falling off a bike. We have to be called inside after dark because we lose track of time. We run around with friends and get into trouble.

When we are young, much of our life is about being social, moving, playing, and exploring. We interact and play with others and get our blood pumping. We are alive! Why then, as adults, should we miss out on this? Why play, move, and interact less?

We close ourselves up in an office to focus; we sit for hours at a time and consider ourselves lucky if we get to the gym twice a week. We are regimented around the clock. We allow routine and societal norms to shape our thoughts and behaviors and tell ourselves that play is only for children.

My clients often say, when referring to recovery and play, "Oh, that would be nice, but I don't have time," or, "Ahh, that would be the day!" Play and recovery should not be treated as a luxury. We can always make room for it, even if it entails just spending time with our family before bedtime.

Make play part of your schedule because it is a necessity. It should be part of your own individual game plan and part of your company's culture.

The same holds true for recovery. Part of adopting a healthy lifestyle involves taking breaks from work, such as to exercise or to stand up and stretch. This is a good start, but recovery should also include downtime, which is indispensable. This is part of fighting against the productivity trap that leads to karoshi. Downtime acknowledges that there is more to life than working hard and completing our to-do list.

Play represents freedom, yet many of us choose to sacrifice that freedom. Play is being carefree, having fun, not worrying about the past or the future, not wondering about tasks undone and boxes unchecked. Incorporate play into your life, whether you take an hour to paint, play tennis, read, learn something new, or go for a hike.

Allocate sufficient downtime, and do not fall into the trap of equating it with idleness. You are allowing your brain (and your vital energy, or prana) to recharge. Recovery should be part of your strategy to work smarter, not harder.

Take the time to be present and engaged with your Self and with others. If you make time for play and recovery, you will develop the habit of experiencing more joy and creativity, so that life does not feel like it is passing you by.

You will foster the childlike ability to see possibilities, opportunities, and solutions with a beginner's mind. You will experience rejuvenation, creativity, and most of all clarity. The things you perceive as problems, the ones that keep you up at night, will cease plaguing you. Instead, you will see the same problems as challenges and opportunities. You will become more productive and efficient. In the absence of stress, fear, and fatigue, your mind will arrive at creative solutions to whatever challenges you face.

The Secret to Staying Young

Sleep is how we recover daily, and it is not a luxury, no matter how busy we are. Think of sleep as your nightly pause, a chance to breathe and reboot. If you have a problem, or a tough decision, sleep on it. Proper rest will refresh your mind and enable it to function at its best. Give your subconscious mind a break, so that your mind can wake up to a clean slate and make mindful decisions.

People often talk about how little sleep they get with a hint of pride in their voice. They say things like, "I really only need four or five hours of sleep per night." A lack of sleep is neither a source of pride nor a badge of honor. It is certainly not sustainable. It compromises our well-being and our effectiveness as leaders.

Working with insufficient sleep is like working drunk. One study found that after participants were awake for more than seventeen to nineteen hours, their performance declined to that of someone with a blood-alcohol content equivalent or worse than that of .05 percent (while .08 percent is the maximum allowed to legally operate a motor vehicle). If you do not sleep enough or well, your thinking will be impaired, your energy will be depleted, and your prana will be blocked. You will make mistakes and function poorly, harming personal performance and business outcomes. As these impacts accumulate, you will eventually crash and burn.

Researchers for the *Harvard Business Review* found a link between adequate sleep and effective leadership. They pointed out that the four most common leadership behaviors of high-performing teams were all hindered by a lack of sleep. Another study found that sleep disturbances and exhaustion resulted in productivity losses that amounted to a cost of $1,967 per employee annually. Similar research by *Virgin Pulse* found that 40 percent of people admitted to dozing off during work at least once a month.

Well-rested people make supercharged employees. They have better memory, make smarter decisions, are more engaged, and are less likely to make serious and potentially dangerous mistakes.

Not all sleep is the same. What we need is restorative sleep that includes REM (rapid eye movement) sleep — the metaphorical equivalent of charging your battery. The brain can function optimally for a maximum of sixteen hours before it needs to go offline and sleep. Exceeding this limit results in sleep deprivation, when the brain's networks start to break down and become dysfunctional.

How do you know if you have had restorative sleep? Dr. Matthew Walker — a renowned neuroscientist and psychologist with whom I worked at the University of California at Berkeley and author of *Why We Sleep* — suggests asking yourself the following question:

Can you wake up without an alarm clock feeling refreshed and not needing caffeine or other stimulants to function for the rest of the day?

If you can answer yes to this question, congratulations! You are getting restorative sleep. According to Dr. Walker, restorative sleep can improve your mental clarity, creativity, mood, performance, immunity, and even aid in weight loss. Sleep is the single most effective thing you can do to reset your brain and body health each day.

Of course, as I discuss in chapter 3, food is also important for maintaining well-being and operating at full capacity. The types and the quantity of food you eat play a vital role in your cognitive abilities, daily energy levels, and overall health. If you do not take care of yourself, you are going to end up sick or on what I call "the most expensive bed in the world" — a hospital bed.

What will you choose: restorative sleep in your own bed or sleepless nights in the world's most expensive bed? As one anonymous aphorism puts it: "A healthy person has a thousand wishes, a sick person only one."

You cannot be open to possibility when you are not taking care of yourself. To avoid burnout, make a choice to infuse your routine with recovery and play, but the secret to staying young starts with restorative sleep: This allows your Self to be present, curious, and well-rested, just as you were as a child.

The Power of Downtime

Boredom can be an important source of creativity. This is just one of many instances of how the brain thrives on downtime and craves the opportunity to recover, recharge, reset, and reboot.

Interestingly, insight into the importance of downtime has its roots in the work of early sleep-research pioneers. Until the discovery of REM sleep, it was assumed that sleep was mostly a passive activity. Now we know the REM state is so important it has been dubbed a "third state of being."

These same researchers found that our sleep cycles are part of a larger "rest-activity cycle" that extends to our waking hours. The human brain thrives on a rhythm where we alternate between effort and recovery, focus and unfocus.

As essayist Tim Kreider wrote in the *New York Times*: "Idleness is not just a vacation, an indulgence, or a vice. It is as indispensable to the brain as vitamin D is to the body." Idleness is an essential form of recovery.

What might be seen as idleness or daydreaming is what researchers call our brain's *default mode network* (or DMN). Scientists used to dismiss DMN as a "doing mostly nothing" state, but now we realize that, just like our REM state during sleep, our brains are highly active and perform critical restorative functions during these periods. The DMN is especially active in the most creative people.

In other words, we operate best when we allow ourselves to alternate between periods of highly structured focus and more unstructured periods of recovery, rest, and downtime. (Chapter 11 discusses focus and flow in more detail.)

Playful Entrepreneurship

While working at Apple, I quickly discovered what playtime looked like for Steve Jobs, and how it was one of the keys to his success as a great innovator. Whenever someone was looking for Steve, or whenever he could not be reached on the phone, there was only one place he would almost unerringly be found: in the office of Jony Ive, Apple's former chief design officer.

In Jony's studio, Steve relished brainstorming and playing with Apple's prototype products, or his "toys," as he called them. If he could have, he would have spent his entire week playing with his toys.

Steve would turn off his phone whenever he was with Jony. We would lose our minds trying to get in touch with him, trying to get him to his meetings. At some point, we would have to call Jony's office and enlist his help in dragging Steve away from his playtime.

Steve's playtime occurred inside the office, but it still gave him high energy because it was outside his day-to-day operations and executive responsibilities. His time with Jony gave him the space and occasion to laugh, imagine, create, and feel a renewed sense of freedom.

Entrepreneurs, innovators, and leaders know that work itself can often be a type of play. Creating a culture of learning can inject a sense of play into the workplace, which results in happy, healthy, and engaged employees. My wellness programs include a variety of fun impromptu challenges (such as, gratitude, habit building, or wall sitting challenges).

While it is desirable to incorporate play into our workdays, play outside of work is just as essential. We need time to unplug. Play in the workplace has an objective in mind; outside of work, play is its own objective, its own reward.

Whether you go to a park with your children or go for a run, play means getting away from stressful environments and getting away from work, even if you are fortunate enough to have fun at your job.

I had a client named Jake who was the CEO at a Fortune 500 company and sat on the boards of two other companies. He was going through an ugly divorce, working long hours, and sleeping poorly. This caused him to wake up in the middle of the night with panic attacks. His stress levels were high, and he was on the verge of burnout. He was making poor decisions; he felt isolated and was lacking support and accountability.

I started Jake on a basic mindfulness program: Since he had minimal experience with meditation, we began with two minutes per day and gradually increased the time. His mindfulness practice allowed him to pause and realize that he needed to make big changes in his life. We worked on making exercise (he preferred tennis and cycling) a regular, scheduled part of his weekly routine. Combined with sleep hygiene tools (see this chapter's Action Steps), these small mindful habits produced dramatic results over time. I worked with him on other things as well, but allocating play and recovery helped make those other changes possible.

Do you allocate play and recovery time, get restorative sleep, and eat mindfully? What do you do to feel rejuvenated, to rest and reboot, to play? How do you tap into your creativity in order to gain new perspectives, new ways of thinking, and new ways to solve problems? Finally, what new things might you start doing to foster a spirit of play?

Creativity is clarity, and it only comes if we truly allow our Self the play and recovery time necessary to be the CEO of our well-being. We were born to let joy and rejuvenation flow through us. We should not live life exhausted and stressed.

We were born to play.

New Heights, New Perspectives

One of my favorite photos of myself was taken in Yosemite National Park. I am doing a backbend on the "diving board" of Half Dome during a much-needed weekend getaway with my then-boyfriend. I was working in pharmaceutical sales and needed the time away from my run-of-the-mill daily grind.

We took our time climbing to the top of Half Dome, reveling in nature. There was no point in rushing. It was not a race, and the climb was not intended to be exercise. Our only objectives were to have fun, recover from work stress, connect with nature, and connect with each other.

When we finally reached the top of the mountain, I looked across the landscape and suddenly felt so light. I found myself in awe of Mother Nature's beauty. I was at 8,600 feet and felt a sudden playful inspiration to do a backbend in one of the most beautiful places in the world so that I could see it from a different perspective, from the bottom up.

Fear of judgment, all my stress, exhaustion, and frustrations — these feelings all escaped me. I lost any sense of time. I felt strong, accomplished, connected, and a deep sense of gratitude in my backbend, breathing the fresh air, at the top of the mountain. I anchored this feeling by being fully present to it.

After returning home, I consciously incorporated that strong mountaintop feeling into my everyday life. The photo was and still is a constant reminder. I was revived, ready to hit the ground running. Unplugging gave me the chance to reconnect with my Self, my partner, and nature. I allowed space to open up in my mind, generating greater clarity and creativity. I worked fewer hours more productively, breaking sales records in a challenging market. I was laser-focused and monotasked instead of multitasked, and I was better able to handle daily stresses.

Whatever you do for play and recovery, the goals are the same. Instead of connecting with nature or practicing yoga, you may prefer watching a film or calling and connecting with a loved one. The key is making this kind of activity a part of your must-do list that cannot be ignored.

I had a client who used to take guitar lessons but stopped because it was no longer a "priority." I encouraged him to once again make time for an activity that gave him great joy, and this created ripple effects in his life. The point was not to become a great guitarist but to use music to rejuvenate. I help clients reframe playful activities so they see them as equally important as a big meeting at work.

As human beings, we can only focus on so much. The thinner we spread ourselves, the harder it is to be creative and to perform at the top of our game.

Take a pause. Take a breath and reset. Take time for yourself, and for passions or hobbies independent of work.

If you do those things, you will be open to creativity, productivity, and clarity. You can take your life, both professional and personal, into your own hands. At the same time, you are modeling mindful rest and play for your colleagues and employees, which will hopefully encourage them to incorporate more play and activities that promote recovery time.

Play and Learn at Work

Happy and healthy employees are more energized and engaged, which leads to improvement in job performance and better business outcomes. Employees who say they have supportive superiors are 1.3 times more likely to stay with a company and are 67 percent more engaged.

Fostering a culture of learning in the workplace goes a long way toward creating that kind of engagement, and learning and play go hand-in-hand in this effort. Just like play, learning is about staying connected to our creative Self and not slipping into autopilot.

The concept of the "learning organization" was introduced by Peter Senge in the 1990s. More recently, Harvard Business School professor Amy Edmondson has written extensively about the building blocks of a culture of learning, and she stresses some of the same things I focus on in my wellness programs.

Edmondson writes about creating time for reflection: "When people are too busy or overstressed by deadlines and scheduling pressures, their ability to think analytically and creatively is compromised. Supportive learning environments allow time for a pause in the action." Mindfulness, learning, and wellness should all be part of an integrated approach.

A learning organization provides employees with resources to build new skills: This includes not just workshops, classes, and seminars but ongoing coaching and mentoring. This kind of investment in employees pays off in the long run by enhancing the ability to attract and retain top talent.

Finally, a learning organization gives employees the freedom to play with new ideas: to take chances and explore out-of-the-box possibilities. Google pioneered the 20% Project; this allows employees to spend up to 20 percent of their time on pet projects. That spirit of freedom and play has since been taken up by other companies. LinkedIn has [in]cubator, Apple has Blue Sky, and Microsoft has the Garage.

What all share is the idea of encouraging employees to adopt an entrepreneurial spirit and to think like their own startup. This empowers employees to be more creative and innovative while having fun.

According to a *Virgin Pulse* survey, new employees are thirty times more likely to leave if they do not believe they can realize their career goal, and 53 percent of employees say the top reason they love their company is because of interesting, challenging work.

Learning and growing are as essential to well-being as exercise, sleep, and nutrition. The more time a person spends learning something new, the better their cognitive function and overall mental well-being.

Invest in employees, and they will treat the company well. This helps propel any business to new heights, uncovering new opportunities for growth, innovation, talent, and success in a market that might otherwise be prone to the productivity trap.

Richard Branson, founder of the Virgin Group, business magnate, investor, and philanthropist, spoke to *Inc.* magazine about the win-win situation of customer, employee, and company health and happiness.

> If the person who works at your company is 100% proud of the job they're doing, if you give them the tools to do a good job, they're proud of the brand. If they were looked after, if they're treated well, then they're gonna be smiling, they're gonna be happy, and therefore the customer will have a nice experience. If the person who's working for your company is not given the right tools, is not looked after, is not appreciated, they're not gonna do things with a smile, and therefore the customer will be treated in a way where often they won't want to come back for more. So, my philosophy has always been, if you can put staff first, your customer second, and shareholders third, effectively, in the end, the shareholders do well, the customers do better, and you yourself are happy.

When employees are treated with respect and are supported to actualize their goals, even those goals outside the workplace, they will be happier and more engaged, and subsequently, they will perform better. The business will thrive as a result.

It all starts with you. How will you choose to go about your day? How will you reboot your mind, body, and creativity? Simple. Make it a priority. Treat these nonnegotiables as you would treat important meetings.

Pause.

Breathe.

Choose to allocate play and recovery time in your day.

BUSINESS HACKS

Learn Something New

If you run a business or manage others, implement an initiative to allow employees time to work on new and different projects to expand their horizons and creativity. Provide them with meaningful assignments and opportunities to develop themselves further through seminars and developmental skill workshops.

Seek to understand the goals of employees. Encourage them through open communication and support and by showing genuine interest in their lives. Make an effort to ask individuals if they have any career or personal goals they want to share with you, without pressuring them into doing so. Ask: "How can I support you or make adjustments that would help you achieve your goals?" This allows the employee to take ownership of the solution.

Take sincere responsibility and follow up. Just as with professional goals, personal goals can contribute to your team or to the company. Allowing employees the freedom and opportunity to pursue their personal growth results in increased happiness, creativity, and work performance.

Give employees "well days" or "exploratory days." Designate a certain number of hours per week or per month at work to explore non-work-related interests and learning opportunities.

Read Voraciously: Leaders Are Readers

Leaders need loads of general information to keep perspective and seize opportunities, and reading is one of the most efficient and effective ways to acquire information. Reading does more than give us a toolbox of ideas. It upgrades our analytical abilities, especially our judgment and problem-solving skills. Improving focus, youthfulness, and relaxation, reading can reduce stress levels by 68 percent, according to research conducted by the University of Sussex. That is more relaxation than listening to music or taking a walk.

Create a "read" file or bookmark articles you receive or come across. Dedicate time each day to increasing your knowledge. Share articles and books with colleagues or your team.

During lunch, once a month, create a workplace book club. Encourage discussion of industry-related topics or personal development books. Enlist different volunteers to lead discussions and encourage everyone to speak up. It is a great opportunity to share ideas and sharpen analytical skills and for team connectedness.

Being a serious reader is an effective way to develop essential leadership insights and qualities. If you want to lead, you must read.

Walk and Talk

For meetings, avoid boring conference rooms if possible. Research finds that walking meetings increase creative thinking and productivity when compared with traditional sit-down meetings. A maximum of three people for a walking meeting is recommended. To record what is said, use the audio notes feature or the voice memo application on your phone.

I first experienced walking meetings during my time working alongside Steve Jobs at Apple. He loved to walk while discussing crucial matters. Walking is playful by nature. Get the body moving, and you will get the creative juices flowing as well. Walking also helps us to recover from long stretches of sitting.

Spend Time in Nature

Organize soccer or softball leagues, or even something as simple as a company picnic. It is no new concept that humans are healthier, both emotionally and psychologically, when we spend time in nature. The connections made outside of work will result in higher productivity and happiness at work.

Provide Flexible Work Schedules and Generous Paid Time Off

To help employees avoid burnout, employers should provide flexible work schedules and ample time off to reduce stress when employees feel a need. Your employees' stress may not necessarily be work-related. They may be juggling other life responsibilities at the same time. As a result, your employees will keep stress levels low and efficiency levels high.

ACTION STEPS

Practice Good Sleep Hygiene

Healthy sleep habits promote healthy sleep so that you can perform at your best and be at your best.

- Maintain a consistent sleep schedule. Rise and retire at the same time each day. Make this your routine, even on days you are not working. This is the single most effective habit if you choose only one way to improve your sleep.
- Never sacrifice sleep. Make sure you sleep for a minimum of seven hours, but eight hours per night is the recommended average.
- Establish a relaxing bedtime routine to unwind and prepare your mind and body for sleep. Practice relaxation techniques such as meditating, stretching, reading, writing in a journal, taking a hot shower or bath, or anything that takes your mind off the stresses of the day before you lay down.
- Limit light exposure at least thirty minutes before bedtime to help regulate your sleep cycle. This includes televisions, phones, tablets, e-readers, laptops, and gaming devices. The blue light emitted from these devices is similar in wavelength to daylight and can trick your circadian rhythm, delaying the release of melatonin, a hormone that promotes sleep.
- Avoid large meals shortly before going to bed. Eat earlier in the evening, and if you are hungry before bedtime, limit your-self to a light snack. Your body will not only expend energy digesting overnight instead of restoring itself, it will not di-gest as properly while lying horizontally.
- Exercise regularly during the day and not close to bedtime.
- Reduce fluid intake and avoid alcohol before bedtime.
- Refrain from working in bed. Your bed should only be used for sleep and sex.
- Do not go to bed unless you feel sleepy. If you do not fall asleep after twenty minutes, or you fall asleep and then wake up and cannot fall back asleep after twenty minutes, get out of bed. Avoid associating your bed with wakefulness instead

of sleep. Go into another room and do something relaxing or listen to meditation music or binaural beats for sleep.

- Ensure that your bedroom is conducive for healthy sleep. It should be quiet, dark, comfortable, and cool (65–67 degrees). Additionally, it should be an electronics-free zone.
- Keep your alarm across the room, and preferably use a clock, as opposed to your phone's alarm. Having your phone close to your bed makes it too easy to check your email as soon as you wake up or before going to sleep. Doing so creates unnecessary anxiety. Placing your alarm clock out of reach also forces you to get up on time, thereby breaking the habit of hitting the snooze button.

Play in Your Sleep

Explore your imagination during sleep. We all dream, but not all of us remember our dreams. For high-frequency dreamers who can recall their dreams at least once per night, analyze your dreams to spur new creative channels. If you would like to remember your dreams better or more often, tell yourself before going to bed: *I am choosing to recall my dreams tonight.* Be intentional. Keep a journal and pen beside your bed to write your dreams down as soon as you wake up. Many artists such as Salvador Dalí and Vincent van Gogh have credited bursts of creativity from their dream state. Diving down into your unconscious in your sleep state can provide fresh new material that is naturally more visual and intuitive. On the flip side, when you try to come up with something during your waking state, it usually comes from your thinking mind, which often regurgitates previously processed, known material. Try it tonight.

Schedule Personal Time into Your Calendar

Allocating personal time for recovery and play is a vital way you can care for yourself. Schedule that time in your calendar, just like work meetings. Note time with your partner, family, and friends; mark time for yoga or boxing classes, meditating, biking, hiking, running, or reading. Hold space for free time. If that time is not set aside in your calendar, if you do not see it regularly, it is easy to skip it or forget it. Out of sight is out of mind. If meetings are important enough to go into your calendar, so are you.

- Playtime is an opportunity for your brain to switch from a highly focused, goal-oriented, and often pressurized mode to one that revels in the moment, free of pressure and expectations and without worry about the past or future.
- Making time for play is essential for clarity and creativity. In turn, play enables you to see solutions to problems that have been looming over you. Equally important, play is fun!
- Recovery goes beyond rest and sleep to include a range of downtime activities critical to restoring your brain and energy reserves.
- The secret to staying young starts with adequate sleep, allowing your Self to be present, curious, and well-rested, just as you were as a child. You were born to play and let joy and rejuvenation flow through you. Allocating play and recovery time in your adult life is necessary to live your best life.
- Sleep is a daily way to recover. Getting seven to nine hours of sleep is equivalent to rebooting your brain. Restorative sleep results in improved mental clarity, creativity, performance, mood, immunity, and weight loss.
- A learning organization provides employees with resources to build new skills. Invest in employees and they will treat the company well. When employees are treated with respect and are supported to actualize their goals, even those goals outside the workplace, they will be happier and more engaged, and subsequently, they will perform better. The business will thrive as a result.

CHAPTER FIVE

AVOID UNNECESSARY STRESS

THE SEVEN A's

Adopt

Allocate

AVOID

Alter

Adapt

Accept

Attend

Does stress cloud your mind and impair your judgment, making you see the different departments of your life through a distorted fun-house mirror?

Working with leaders from small startups to large global companies, I find the same story is true for everyone. Managing stress is a daily reality. Decision-making is constant. You wear many hats, each with its own pressures and responsibilities. What happens when your clarity and creativity, your ability to make good decisions, become blocked by stress? You learn how to tap into good stress and avoid bad, unnecessary stress by using what I call the *ACE Method*.

Avoiding unnecessary stress, the third of the Seven A's, does not mean disregarding or downplaying the stresses you experience. It also does not mean avoiding the symptoms of stress (in fact, quite the opposite). Finally, it is not about getting stuck in a negative or fearful attitude toward stress.

Avoiding unnecessary stress includes one or all of the following strategies:

- Clearly distinguishing between productive stress and unproductive stress.
- Embracing productive stress and putting it to work for you, and when possible, converting unproductive stress to productive stress with a mindset upgrade.
- Mitigating unhealthy stress by avoiding stressful situations and the vampires who suck your energy. If you cannot avoid a particular situation or person, let their presence teach you patience and compassion. Stressful people and situations can also be our teachers.
- Separating what you can control from what you cannot control and letting go of the latter.
- Cultivating a culture of wellness in the workplace and leading by example as the CEO of your well-being. This serves as a kind of protective shield for the inevitable stresses that we all must confront.

Unnecessary stress clouds our mind and judgment, hindering us from making the right decisions for ourselves, our relationships, our career, our finances, and so on. One wrong decision can lead to another, creating a potentially catastrophic domino effect.

In the end, we can find ourselves standing amid chaos, scratching our head and wondering where it all went wrong. Avoid that situation. Cultivate a state of clarity and creativity before making a decision. Pause. Breathe.

Having a clear and sharp mind lets you see the bigger picture and the consequences of each choice. Choose to self-direct, and by anticipating and preventing future stress, save yourself the trouble of picking up the fallen dominoes.

ACE Stress Using the ACE Method

If you do not experience any stress, you are dead. Stress is inevitable and a natural part of life. Stress can fuel us in high-stakes situations, and it can save our life during a crisis. Let us take a closer look at stress — at what it does to our mind and body, and when it can and cannot be channeled productively. It is critical to understand that there are three different types of stress: acute stress, chronic stress, and eustress.

Acute stress is *necessary stress*. It is a short-term spike of adrenaline that energizes us to act quickly and decisively in a challenging or threatening situation, like jumping out of the way of a speeding taxi. In the face of a perceived threat, our dominant emotion is often fear: the fight-or-flight response. Acute stress functions as an invaluable survival mechanism. However, if the threat is unremitting, acute stress can turn into chronic stress. If we can reframe the threat or challenge as an opportunity, we can prevent acute stress from spiraling into chronic stress by converting it to *eustress*, the desirable and productive type of stress. To a great extent, how we experience stress is a matter of the mindset we choose to adopt.

Chronic stress is *dangerous stress*. It is often prolonged and characterized by hopelessness, helplessness, and uncertainty. Chronic stress (also known as distress) is unnecessary and can be avoided with an upgraded mindset. Research shows that chronic stress can contribute to the development of major illnesses, such as heart disease, depression, and obesity. It also causes us to unwisely operate on autopilot, preventing us from anticipating stressful situations that could be avoided. It blocks our prana from flowing freely and depletes our energy.

Eustress (pronounced "you-stress") is *desirable stress*. It is the drive that energizes us to reach for fulfillment and success. Eustress is a moment-to-moment experience of well-being as we strive for new heights, giving us the energy to perform effectively. It is a feeling of being in the zone or in the flow. Eustress is a productive tool you can put to good use to increase your focus and fuel peak performance.

When we experience chronic stress, we have fallen into a trap, most likely due to an unresolved, challenging situation. We might feel helpless or hopeless, as though we are looking through a fogged-up lens.

Chronic stress does not have a productive function, like eustress or acute stress. It does not save us by signaling danger; it does not help fuel peak performance. Instead, chronic stress puts our life at risk by manifesting disease. Unchecked, chronic stress can lead to premature death or karoshi: death by overwork.

This is where mindful choice comes into play. For many, continuing to live in chronic stress is a choice, even if we do not make that choice consciously. It is a default choice or a failure to identify options. We are not aware that we have a choice, and so we feel as if a situation is happening to us. We are passive or reactive, instead of being proactive or responsive.

In order to make that mindful choice, we have to see the situation clearly. When people say they are stressed, they are referring to their physical, mental, or emotional response to a demand, threat, or event. They are not referring to the actual demand, threat, or event itself. In other words, they have not identified the stressor itself. Instead, they simply see an overwhelming situation.

The ACE Method is a new way of reframing stress. It is an effective way to upgrade both your mindset and behavior. The ability to distinguish between different kinds of stress (acute, chronic, and eustress, or ACE) allows you to perceive stress as a challenge, rather than an obstacle. Once you understand the type of stress you are facing, you can identify the actual stressors and their source and take empowered action. You can embrace and harness the *desirable stress* and mitigate or avoid the *dangerous stress*.

We ACE (acute, chronic, eustress) stress using the three-step ACE Method through *awareness*, *change*, and *empowerment*.

- **Step 1:** Be aware of the signs and symptoms of the stressor(s). Identify the type (acute, chronic, eustress) and the source of the stress.
- **Step 2:** Change your mindset. Choose to reframe the stress using an upgraded mindset so that you can identify your options or opportunities — both in mindset and behavior.
- **Step 3:** Take empowered and effective action.

The goal is to make the most of the situation by moving between acute stress (necessary stress) and eustress (desirable stress) while choosing to avoid the trap of chronic stress (dangerous stress). See the diagram on the next page.

We always have a choice. What we are feeling and thinking could be acute stress or eustress, which we can use to our advantage. Even when we are already experiencing chronic stress, it is not too late to pivot and change course.

THE ACE METHOD DIAGRAM

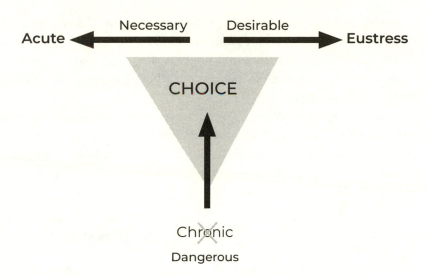

On an organizational level, a strong company culture of wellness that helps employees thrive and lead fulfilling lives empowers them to cope with stress healthfully, mindfully, and proactively.

Signs and Symptoms of Stress

In order to avoid chronic stress, you need to first be aware of and identify the stressors. You will never be able to identify the stressors if you are oblivious to the signs and symptoms of stress. Once you have pinpointed the culprits, only then can you map out the bigger picture and determine the next steps to take.

As a young and excited new employee at Yahoo!, I thought it was a perk to have free access to junk food from vending machines. There was more Cheetos dust in the air than productivity. At that stage of my career, it did not cross my mind that going to happy hour on Thursday nights and showing up to work the next day hungover was not the best idea. My colleagues went out multiple nights per week, making it the norm.

In addition to alcohol and junk food, we are faced with many other kinds of addiction: tobacco, drugs, gambling, video games, sex, shopping, work, and even technology. Reliance on various toxic behaviors can be seen across many organizations in response to unhealthy stress. Sound familiar?

Oftentimes, we do not know we have slipped into chronic stress because it slowly creeps up on us and becomes our new norm. We fall into certain behaviors and habits that might at first be responses to short-term stress. By numbing our perceptions, they blind us to the warning signs of chronic stress.

This is why we sometimes do not recognize we are on the fast track toward rock bottom, which is why chronic stress is considered *dangerous stress*. It is the stress that kills. Take a look at the chart below. If you experience some of these signs and symptoms for a prolonged time, you may have fallen into chronic stress.

Mental	Emotional
• Memory problems • Inability to concentrate • Poor judgment • Constant worry • Anxious or racing thoughts • Shift in mindset, values, beliefs, expectations, goals (either losing them or being unrealistic)	• Feeling down, helpless, and hopeless • Overwhelmed • Irritable (short-tempered), pessimistic, or other changes in attitude or mood • Anxious or agitated • Indecisive
Physical	**Behavioral**
• Change in breath (such as shallow, sighing) • Digestive issues • Aches and pains • Frequent colds and illnesses • Nausea, dizziness, or headaches • Loss of sex drive	• Increase or decrease in appetite • Nervous behavior/habits • Difficulty or irregular sleeping • Excessive use of alcohol, cigarettes, drugs • Defensive and/or overreactive • Withdrawing from others • Feeding your Inner Critic

Knowing that stress has the potential to become chronic is the first step to identifying stressors and learning to avoid them.

Identify Stressors

Once we take the time to be mindful of the effect stress is having, we must then identify the source of that stress: the stressor.

In today's world, stress comes at us from all directions. It can originate in our professional lives, our personal lives, or a combination of the two. The source of stress can be things beyond our control (like traffic) or things within our control (like unhealthy habits). Moreover, the overload of information we are subjected to the moment we power up our smartphones or computers is its own form of stress.

Business leaders and entrepreneurs frequently (if unintentionally) invite stress into their lives. On a daily basis, they make big decisions and take big risks. They are responsible for the livelihood of their employees and are responsible financially to their stockholders or investors. These obligations bring long hours and the challenges of setting and maintaining deadlines, managing a team, and mediating conflict.

What about the other areas of life: relationships, finances, major life changes, or the loss of a loved one? Relationship problems and not having enough time for loved ones can weigh heavily. Just as stressors from work can affect our home life, personal stressors can cross over and affect our work life.

Financial stress is the number-one stressor in the United States, and it includes worries about debt, healthcare costs, and student loans. Based on my experience with clients, one prevalent stress is a lack of time and resources. When you feel pressed for time or money, the immediate reaction might be to compromise other areas of your life. You might pull from time with family, from time for sleep, and from your self-care to make up for not having enough time for work. This will take a heavier toll than you expect, not just in your personal life but also in your professional one.

Leaders are in charge of making the decisions that will impact others and the company. They are responsible for leading others in the right direction. However, whatever your professional role, you will not be able to find the right direction if you are not the CEO of your well-being.

Practicing the first two of the Seven A's — adopting a healthy lifestyle and allocating time for play and recovery — will help you avoid unnecessary stress. Instilling a culture of wellness in your team or company can safeguard them and increase resilience in stressful times (see "Cultivate a Culture of Wellness," page 100).

The success of a company boils down to its people, their well-being, and the ability to perform well, and that includes you.

Break the Cycle

Imagine you are in a meeting with potential investors to raise capital for your company and the conversation takes a turn for the worse. You are keenly aware that your company is on the line, and you believe this meeting is going to either make or break it. Your hands are sweating, your heart is racing, and it feels hard to breathe. You are experiencing acute stress, which is healthy and necessary.

Now let us look at how, if you are not careful, that necessary, in-the-moment stress can turn into chronic stress. Say the meeting does not go well. Afterward, you continue to ruminate over what went wrong, playing it over and over in your head. Further, you feel you have exhausted your options. You have had countless investor meetings to no avail, and now your company is running out of money.

Of course, you do have other options, which is always the case. However, you do not take the time to identify them, you are not thinking clearly enough to see them, or perhaps you are too attached to one desired outcome, blinding your peripheral vision, leaving you with a limited mindset. Instead of directing the energy of your acute stress into decisive action, anxiety takes over. Weeks turn into months and you feel increasingly hopeless and helpless. It becomes challenging to focus on your day-to-day work and decisions. You let what should have been acute and in-the-moment stress become chronic stress by not taking action to self-correct.

As this continues, you unconsciously dig yourself further into a pit of chronic stress. According to the American Psychological Association, stress starts becoming chronic when it begins "interfering with your ability to live a normal life for an extended period." Extended chronic stress is what becomes dangerous.

Do not allow acute stress to become killer chronic stress.

The key is to convert acute stress to eustress using an upgraded mindset. Stress can actually work for you instead of against you. Eustress is the fuel that can keep you at the top of your game when you most need it. You just have to put it to good use.

Putting acute stress to good use means, first and foremost, reframing your stress reaction as positive energy to be harnessed. Studies show that a positive mindset toward a challenging situation changes your hormonal response to it. Ask yourself if you are framing the situation as a threat or as a challenge.

In the hypothetical situation above, an entrepreneur with a negative and limited mindset would view each meeting as a threat and might focus solely on all the things that are going wrong, believing that each investor rejection is lessening their chances for success. However, an entrepreneur who chose a positive, challenge mindset would view each pitch meeting as an opportunity to improve their business, even when an investor says no. Each presentation would be a chance to refine their message, build new relationships, and make a good impression on someone who might recommend this business opportunity to others (or even change their mind and invest in the future).

Take another example: Imagine that a company's profits are declining, its resources are dwindling, layoffs have occurred, and morale is down. As the CEO, you know you must develop a new business strategy to save the company, but you wonder: *Is it already too late?*

The situation may be dire, but it may also be an opportunity. Pain can sometimes be our greatest teacher (which is the focus of chapter 10), and if you avoid falling into debilitating chronic stress, you might be able to identify the solution and opportunities within the substandard situation. This may be an opportunity to make a bold pivot: Perhaps it is time to cut a less-productive division, to invest in research and development, or to reinvent your company altogether.

Once we upgrade our mindset, putting acute stress to good use and converting it to desirable eustress, we are ready to take empowered and effective action.

One of the defining characteristics of anxiety and chronic stress is a sense of not being in control. People who feel this way have what psychologists call an external *locus of control*; they see life as something that happens to them. Someone with an internal locus of control feels in charge of their own life. This is what being the CEO of your well-being means.

You can regain a sense of control by being proactive, rather than passive or reactive.

Consider Rob, a client of mine in his midforties who is a founder and CEO of a technology startup. Rob described his stress level as "off the charts." He said he felt he was "running around dealing with a million things at once, but with no game plan." He was particularly challenged by making decisions, which he inevitably put off, especially when it came to hiring and scaling the business. He was paralyzed by chronic stress and holding back his company. A board member observed how these delayed decisions were slowing the company's growth and told him that he needed to step it up and make confident decisions in a timely manner.

I worked with him to create an effective approach and strategy. To avoid the paralysis of chronic stress, we broke up the hiring process into discrete stages and identified the goal in each step. Rob found it easier to make these smaller decisions, and he started making decisions faster. As this led to positive outcomes, he trusted his instincts more.

Once Rob had a structure and a strategy in place, the pressure to make quick and strong decisions became productive, energizing eustress. He no longer experienced ongoing, debilitating chronic stress. His increased decisiveness gave him a greater sense of control, which in turn empowered him to make other mindful decisions affecting his well-being. He used the ACE Method and dug himself out of his pit of chronic stress.

Taking what at first seems like an overwhelming situation and breaking it up into incremental, manageable steps puts us in the driver's seat. I offer more on this below and in the next chapter.

Make Stress Your Friend

It might seem counterintuitive to write about embracing stress in a chapter about avoiding stress. However, this one of the Seven A's is "avoid *unnecessary* stress." It is impossible to avoid all stress, but we can avoid the chronic, dangerous stress that undermines our lives and effectiveness. This type of stress is unnecessary, and it arises when we have a limited mindset about stress.

In other words: *It is not stress itself that kills us, but our perception of stress.*

Solid science backs this up. In 1998, researchers looked at thirty thousand US adults and assessed both their stress levels and their attitudes toward stress. Then they tracked their mortality rates over the next decade. Those with high levels of stress who also believed stress was harmful to their health had a 43 percent higher risk of premature death.

Those with high-stress levels who did not view their stress as harmful did not have a corresponding high mortality rate. In fact, their risk of death was the lowest in the study, even lower than those reporting very little stress.

Body chemistry helps explain this initially surprising disparity. Our adrenal glands release two major hormones — cortisol and DHEA — during what is called a *stress response*. Cortisol has some positive short-term effects, but it also suppresses other functions and can wear us out over time. DHEA, on the other hand, counters those negative effects and enhances brain growth, wound repair, and immune function.

The ratio of these two hormones is called the *growth index* of our stress response. Those with a high growth index not only survive stress well, but they also thrive under it. An upgraded mindset about stress triggers higher levels of DHEA, and thus a higher growth index.

Neuroscientist Ian Robertson studies stress and has found that our brains release a number of other chemicals under stress, including noradrenaline. While it is not good to have very high or very low levels of noradrenaline, "there's a sweet spot in the middle where if you have just the right amount, the goldilocks zone of noradrenaline, that acts like the best brain-tuner."

How do you tap into the beneficial effects of stress and make it your friend?

One thing to avoid is trying to fight your body's physiology. You must first acknowledge what you are going through in the moment. If your adrenaline is pumping, you must work with that natural response, not against it. Instead, you can choose the path of least resistance and allow your body's natural process to work for you. Then, you can upgrade your mindset and reframe your stress response in a positive, not a negative, light.

This is where asking if a problem represents a challenge or a threat comes in. Your answer reveals two different mindsets and leads to two different stress reactions. A positive, challenge mindset is likely to produce a constructive course of action. A threat mindset leads to fear and defensive reactions or inaction.

I have seen clients do both. For one client, a challenging deadline was an opportunity to be creative, to have a clear vision for the desired outcome, and to feel invigorated like an athlete in the Olympics. Another client would end up feeling overwhelmed and anticipate failure.

Stress is what we make of it.

Imagine you have an upcoming product launch and must speak in front of thousands of people, including the company's executives. Before delivering your keynote speech, you realize you are amped up. But how do you label that feeling, that stress response? If you label it as "excitement" as opposed to "anxiety," this reframing will go a long way toward helping you harness the positive energy of eustress, which is the positive stress that boosts your energy and helps you succeed.

You might be skeptical that a simple cue like this can change your mindset. However, Dr. Alia Crum, a researcher at Columbia Business School, has studied short interventions like this and found that they work. "Stress is paradoxical," she says. "On the one hand, it can be the thing that hurts us most. On the other, it's fundamental to psychological and physical growth. Our belief system, the lens through which we choose to view and approach stress, will shift the outcome."

This is a prime example of how *Pause. Breathe. Choose.* can be applied in a practical way within the ACE Method.

Pause. Step back. Do not get swept up in the emotions of the moment. Become aware of your body's natural stress response.

Breathe. Upgrade your mindset and identify the opportunity. What are you excited about, as opposed to anxious about?

Choose. Embrace the opportunity and put the energy of the moment to good use.

Mindful Self-Check-Ins: Be Present to Stress

Remember, avoiding unnecessary stress does not mean suppressing stress or ignoring its symptoms. Doing so will only start a vicious cycle where you create more stress in the long run, while denying yourself the positive benefits of short-term stress.

Sometimes chronic stress begins with short-term acute stress. It can also emanate from a stressor in your personal life, the loss of a loved one, or the ending of a relationship. You might feel stuck and hopeless, as if there is no way out. You may not even realize you are sinking into chronic stress until you have hit rock bottom. In these cases, ignoring or trying to avoid stress will not help. You already feel chronic stress, and the only way to transform it is to be fully present to it.

This was demonstrated by a University of Rochester program to reduce burnout among medical professionals. Understandably, some physicians respond to difficult situations involving pain, suffering, and death by distancing themselves emotionally. Yet in the long run, this coping mechanism actually increases the risk of burnout.

The Rochester program experimented with a mindfulness program that taught participants to be fully present to the emotions and sensations of the moment, however difficult they might be. At the end of the year-long program, the scores of participants on a test assessing depression and anxiety had dropped dramatically.

Similarly, a central component of my wellness programs is what I call a *mindful self-check-in*. I encourage clients to take an inventory of themselves by first taking a pause and then asking themselves the following questions:

- Am I breathing?
- What am I thinking?
- What am I feeling, both emotionally and physically?

Through your breath, this kind of mindful self-check-in enables you to become fully present to any difficult or challenging emotions you might otherwise be tempted to suppress. It also allows you to notice negative thought patterns (like your Inner Critic; see chapter 6). Awareness of the structure of your subjective experience is the first step toward making better choices.

The psychological framework for these mindful self-check-ins is called "relative weight of importance and duration" (or RWID). It is not enough to simply flag negative thoughts, although that is a start. The next step is to notice the weight and importance you attach to certain thoughts and also how much time and space they occupy. If you notice these patterns in detail, and then make an effort to shift to an upgraded mindset, you can ultimately rewire your thought patterns.

I address acceptance in chapter 8, but the first step to altering any situation is to pause and step back, then breathe and become aware of how your body and mind are responding. When you can accept both the reality of the situation and your response to it, you can move on to assess what you can and cannot change.

It is through a lack of mindfulness that chronic stress becomes dangerous (and deadly). Instead of taking effective action, we feel hopeless, tired, lethargic, clouded, irritable, and moody, along with other symptoms of long-term stress.

Awareness, on the other hand, by using mindful self-check-ins, lets you harness the energy of acute stress and eustress in order to find a solution, move forward, and avoid dangerous chronic stress. Even taking small positive actions can shift your mindset and move you in the direction of your goals. Again, these are the keys to the ACE Method:

1. Be aware of how stress is affecting you.
2. Change your mindset and identify your options or opportunities.
3. Take empowered and effective action.

If you have a deadline coming up, do not let stress conquer productivity and creativity. Instead, think of one small step you can do to move in the right direction. Break up tasks into small, doable actions. One by one, you will get closer to achieving your goal without feeling helpless, hopeless, or overwhelmed by chronic stress.

By learning to put the ACE Method into action, you will gain the awareness and tools to effectively handle perceived threats and challenges. You will be happier, healthier, more creative, and more in control of your life.

If we want to live longer, we must avoid a limited mindset about stress. For instance, we often worry about things that never actually happen. When we ruminate on future possibilities, we must ask ourselves: Why spend time and energy sacrificing our well-being and the well-being of our companies on something that may never occur?

We can dedicate ourselves to what is really important and what gives us joy and fulfillment. We can choose to take empowered action. We can recognize stress and put it to more effective, purposeful, and productive use.

Will you remain open to experience prana flowing freely?

Will you live in aspiration or die in desperation?

Do not limit yourself. Choose an opportunity mindset rather than a threat mindset.

Pause.

Breathe.

Choose to ACE stress by tapping into the positive energy of eustress and taking preventative steps to avoid unnecessary chronic stress.

BUSINESS HACKS

Be Proactive

Instead of merely reacting to events as they happen, consciously engineer your own events. Proactive people are rarely caught by surprise because they learn to anticipate problems and events. They are always on their toes and several steps ahead.

Understand how things work, look for patterns, and recognize regular routines, daily practices, and natural cycles in your business without becoming complacent. As you do this, remember not to rely only on the past to anticipate future outcomes. Use your imagination, creativity, and logic to come up with different scenarios of how events may unfold in order to avoid unnecessary stress.

Flip a Coin

Often, we procrastinate on projects because we are indecisive about how we want to approach them. To simplify this problem, just flip a coin. This will force you to make a decision in a few seconds. You do not have to accept the results of the flip. Just knowing how you feel about the result will reveal your real feelings about the situation and what to do.

Divide and Conquer

Avoid future stress by delegating responsibilities to people you entrust to deliver outstanding work. Know people's strengths so you can optimize efficiency and the quality of the job at hand.

Make sure you do these three things:

1. Clearly communicate the task and expectations.
2. Check for their understanding.
3. Provide timelines and support.

Also, know when to say no to tasks, and do not try to address every disruption that occurs. When explaining why you are declining something or someone, try replacing "I can't" ("I can't finish that in time," "I can't find enough people to help") with "I don't" ("I don't have enough time to do that job well right now," "I don't have the resources to finish by that date"). According to the *Journal of Consumer Research*, "I don't" is much more effective and empowering than "I can't."

There is nothing wrong with setting limits. Only you know how many productive hours you have in a day. Taking on too much not only raises your stress level, but your work ethic and effectiveness will likely decline as a result.

Cultivate a Culture of Wellness

Chronic stress makes it nearly impossible to filter out noise and chaos and to focus on what matters. This is true for anyone, no matter what your role in a company, and it hinders the performance of even the most stellar employees. As the CEO, do not underestimate the negative power of chronic stress and the impact it has on you, your employees, and your business.

The goal is for everyone to thrive, not just survive, which is why it is paramount to cultivate a culture of wellness. As a leader, you have the power to directly influence the lives of your company's employees, so promote a culture that focuses on their needs and desires. Build individual and team resilience by incorporating stress management workshops and giving employees the time and space to wind down. Prioritize wellness as central to the company's culture, and model healthy habits yourself.

Implement these strategies for yourself, and it will influence others to move in the right direction. As an executive, consider all elements of your employees' lives through wellness assessments and comprehensive and holistic employee well-being programs to ensure the most significant impact.

ACTION STEPS

Stressors Checklists

In the following checklists, check off the stressors you are feeling that may be slowly piling up to become chronic stress. Or write or type them into a list in a notebook or app. The lists of personal stresses can apply to every reader, and the subcategories apply to specific roles. Then, you will use your responses in the next Action Step, "Create a Stress Action Plan."

EXTERNAL PERSONAL STRESS

- ❏ Finances
- ❏ Work or career
- ❏ Health and well-being
- ❏ Relationships
- ❏ Lacking work-life engagement
- ❏ Political, social, and environmental anxieties
- ❏ Media overload
- ❏ Major life changes
- ❏ Traumatic event

INTERNAL PERSONAL STRESS

- ❏ Chronic fears or anxieties
- ❏ Limited or fixed mindset
- ❏ Negative beliefs, or unrealistic expectations or goals
- ❏ Conflicted or neglected values
- ❏ Uncertainty and lack of control

INTERPERSONAL STRESS

- ❏ Conflict, lack of trust, and confrontation with others
- ❏ Overcoming job-related constraints to maintaining interpersonal relationships
- ❏ Building and maintaining relationships
- ❏ Style differences in communication, leadership, parenting
- ❏ Performance concerns with your direct reports

FAMILY AND CAREGIVER STRESS

- ❏ Overwhelmed with demands and pressure
- ❏ Adrenal fatigue
- ❏ Lack of time
- ❏ Feeling "on-call" constantly as a caregiver
- ❏ Keeping up with doctor visits and medication
- ❏ Chauffeuring

EMPLOYEE STRESS

- ❏ Workload and overwhelm
- ❏ Level of responsibility
- ❏ Lack of skills and capabilities
- ❏ Lack of career development
- ❏ Overall job dissatisfaction
- ❏ Communication issues
- ❏ Office politics
- ❏ Management style issues
- ❏ Job security
- ❏ Presenteeism (working while sick or otherwise compromised) and burnout

LEADERSHIP STRESS

- ❏ Lack of resources and time
- ❏ Recruiting and retaining top talent
- ❏ Developing and inspiring your team
- ❏ Heavy workload and responsibility
- ❏ Managing stakeholders
- ❏ High expectations
- ❏ Personal insecurity — impostor syndrome
- ❏ Team and collaboration issues
- ❏ Lack of clarity and direction

STARTUP STRESS

- ❏ Raising capital
- ❏ Building a stellar team
- ❏ Limited resources and time

- ❏ Multitasking and wearing too many hats
- ❏ Instability and uncertainty
- ❏ Achieving milestones
- ❏ Pressure to prove yourself
- ❏ Market research
- ❏ "Do-or-die" mindset
- ❏ Launching a product
- ❏ Building a customer base
- ❏ Fear of "failure"

Create a Stress Action Plan

To help clients manage valid stress and avoid unnecessary stress, I have them develop a Stress Action Plan (SAP).

In a notebook or in an electronic spreadsheet, create two columns. Title the left column "Stressors." Using the stressors checklists above, list all of the things that are causing you stress or keeping you up at night; include everything you can think of. Then, one by one, for each item listed, ask yourself, "Is this stressor 100 percent true? Is this something I have control over? Is this something I can take action to rectify?" If the answers are no, cross it off. Dispute any irrational thoughts that are self-induced stress responses with facts. For instance, valid stressors might be that you have too much on your plate and feel you are spreading yourself too thin, or you had a negative encounter and are avoiding that person because you feel bad about it. An unnecessary stress to cross off would be worrying while waiting for the results of medical tests. This is an example of stressing in vain because you have no control over the results.

Another way to evaluate each stressor is to determine if it is from the past, in the present, or might possibly occur in the future. If the stressor is from the past, there is no way to change the past, but you can change your current self-induced internal stress response to it. For a stressor in the present, it is more likely you can take direct action to rectify the situation causing the stress. Since we cannot foresee the future with 100 percent accuracy, future stress is mostly subjective. It is fear over what might happen, which we cannot control, and this would be a stressor to remove from your Stress Action Plan.

Worrying is like punishing yourself for something that has not happened or might never happen. Stressing about things you cannot control is a waste of time.

Next, title the second or right column "Actions." For each of the remaining items in the left "Stressors" column, write one or two small steps you can take today to mitigate that stressor. Ask yourself, "What can I do about this? What action can I take to change this from being a point of stress to being an accomplishment?" For example, if you have too much on your plate, the first action step might be to make a list and prioritize all your responsibilities in order of urgency and importance. Next, you might identify any items that you can get help with or delegate to someone else to lighten your load. Other steps could be identifying and asking appropriate people to help you, and so on. In the example of the negative encounter, the first step could be to objectively reflect on what happened, to put yourself in the other person's shoes to better understand their perspective and modify any limitations of your own. A second step might be reaching out to talk with that person.

Creating a Stress Action Plan helps you refrain from spiraling down a rabbit hole (for more examples, see "Assess, Act, Alter," pages 112–14). For the things you cannot control, there are no actions to take, so accept this and let go of unnecessary stress. Focus on the items you do have control over and take aligned action, which uses your energy more productively and purposefully.

This exercise not only helps identify valid stressors and avoid unnecessary ones, but it also develops an action plan to transform your state of stress into a state of accomplishment.

Practice Mindful Self-Check-Ins

Throughout each day, choose to practice mindful self-check-ins (see "Mindful Self-Check-Ins: Be Present to Stress," pages 96–98) to assess the state of your body and mind. Ask yourself the following series of rapid-fire questions:

- *Am I breathing?*
- *How is my posture? Am I hunched over, sitting, or standing tall?*
- *Am I frowning or clenching my jaw?*
- *Am I thirsty?*

- *Am I tired or energized?*
- *What am I feeling?*
- *What is on my mind?*
- *What do I smell?*
- *What do I see?*
- *What do I hear?*

You may be surprised by what you can learn about yourself through these regular mindful self-check-ins. Practice every hour or so. I recommend using a periodic vibrating smartwatch or phone alarm to serve as quick reminders.

Avoid People Who Stress You Out

There are certain people at work and in life who act like vampires, sucking the energy out of us. What can you do about this?

As CEO of your well-being, evaluate those around you and either promote, demote, or terminate your relationships as necessary. For the people in your life who increase your energy and joy, *promote* your relationship by spending more time together. When you identify someone who drains your energy and causes you stress, choose to either *demote* or *terminate* that relationship depending on the toxicity levels. Demoting someone simply means spending less time with them or decreasing your encounters. However, when someone causes you lots of stress frequently, it could be time to cut ties and terminate the relationship if possible.

When you cannot avoid certain people — whether coworkers, your boss, or your in-laws — reframe their presence for yourself and consider your encounters teachable moments. Think of them as high-value educators, teaching patience and compassion.

Share Your Stress

Let the people in your life — family, friends, coach, doctor — know about your stresses. Sharing the burden can be therapeutic and lighten your load.

You are not alone, and you do not have to be if you choose to be open and share.

Be Mindful of Your Environment

Take control of the space around you to better manage your stress. For example, if commute traffic is a prominent stressor, choose to drive a less-crowded route, even if it takes longer. If you do not like the feeling of rushing out the door to be on time, wake up ten to fifteen minutes earlier to give yourself extra time to get ready.

Disconnect from Technology during Crunch Time

When you need to, allow yourself to completely disconnect from technology in order to eliminate distractions. Whether meeting a deadline in the eleventh hour or prepping for an important meeting or presentation, when you disconnect from technology, you will be able to fully focus.

Apply the Ninety-Second Rule

Sometimes our stress does not come from massive, looming projects but instead from a pileup of smaller tasks. Alone, each seems easy, but taken together they become daunting. To keep your list of tasks from compounding and becoming a source of stress, use the ninety-second rule. If a task takes ninety seconds or less to complete, do it immediately, when possible. The satisfaction of completing it and not adding it to your long list of "I'll do it later" items will give you a sense of achievement and boost your productivity.

KEY TAKEAWAYS

- Stress is natural and inevitable. Avoiding unnecessary stress does not mean disregarding or downplaying different stresses. It means clearing your life of the stress that can be identified as negative or unnecessary. There are valid times to be stressed; framed positively, stress can be a source of energy and focus. At other times, stress is dangerous and must be avoided.
- There are three different kinds of stress: acute stress, chronic stress, and eustress. Necessary acute stress is the short-term spike of an adrenaline rush that results from unpredictable challenges or threats. Dangerous chronic stress is characterized by its prolonged nature and by feelings of hopelessness, helplessness, and uncertainty. It is the ultimate killer stress. Positive eustress is the drive that energizes us to reach for fulfillment and success.
- Stress refers to an individual's physical, mental, or emotional response to a demand, threat, or event. Remember, stress is *not* the actual demand, threat, or event itself. Stress arises from the perception of a situation being overwhelming or out of one's control.
- Stress management is about ACE-ing (acute, chronic, eustress) stress using the three-step ACE Method (awareness, change, empowerment). The ACE Method is a new way of reframing stress that effectively upgrades both mindset and behavior. The first step is to be aware of your body's natural stress response. The second step is to change your mindset and identify your options or opportunity. The third step is to take empowered and effective action.
- The ultimate goal is to ACE stress by moving between acute stress (necessary) and eustress (desirable) while choosing to avoid the trap of chronic stress (dangerous).
- Chronic stress hinders a person's ability to make strong decisions. This is a skill successful leaders cannot afford to neglect. Chronic stress allows crippling anxiety to set in, preventing us from taking proactive and preventative measures

to address the source of stress. It sinks one into a state of distress, a state that is both slow and deadly. The choice is yours: *Live in aspiration or die in desperation?*

- A significant part of avoiding unnecessary stress is avoiding a limited mindset about stress. Reframing chronic stress as acute stress and eustress is the first step toward harnessing their positive energy. A mindful self-check-in — or paying attention to the relative weight of importance and duration of stress-related thoughts — is a useful tool for rewiring our mindset about stress.

CHAPTER SIX

---·---

ALTER
THE SITUATION

---·---

THE SEVEN A's

Adopt

Allocate

Avoid

ALTER

Adapt

Accept

Attend

Take a step back.

Pause.

Breathe.

Do you feel stuck? Is there a situation at work, in your relationships, in your personal or professional growth and development, or with your self-care that you want to change? Are you working meaningless long days? Are you sleeping less? Are you under high pressure and stress? Do you find yourself feeling overwhelmed rather than exhilarated as you approach a new product launch or project?

Maybe your company is flourishing, but you have not tucked your children into bed in weeks. Perhaps you just landed a prominent investor, but you skipped lunch today because your meetings were scheduled back-to-back. Or maybe you appear to be successful, but on closer inspection, you are merely surviving, not thriving.

Something needs to change. There is no point in being professionally ambitious if you cannot be energized by the challenges such ambition brings or if you cannot enjoy the journey.

When people hear what I do for a living, they often smile and respond, "What does being an executive wellness coach and corporate wellness consultant entail?" Then they invariably ask if I help only with nutrition and fitness, since that is what they tend to associate with wellness. However, I teach my clients to adopt a holistic (whole-person) approach to well-being. I coach them to be energetic, engaged, and fulfilled in *all* areas of their lives. Addressing only one aspect of well-being — whether in our personal lives or in our company — is never as effective as a holistic approach.

When you make changes to improve your well-being, are you approaching it holistically? Or are you just changing one area of your life, like diet or exercise? All departments and levels of well-being are interconnected: emotional, physical, social, mental, occupational, environmental, purposeful, and financial. Are you using changes in one area to trigger changes in another?

At home and at work, one thread holds this work together. If you do not attend to your health and well-being, it does not matter who you are, who you know, what your status is, how much you have, or what milestones you have reached. You can still be miserable. But if you can step up and make mindful choices to alter situations that no longer serve you and take control of your well-being, you will be more fulfilled, happier, and more successful.

In other words, the fourth of the Seven A's flows from the previous three. You can actively choose to:

- adopt a happier and healthier lifestyle
- allocate downtime, restorative sleep, and time for play
- avoid unnecessary stress when possible
- alter the situation when necessary

Some things cannot be changed, and sometimes you will feel stuck. How you address the challenges you face, however, is always a choice.

As with stress, our mindset plays a significant role in shaping our response, and quite often, our first and most important action is to shift our mindset.

In other words, altering how we communicate — both internally with ourselves and externally with others — plays an influential role in altering stressful situations for the better. You have the power to pause, breathe, and choose what is best for you.

Finding Your Way

Why would you want to change? Why alter a situation, your business strategies, or your life? The answer is simple: *The ultimate wealth is to become the CEO of your well-being.* For me, this means having the vital energy to do what makes me happy, live with intention, have deep connections with my Self and others, and live healthily and mindfully.

In broad terms, if you are living in stress and fear, how can you replace those detrimental emotions with love and joy? We shift the experience of our disempowering emotions to empowering emotions. No matter where you are at this moment, this chapter will help you take the small steps that lead to changed habits and mindsets. Many roads lead to mindfulness, and every route and map is different and unique.

If we want to reach a certain destination, do we choose to fly, drive, take a train, walk, hail a taxi? It really depends on where we are starting from. Further, what if we hit traffic or our flight is canceled? We can find another route or catch another plane and still get there, right? Obstacles can make us change our plans and cause delays, but we can still reach our destination.

The same is true with your well-being. Detours, delays, and bumps in the road happen. You may have to revise your route, but you will still find your way from point A to point B. You can build new mindful habits by making decisions according to the Seven A's.

Our minds are constantly in chaos, trying to find order. We are overworked and overstressed. Consider how you feel at 4 PM on a typical Thursday. Irritable? Short-tempered and overwhelmed? Fatigued? All of these are symptoms and signs of stress, which if unaddressed can lead to chronic stress and, at times, karoshi.

If you are already mired in this kind of deadly chronic stress, and you cannot avoid the situation that is causing it, then you must alter something. As we have seen, a key component to chronic stress is a sense of not being in control. Proactively altering the situation is the first step toward controlling your own destiny.

Assess, Act, Alter

In order to alter the situation, you must first assess and understand what is going on, and then find the means of change, whether it is a mindset upgrade, a behavioral upgrade, or both. If you can recognize what is causing this unhealthy state, you can alter the situation for the better and live up to your highest potential.

Although we can alter almost any situation, we can also, often by default, choose to remain in a state of negativity. We can choose to let distress dictate how we live daily and write it off as part of the job or part of life. But there is no reason to stay hopeless and helpless in chronic stress, even when it seems like we have been there forever and there is no way out.

Because each stressful situation is different, each solution is different. For example, imagine a successful and seasoned entrepreneur named Kate who has been experiencing things going downhill for the past eight months. Sales are decreasing, the release of reviews is looming, and resources are declining.

Kate knows she and her company are in a state of chronic stress. She feels powerless to change it, stuck in a pit that is dangerous not only to the success of her business but also to her health.

Despite this awareness and the desire to get out of it, every time Kate tries to alter the situation, using strategies she knows, it does not work. The dominoes fall back on her. She feels exhausted, overwhelmed, and pressured by the lack of time. Every effort to relieve one stress just makes stress pop up elsewhere.

However, no matter what the issue is, or whether the source of stress is known or unknown: There is always a way to manage cost, time, efficiency, and resources to improve it. The key is to correctly identify the stressor, assess the situation, and determine your options. There are always options. Then take effective action, and keep taking action until you see an improvement. A one-size-fits-all approach does not work.

Identifying stressors and action steps is what the Stress Action Plan does (see pages 103–4). Let us look at it again using the example of stressed-out Kate.

Kate has already identified the stressors of the declining sales and resources. She must assess the situation and clearly formulate desired and specific outcomes. For example, some goals might be: prioritize restorative sleep and exercise; increase month-over-month revenues by 10 percent; reduce monthly customer churn to less than 1 percent; increase units sold and profit margins by 10 percent; and increase customer lifetime value by 10 to 20 percent year-over-year. The next step in assessing is knowing the reason why you must achieve these outcomes. What drives you? Changing the trajectory of the company's revenue would save the company from decline. Next, identify the action steps for each goal and then take consistent, aligned action. If the action you take does not work, alter your approach. Do not alter the goal. Continue to alter the approach until you achieve and surpass your goals.

How do we identify the stressor?

First, what are the individual thoughts that give rise to stress? Is it thinking about an upcoming meeting? Is it a nagging suspicion that you are not doing your best? Is it specific, like the fact that one department has needed help for a while and you cannot find the right person for the job? Are you neglecting your relationships?

Often, the act of simply writing down stressors with a few possible ways to alter the situation can help mitigate the stress.

What if a vague, stressful daily thought continues to plague you? For example: *I should do a better job leading my team.*

- Talk with someone from each department every week to discover their current challenges. Ask them how they can be supported better.
- Ask those around you, "What is the one thing you would change about your average workday?"
- Ask yourself, How could I have made today better?

This process of assessing and identifying what is causing you chronic stress and making a list of ways to alter the situation are steps in the right direction. Keep in mind that the decision to make a change is instant, but the outcome of the change itself does not occur instantaneously in one leap. You have to break the goal down into achievable chunks, putting one foot ahead of the other. Research in fields from airline safety to hospital emergency rooms has shown that the humble checklist is one of the most powerful and underappreciated decision-making tools.

More Than Talk: Strong Communication and Culture

Sometimes the most significant source of stress in our lives is how we communicate (or do not communicate) with others and with ourselves. Just as altering our mindset can be the first and most important step in altering a situation, making mindful choices about how we communicate can have a powerful transformational effect in our lives and our company's culture.

Strong communication is never just talk. Communication is connected with mindset. How we communicate reveals how we think about and how we interact with the world. Truly connecting with others starts with a heightened sense of situational and contextual awareness. This means understanding someone's environment, circumstances, moods, attitudes, values, and concerns. Great communicators not only read their environment and other people well, but they possess the uncanny ability to alter their communication style accordingly.

Be mindful of your own communication style, the communication styles of others, and find common ground. Resolving conflicts, which are often at the heart of most stressful situations, is easier when we have a flexible mindset and can view the world through different lenses.

Skillful communication is also a characteristic of strong leadership. Effective and empathetic communication and listening skills distinguish great leaders from good ones. This is especially important in a changing economy where companies with rigid, top-down leadership are losing competitive ground to those with a more flexible and collaborative corporate culture.

Working with clients to alter how they communicate is a significant part of how I empower clients to alter stressful situations and become more effective leaders. When I helped my client Rob (see "Break the Cycle," pages 92–94) improve his decision-making process, I urged him to assign what I call a *senior devil's advocate* to help him with big decisions, such as a major acquisition, in order to test potential outcomes and identify any red flags or weaknesses. Rob wanted an unbiased sounding board outside of his professional network, and he called me his "silent advisory board." In essence, I encouraged him to make his big decisions a conversation rather than bottle them up inside.

One useful way for leaders to get a panoramic view is to conduct a 360-degree review; this process gathers feedback on someone's leadership from employees, subordinates, colleagues, and supervisors, and includes a self-evaluation. I completed a 360-degree review with another client, Jake (see "Playful Entrepreneurship," pages 74–75), to help uncover his blind spots. Jake was going through a painful divorce, which he knew was impacting his work, and the feedback revealed communication breakdowns caused by limiting beliefs and unhealthy habits. At times, Jake's team felt he dismissed alternative options or contrarian points of view. To help rectify this, Jake altered his communication style and made room for more collaborative brainstorming and decision-making. He upgraded his *monologue style* of communication to a *dialogue style*, involving active listening and keeping the feedback loop open. The result was a stronger company culture, which improved business outcomes, and this reduced Jake's stress by creating a more communicative, cohesive team.

Mindful communication in our personal and professional lives can go a long way toward altering stressful situations. Moreover, we must pay attention not just to how we communicate with others, but how we communicate with ourselves.

Two Dogs: Inner Coach Versus Inner Critic

There is a Cherokee legend that describes two wolves inside of us that continually fight each other. I use a similar story with clients, using dogs as examples.

Imagine that one dog represents positivity, eustress, and a growth mindset. This dog gives you motivation, clarity, confidence, energy, and joy. The other dog represents negativity, distress, and limiting beliefs. This dog is demotivating, disempowering, fearful, and insecure. When you look in the mirror in the morning, this is the inner voice that says:

- *I'm fat.*
- *I'm losing my hair.*

- *I have bags under my eyes; I look tired.*
- *I'll probably blow my presentation today.*

In the Cherokee legend, a boy asks his grandfather, "Which wolf will win?" The grandfather replies, "The one you feed."

The dog you feed is the dog that wins. The behavior and mindset you allow yourself to listen to and adopt is the one that conquers your life. Think of these two dogs as your *Inner Critic* and your *Inner Coach*, competing against each other.

You hear your Inner Critic barking at you all day:

- *I did that wrong.*
- *I procrastinated too much.*
- *I lost the deal.*
- *I didn't try hard enough.*
- *I knew I was going to fail.*
- *I'm not good enough.*
- *Nothing ever goes my way.*

What about your Inner Coach? If you listen, your Inner Coach says things like:

- *Breathe.*
- *Choose to be happy. What am I grateful for today?*
- *Ditch the ego and be present. Be here now.*
- *Be curious.*
- *For every challenge, there's an opportunity for growth. What's the lesson?*
- *Let go of fear and replace it with love.*
- *Don't give up. I've got this.*
- *I have the power to change anything in my life I don't like.*

But do you ever hear that voice? Is that dog sleeping, or are you not listening? Many people never feed that dog.

How about, if something does not work out, instead of telling yourself, *I did that wrong,* you said, *Next time, I'll try a different approach.*

Instead of *I procrastinated,* think: *Now I know I should have made this a priority.*

Instead of beating yourself up over mistakes made or opportunities missed, how about allowing your Inner Coach to override your Inner Critic? That Inner Coach will help you do better; it reminds you that one experience prepares you for the next time. It tells you how you did your best, but things simply fell through. (We cannot win all the time!)

Be mindful and realize the difference between feeding your Inner Critic and your Inner Coach. We grow accustomed to listening to our Inner Critic. It is almost as if we are unaware of how powerful and dominant that voice is. Like being on autopilot, it becomes an unconscious choice, a default mode we must snap ourselves out of. We can only snap ourselves out of it, however, if we are aware it is happening in the first place.

I quite literally helped my client Jake snap out of this habit. I had him wear a rubber band around his wrist, and I asked him to snap it every time his Inner Critic spoke. Whatever the Inner Critic said, Jake was supposed to say "and," then follow with a more positive, constructive thought. For example, if he thought, *I screwed up the numbers in that presentation*, he would snap the rubber band and say: and *I will always double-check the numbers for future presentations; I have learned from my mistake.* Over time, he snapped himself less, and eventually no longer needed the rubber band. As he fed the good dog, he starved the bad dog.

The voice of our Inner Critic is a kind of verbal abuse that wipes out our confidence, our spark in life, our energy, and our motivation. It is the mindset of our evil alter ego. Know that the mindset we feed is the one that will conquer our day.

Are you going to continue feeding the negative dog until its barking is the only thing you hear? Will you ignore the dog that bestows positivity until it eventually dies of starvation and neglect? Alter your mindset to one of can-do energy and positivity, and feed the dog that will help you thrive.

We know that a big part of avoiding unnecessary stress is avoiding a limited mindset about stress. In the same way, the first step in altering a situation that may be holding us back is changing the lens through which we view it.

When we view the world through the eyes of the Inner Coach, we feel in control of our own destiny, and we view challenges as opportunities, not threats. We harness the positive energy of acute stress and eustress and can avoid chronic stress. We see ourselves as constantly evolving and focus on improving incrementally.

This is why seemingly small changes have a snowball effect and turn into big changes. Identifying potential stressors, putting together a Stress Action Plan (see pages 103–4), and then implementing that plan becomes a habit or a mental muscle that grows stronger with repetition. Over time, that repetition can rewire the brain, upgrading from a limited mindset to an opportunity mindset.

Once you learn to alter your mindset, you can alter your situation in a deep and lasting way and truly become the CEO of your well-being.

Small Changes, Big Results

Another client, Peter, loved to have a New York bagel with cream cheese and coffee every morning. However, during our sessions, he would often complain about hitting a wall midmorning and about gaining thirty pounds over the years.

In response, I challenged him to a breakfast experiment. I recommended that he replace the bagel with a green juice, one that contained 80 to 90 percent vegetables and 10 to 20 percent fruit. This one small, daily action completely changed the course of his life. Initially, he reported feeling an increase in his energy. Within six months, he had lost twenty pounds. He started going to the gym, his energy and confidence skyrocketed, and he found himself in a fulfilling, healthy relationship. As part of my Upgrade Method, I encouraged him to consider each small change as a stepping-stone to larger changes.

Another client, Mark, was a smoker. His trigger was a specific gas station near his girlfriend's house. Every Sunday night, he left her house and stopped at the gas station on the way home to buy a pack of cigarettes. I challenged him to avoid turning into the gas station. Instead, I gave him an alternative destination, Whole Foods, and told him he could only shop the perimeter of the market, where all the fresh food is located. Whenever he had a cigarette craving, he ate a carrot; this helped occupy his hands and mouth with a healthier habit. The active choice to bypass the gas station every Sunday and go to Whole Foods instead helped him quit his life-threatening addiction. He experienced how avoiding a negative trigger and replacing an unhealthy habit with a healthy habit allowed him to kick a destructive habit. That one change also set in motion other changes: He could bike longer distances without shortness of breath or feeling fatigued, and this led him to improve his diet and eventually to quit drinking alcohol, since alcohol was a trigger that made him crave cigarettes.

One mindful choice begets another.

I always emphasize the importance, when making choices about small things, of keeping your eyes on the big picture. Even the smallest actions can create ripple effects that significantly impact your life. Do not underestimate the power of small changes to create big results.

By being proactive, we take charge of our lives and our well-being. We act out of love, not out of fear. We feed the good dog.

The Golden Handcuffs

In our lives, we are not always overworked or overwhelmed by stress. Sometimes we feel bored, unfulfilled, dissatisfied, or perhaps even trapped by the monotonous routine of everyday work and life. When this happens, we must step back and recognize what in our current situation no longer serves us, and then choose to self-direct and alter it.

During my time in pharmaceutical sales, I felt restricted by the job's "golden handcuffs." The corporate benefits were amazing: all-expenses-paid trips, a corporate credit card, a company car, generous vacation time, good salary, and excellent health insurance. Most importantly, I had autonomy.

Nonetheless, after a couple of years, I found myself in the same place as when I had worked at Yahoo!: I was hitting my snooze button every morning and could not find the energy, desire, or motivation to start the day. My job did not bring me a sense of purpose. This routine slowly chipped away at me, dampening my motivation and the youthful, enthusiastic spark I once had. I only experienced fleeting moments of happiness during weekends and vacations.

Many people find themselves in a similar bind, not wanting to risk what they have to aim for something better. On the surface, it seemed like I had a dream job: all the perks and benefits one could ever want, and a salary on the rise.

It took me a long time to take action. I worried I would never find another job with such great benefits. There was no denying that this pharmaceutical company treated its employees well. However, the realization slowly dawned on me that I was not merely hitting the snooze button every morning. I was asleep at the wheel, coasting on autopilot through my life. That was when I chose to alter my situation by doing something drastic.

I broke free of the golden handcuffs and left my job to pursue my passion and my purpose.

Up to then, I had altered some of my habits and adopted a healthier lifestyle. That was a start, but it did not alter the heart of the problem. The real problem was that my job was not aligned with a higher sense of purpose (which I explore in chapter 12). I realized that I did not want to settle for working at a job merely for the paycheck. I made a conscious decision to shift to a purposeful mindset and take aligned action.

With my own clients, a telltale warning sign is when they can no longer recall the last time they did not feel battered by constant stress. When chronic stress has become the norm, the bad dog rules. Clients think their lives are falling apart, and they surrender to a negative pattern: unfulfilled, unmotivated, and living on autopilot. They slowly slip into this state without realizing it.

This is when stress can become fatal. If you cannot remember the last time you felt happy, energized, and excited, or if you cannot recall the last time you had a good night's sleep or got through a day without feeling depressed or irritable, then it is time to alter both your mindset and your situation.

Ask yourself: *How long has it been since I was excited about my life, my career, my friends, my family, and myself? Has it been months or even years?*

Remember, no matter how stuck you feel, or for how long, you have the choice, the ability, and the strength to pull yourself from chronic stress and alter your situation.

Before leaving my pharmaceutical job, which was a big daunting change, I made several incremental changes that slowly and gradually altered my mindset and situation. Those small changes planted the seeds for larger ones to come. If we feel like we are drowning, it is often better to make smaller choices to be more mindful and improve the quality of our life before attempting to make big changes. For instance, taking action to alter our situation could actually make things worse if our minds are muddled and exhausted and we cannot see the right choice clearly. This is why adopting a healthy lifestyle is so important. It provides clarity and keeps us at the top of our game. Everything is interconnected. Our well-being must be approached holistically. Small upgrades and incremental improvements in our health and well-being create a chain reaction that prepares us to make the big changes we need.

When Tibetan lamas refer to their "mind," they point to their heart. Mind *is* heart. Ensuring that your mind and heart are connected is vital in choosing how to alter your situation. This is where listening to your Inner Coach and feeding the good dog come in. As you improve your mindset, you become increasingly happy, energized, and empowered, and this helps you identify your stressors, what is wrong in your situation, and how to fix it. When you are aware of where you are and where you want to be, and you are ready and willing, you can take the necessary steps to get there. If you are in a situation that is not serving your highest good, pause. Step back and assess. Identify options and actions. Pay attention to how you communicate with yourself and with others.

Breathe. Be present with your Self and the moment. Recognize change as an opportunity, not a threat.

Choose to alter your mindset and situation for the better.

BUSINESS HACKS

Alter the Way You Communicate

One thing that sets a good leader apart from a great leader is their ability to communicate. While social media has created new modes of instant communication, your ability to communicate and connect in a meaningful and personal way remains critical in building trust and credibility in the workplace.

According to a therapeutic and philosophical technique called *neuro-linguistic programming* (NLP), the four preferred communication styles are *visual, auditory, kinesthetic,* and *auditory digital*:

1. Visual communicators *see* the world. They learn through imagery, not through long, verbal instruction. For them, a picture truly is worth a thousand words. They respond well to slides, videos, and images better than written reports. Alter your language to include more keywords such as *look, see, focus,* and *notice,* or phrases like *bird's-eye view, see a light at the end of the tunnel, lighten up, in view of, in light of,* or *keep an eye on.*

2. Auditory communicators *hear* the world. They respond well to spoken instructions and conference calls. Choosing the right words and tone of voice, in this case, is imperative, as well as being aware of noises that might distract an intent listener. They are good at understanding steps or procedures, so take time to structure your message carefully and logically. They like to be told how they are doing and are interested in whether or not your communication sounds right. They tend to use keywords and phrases such as *listen, resonate, hear, on that note, can't hear myself, it speaks to me, rings a bell, lend me your ear, sound good?*

3. Kinesthetic communicators *feel* the world. They learn by doing and through hands-on experiences. They are not the most succinct communicators, and instead trust their gut feeling. They learn and remember things by walking through the process, and they respond well to words and phrases

such as *touch, feel, grasp, smooth, firm, get a grip, tapped into, blown away, hand in hand, get a hold of*, and *can't put my finger on it.*

4. Last, auditory digital communicators are a combination of the other three common types. They take great care in learning the meaning behind words and look specifically at whether or not the message is crystal clear, no matter how it is presented. They like to analyze communication for deeper meanings and messages. They respond well to words such as *think, learn, understand, process, consider,* and *change.*

Whenever you communicate, look and listen for clues (keywords or phrases) as to which type another person is so you can communicate using their preferred style to be on their wavelength. Experiment by matching and mirroring predicate words from each style, and notice which words they respond to most. Know your audience's preferred communication style and adjust your message accordingly. When in doubt, use all four styles in both your written and verbal communication. No one is 100 percent one style, but we all develop preferences. Take the time to learn the preferences of others and optimize your messages to build stronger relationships.

Sharpen Your Reframing Skills

Think of reframing as a mental way of hitting the reset button, just as your breath is a physical way to reset. Make that reset a regular habit in how you apply *Pause. Breathe. Choose.* When we change the conceptual and emotional framing of a situation or experience, we change its entire meaning. Reframing is a choice to see a problem or situation in a different, more constructive way. Choose to view issues, weaknesses, and roadblocks as opportunities. There is an upside to every downside if you are open to exploring it.

How you frame things is connected to your inner dialogue, or how you talk to yourself. Altering how you communicate has both an external and an internal dimension. When you frame difficulties positively as challenges and opportunities, you start listening to your Inner Coach instead of your Inner Critic.

Take Breaks Every Ninety Minutes

Research indicates that working in ninety-minute intervals is a prescription for maximizing productivity. Doing so aligns us with a deeper rest-activity cycle that is embedded within all of us.

If you begin to lose focus, take a walk, drink some water, stretch, do something to alter your situation. Make an effort to alter your tasks, and switch projects every ninety minutes, giving your brain a break from one point of focus to another.

This is a small mindful habit that can create ripple effects. It gives us a chance to stretch, move, and take a break from sitting. It prompts us to step back from the task at hand, become more aware of ourselves, and avoid slipping into autopilot. Similar to regular mindful self-check-ins, these periodic breaks should be an essential part of your mindfulness tool kit.

ACTION STEPS

Quiet Your Inner Critic

The first step to quiet your Inner Critic is a surprising one: Do not try to stop it or control it. Remember, what you resist persists. If you are obsessing about a lost business deal or a conflict with a colleague or spouse, whatever you do, do not tell yourself, *I have to stop thinking about this.* Instead, notice that you are in a vicious negative cycle and own it. Tell yourself, *I'm obsessing about my lost business deal.*

Noticing your thoughts in a nonjudgmental manner and accepting them without trying to control or stop them helps tame negative thoughts. Accepting these thoughts can lessen their weight. Getting angry at yourself for worrying, or telling yourself to stop, only adds fuel to the negativity fire.

Once you have accepted a negative thought, challenge it. Perhaps losing the business deal makes you worry about your overall competence, and you are berating yourself about your skills. Ask yourself, *Why would one setback mean that I am incompetent?* You might even ask, *What have I done in the past that shows I am actually very competent and can close deals?*

If you are having trouble challenging your negative thoughts, try this approach. Imagine that your friend is the one who is going through your situation. What advice would you give them? Now think how that same advice might apply to you.

Assess Your Communication

Do you openly communicate with your colleagues, leadership team, employees, family, and friends? Do you talk about your stresses, how they are affecting you, and how they might be changed? When there are disagreements, do you listen empathetically to others?

To increase empathy and openness, practice *Pause. Breathe. Choose.* Put yourself in another person's shoes. Strive to open up and communicate clearly to find a middle ground; avoid weak, one-sided arguments. Remember to listen and have a dialogue, not a monologue.

When we communicate our needs, concerns, and feelings clearly, it leads to clarity, productivity, and effective compromises. When we hold everything inside, our negative feelings often fester and grow. Practice openness in communication the way you train to strengthen a muscle. Self-consciously practice every day, in both personal and professional situations. If you need someone to make a change in their behavior, you must be willing to do the same. Flexibility and deep listening are the keys to excellent communication.

Think about how a relationship in your life could, without clear communication, rapidly go south. How would you choose to alter the situation?

Watch a Cute Puppy Video

Despite what you may think, watching adorable animal videos is actually not a waste of time. It is an effective way to alter your state. Whenever I feel stress creeping in, I pull up a cute puppy or kitten video my father has sent me. This not only brings me great joy and melts my heart, but studies have shown that watching animal videos can be used as a form of digital pet therapy and stress relief. It can also boost energy levels and mood. That said, you want to be mindful not to get sucked into an endless stream of videos, which leads to procrastination.

Look through Different Lenses

If you are in conflict with someone, try a *reverse lens*: See yourself from their perspective. What might the other person be right about? How can you change without conceding to do something you do not want to do? In what ways can the two of you compromise? If someone else is rigid, that does not mean you have to be.

A second approach is the *long lens*: Consider what the situation will look like six months, a year, and five years from now. Are you worrying in vain? If not, what steps can you take to make that long-lens picture look the way you want? Making a list of these steps will help you see the bigger picture. Look at the situation afterward and determine whether worrying was worth it in the first place.

Third, try the *wide lens*: Regardless of the outcome of this issue, ask how you can learn and grow from it. No matter how this situation turns out (because we cannot control everything), how are you going to take this experience and turn it into a lesson, a tool for future use? Even the most stressful situations, including battles we lose, have value in making us more exceptional leaders moving forward.

Viewing any situation from different perspectives — from reverse, long, and wide lenses — helps us gain further insight, promoting greater flexibility and less rigidity. This helps us with many of the Seven A's, especially avoiding stress, altering a situation, adapting to stressors, and accepting what we cannot change.

KEY TAKEAWAYS

- To alter means to make a change. Make the necessary changes in your life to ensure that you are taking a holistic approach to your well-being. Your well-being is the ultimate wealth.

- Assess and understand a situation before laying out the options to make the change. Only then can you act to alter the situation for the better. If you cannot outright avoid a stressor, then you must make a choice to alter the situation instead.

- Altering your mindset is often the first step toward altering your situation. Learn to reframe situations and see them through different lenses.

- As a leader, you will have to make crucial decisions and navigate times of uncertainty. When this happens, avoid feeling overwhelmed or hopeless. Instead, identify the stressor and tackle it in small chunks. Significant changes, after all, do not occur overnight.

- How we communicate with ourselves and with others plays a vital role in how we manage stress. Mindful communication can go a long way toward helping us alter stressful situations. The greatest leaders are the most effective communicators.

- Like two dogs inside of you, competing for attention, you have an Inner Coach (the good dog) and an Inner Critic (the bad dog). The Inner Coach represents positivity, eustress, and a growth mindset while the Inner Critic represents negativity, distress, and limiting beliefs. The dog you feed determines the kind of life you lead. Choose to feed the good dog.

- Do not underestimate the power of small, consistent changes to generate big results. A small change in one area of your life can create ripple effects in other areas.

CHAPTER SEVEN

ADAPT
TO THE STRESSOR

THE SEVEN A's

Adopt

Allocate

Avoid

Alter

ADAPT

Accept

Attend

When an earthquake hits, buildings and structures that are flexible are more likely to survive, while those that are rigid often crumble and fall. On October 17, 1989, the sky was falling in Palo Alto's Stanford Shopping Center. Large tiles fell from the ceiling all around customers in my mother's Benetton store.

Back at home, my brother was watching the World Series on television, and I was on the phone with a friend, when the massive, 6.9-magnitude Loma Prieta earthquake started to severely shake our house in Palo Alto.

We should have done what we were repeatedly taught in school (duck and cover), but we did not. Instead, emotions took over, and we did exactly what we were always told not to do.

My brother's first reaction was to reach up to stabilize our swinging crystal chandelier. I held up a large, original painting that was about to fall. We remained this way until everything returned to stillness. Despite our instinctive reactions, we ended up being fine, though others were injured and killed by this disaster.

The destruction caused by the 1989 quake resulted in stricter building regulations to ensure that structures would be more flexible and better able to survive the next "big one."

Similarly, flexibility and adaptability in our thoughts and behaviors build our resilience reserves, enabling us to thrive. When faced with the unknown, if we cannot avoid or alter our situation, we have no choice but to adapt.

Adapting to Disaster: 208 Super Stressful Seconds

Sometimes you only have 208 seconds before your plane — real or metaphorical — hits the water. This is what happened to Chesley "Sully" Sullenberger, the captain of Flight 1549, not long after taking off from LaGuardia Airport in New York in January 2009. What would you do if you learned that the plane you were flying was going down, with everyone in it? Your crew had done everything imaginable to avoid this outcome, and you had done your best to change the situation, but to no avail. The plane was going down. How would you react? Would you lose your head, panic, and faint? Or would you adapt, put your training to use, and find a way to save everyone?

On Flight 1549, after birds damaged the aircraft's engines, causing them to fail, Captain Sully's initial reaction was disbelief. "I can't believe this is happening. This doesn't happen to me," he remembered thinking. The plane, Sully explained, lost forward momentum almost completely: "The airplane stopped climbing and going forward and began to rapidly slow down. That's when I knew I had to take control of the airplane." He also knew that, unlike every other flight he had flown over forty-two years, this flight would not end with an undamaged airplane on the runway. As the pilot, he was now in charge of his own life and the lives of the 154 people on board. He chose to make a radical mindset shift to adapt creatively to this life-or-death situation. His everyday known routine had instantly plunged into a terrifying unknown, and he had to think outside the box and somehow land the plane safely. He crash-landed on the Hudson River, and all the passengers survived.

None of us wants to be thrown into an extreme, life-or-death situation, and most of the time, life's everyday "emergencies" are less dire. But the concept is the same. When faced with an unexpected stressor or problem, will we be present, calm, and collected, adapt to what is happening, and safely land the plane?

When we cannot adapt, our "plane" will crash.

Sully adapted by quickly assessing the situation. He did not become attached to the obvious option that the control tower recommended, which was to return to the runway. Sully knew they would not make it back, and so he exercised independent judgment. Then he acted quickly and decisively. In hindsight, Sully believes his entire life until then had prepared him to handle that particular moment.

Only with practice and by following the other six of the Seven A's will we be able to apply the fifth A and adapt to the stressors in life. By making conscious choices when faced with any challenging situation, we prepare ourselves for life's genuine emergencies — when our plane is going down and we have 208 seconds to respond and land safely.

Daily Pressures

The daily challenges we face at work and in our personal lives might at first seem unwelcome or make us uncomfortable. These are different for everyone. An entrepreneur might have to cope with the many unknowns related to raising capital or developing and launching products. Executives must balance the company's well-being with that of employees when planning for reorganizations or extensive layoffs. The key is to remain positive, flexible, and curious. Ask: *What can I learn from this situation? Is there something I am not paying attention to?*

Even with work deadlines looming and family demands at home, you have the ability to make mindful choices. You can either let negative energy and anxiety bring you down, making you a less productive and effective leader, or you can remain positive and open and practice adapting to your stressors.

No matter what daily pressures arise, use them as opportunities to practice the Seven A's and assess your overall direction. Be proactive, rather than passively accept circumstances as beyond your control. Assess stressors and convert them into concrete action steps. This might mean focusing on better self-care or minimizing stress by playing more. The right choice in each situation will vary. Sometimes, getting from point A to point B is a simple straight line, and sometimes the most direct path is not the most effective route. But there is always a way to get from where you are now to where you want to be.

You may find yourself toggling between the different Seven A's. This is completely natural. All seven strategies are interrelated and complementary ways of mindfully navigating stress and building resilience.

As always, when unexpected daily stress hits you, take a moment to pause, breathe, and step back. Choose to look at the big picture. Ask yourself: *Will this actually matter in a year?*

Indefinite Vacation

In 1979, when I was two years old and still living in Tehran, my family went on a life-changing vacation to San Francisco. The Iranian Revolution had just broken out, and my parents wanted to escape their harrowing living conditions. Our friends and family were being imprisoned and executed. Everyone was living in fear and chaos.

So my parents decided to take my brother and me on vacation, in hopes that the revolution would die down by the time we were due to make our return. This did not turn out to be the case.

We ended up moving permanently to California. We found ourselves uprooted against our will and taking an indefinite vacation. At first, we were waiting for the revolution to end, and we entered a limbo of not knowing where we would be long-term. However, as time passed, and as my parents had to make the decision to enroll my brother into elementary school, we had no other choice than to stay and adapt to life in the United States.

The unexpected transition was a challenge for my parents, then in their thirties, who suddenly needed to find new jobs. Transferring money from Iran was forbidden, and they had only brought enough money for a few months' vacation. They had to face the fact that we had just accidentally relocated from one country to another, with limited cash and no resources.

The biggest shock was finding ourselves stuck in a completely foreign environment. In Iran, my entire family would gather every weekend at my grandparents' house, and throughout the week, we would see one another regularly. Family and community were always the highest priority. Now that we had been dropped into a foreign culture with few connections, living in an unfamiliar city, we had to start from scratch.

Could we have avoided this? Sure, if we wanted to stay in Iran during the revolution.

Could we have altered it? Not really. We needed to remain somewhere safe, with good schools, away from the dangers of Iran during a revolution. We needed to make our lives work in California, no matter how foreign or frightening.

After weighing our options, my family chose to adapt. We made the best of our situation. My parents reframed our vacation as a relocation for our highest good. They let go of the familiar and embraced the unfamiliar.

Now, more than forty years later, they are happy to call the Bay Area their home.

Resilience through Healthy Habits and Mindsets

As we have seen, our mindset is crucial in our response to stress. If we reframe a difficult situation as an opportunity rather than a threat, we can learn not just to survive stress but to thrive in the midst of it.

Transitions are a common stressor in both our personal and professional lives. Not everyone must flee political persecution and revolution, but change is constant. In today's dynamic and fluid corporate environment, mergers and acquisitions are common. Familiar procedures and lines of command are turned upside down.

How do we embrace such transitions in our professional lives as opportunities? The first step is a mindset shift that approaches disruptive forces as opportunities rather than as threats or obstacles. Then develop a Stress Action Plan (see pages 103–4) and break down each stressor into incremental, manageable action steps. Adapting to change is challenging. Do not attempt it all at once.

One of my clients, Bill, merged his company with another company whose culture was radically different. Instead of letting the weight of chronic stress take over, he first adopted a flexible, positive, and curious mindset. Then he took a step back to understand the big-picture challenge of how to integrate two distinct corporate cultures. He saw an opportunity to take the best of both organizations and to emerge with an improved and smarter company. Then he identified the differences that mattered most. Now he was ready to define, develop, and build a cohesive and robust culture, which is the foundation of any successful business.

The CEO of a company has a significant role. They are not only a leader but also a protector, serving as an umbrella against the storm for those around them. The CEO must take care of themselves and be resilient so that they can effectively take care of their company and their employees, rain or shine.

Mergers and acquisitions are just one of many potential disruptions facing today's business leaders. The word *disruption* has itself become a kind of cliché, encompassing a broad range of factors that can suddenly send Fortune 500 companies scrambling to keep pace with fast-growing startups. As individuals and as companies, we are likely to encounter times when we have to reinvent ourselves. "Long-established organizations are really being rocked to their core," says *Fast Company* cofounder Bill Taylor. "And if they don't adapt, they'll die."

Resilience finds strength in adaptability and flexibility, the same way buildings are more likely to survive earthquakes if they are constructed to move. Rigid buildings resist the force of the quake, absorb the shocks, and can collapse. To survive, they need to be more like suspension bridges, which are made to sway in high winds; they bend but do not break.

Similarly, our first impulse when unexpected change hits is often resistance. We tense up, become defensive and rigid, and hold on to the familiar. Instead, adapting to the stressor means cultivating flexibility. This means letting go of the urge to resist and being open to change. It means assessing and understanding the bigger picture and identifying the pathway to greater possibility.

Building resilience does not happen overnight. Think of it as a savings account that you invest in regularly so that it is there when you need it. You start building your reserve by practicing in small ways every day through healthy mindsets and habits. When you have a limited mindset, your thoughts, feelings, and perspectives become narrow in scope, limiting your options and opportunities. By improving your mindset, your capacity to adapt to stressful situations or crises will grow over time, and it will lead to better health, greater happiness, and more success.

As I say, this means practicing all of the Seven A's. We cannot build resilience without practicing self-care. When we are tired, hungry, and burned out, everything seems more stressful. We can build our resilience reserve by prioritizing restorative sleep, having a daily mindfulness practice, allocating regular physical activity, eating mindfully, emphasizing play and recovery time, and developing strong connections with our Self and others.

Here is more of what upgrading your mindset entails:

- Maintain an attitude of gratitude. Focus on the positive and what is present, not on the negative and what is lacking.
- Feed the good dog: your Inner Coach. Starve the bad dog: your Inner Critic.
- Have compassion for yourself and others.
- Keep things in perspective with the three lenses: wide, long, and reverse (see "Look through Different Lenses," pages 126–27).
- Accept that change is a part of life. Embrace change. Choose to see it as an opportunity instead of an obstacle or a threat.
- Avoid a limited mindset that frames crises as insurmountable problems.
- Revise your narrative and the meaning you attach to it. Revise the map of your journey (see chapter 13).
- Instead of ruminating on the downside, look for the upside. Take inventory of the positive developments in your life. Writing them down makes this practice even more powerful.

Developing these mindful habits and mindsets will go a long way toward building a positive currency you can draw on as needed. Upgraded habits and mindsets can literally rewire your brain, enabling you to thrive and be resilient in ways you might have never thought possible. Remember Captain Sully, who said he felt as if his entire life had been preparing him to respond calmly in a life-or-death crisis. That is what happens when we practice navigating all the unexpected and challenging situations that arise every day. We build the resilience we need for the biggest challenges.

Beyond Resilience

Resilience is essential. It enables us to bounce back and survive a stressful situation. But I encourage you to think bigger, to aim higher. Seek instead to bounce forward and thrive, to harness the energy of change and make it meaningful or purposeful. If we maintain an opportunity mindset and remain flexible, open, and curious, we can adapt to stress and grow stronger and wiser as a result.

The following skill sets and habits will help you achieve resilience and more:

- Develop strong problem-solving skills. Focus on the solution, not the problem. Tap into your curiosity and creativity. A problem can be revealed to be an opportunity if you dive deep beneath its surface.
- Create goals and a clear vision that are tied to a sense of purpose (see chapter 12).
- Face your fears. Venture outside of your comfort zone. Take explorative action.

A major crisis or challenge can create new possibilities, new strengths, and new insights (which is called *posttraumatic growth*; see "How Trauma Gives Birth to Growth," pages 193–95). Nature and our own bodies are full of such examples. When we work out at the gym, we are, in fact, creating intentional trauma by breaking down muscle tissue. Our bodies overcompensate by building up additional muscle, new strength.

Organizations and businesses can also go beyond resilience by identifying and managing risk, and by preparing for VUCA — volatility, uncertainty, complexity, and ambiguity. Many companies know that what works today may not work tomorrow. VUCA is simply disruption, and it happens to everyone. Leaders and employees who have developed resilience and flexibility can adapt to stressful situations and crises and survive.

But the most skillful leaders are similar to judo practitioners: They recognize and anticipate disruptive forces, and they redirect those forces into advantages for themselves. The term *judo* translates as "gentle way" because it takes an opposing force and redirects it, rather than trying to stop it with a comparable force. Judo meets force with flexibility and turns an attack into an opportunity.

To survive and thrive in times of volatility, uncertainty, complexity, and ambiguity, adapt to the stressor. Prepare for the unexpected. Do your best to achieve the best outcome. Remain resilient, flexible, positive, curious, and open.

Pause.

Breathe.

Choose to be flexible and adapt.

BUSINESS HACKS

Develop an Agile Mind

Different situations and different players call for various types of leadership. It is important to first know what your leadership style is before observing the styles of others. Then acknowledge differences and strive to reach a compromise. A middle approach is more effective than being stuck in a my-way-or-the-highway mindset.

The more flexible you are, the more you will be able to adapt and determine the quality of your experience and outcome.

Flexibility expands choice, and rigidity restricts choice. Choose the option that offers more choice.

Here are several exercises to help:

- Stretch your mind. Question your thoughts and words. Refrain from attaching yourself to one way of thinking. Explore different perspectives regularly. Ask yourself, *Am I flexible or inflexible in this situation?*
- Change things up. Change your environment. Take a walk. Take a break. Take a vacation. Change your routine. Change what you eat or alter the order of your day.
- Seek new experiences. Explore an unfamiliar part of town. Travel more. Take a lesson in something you want to learn, like a musical instrument, sailing, tennis, cooking, a new language. Train for an endurance challenge, like a marathon or a Tough Mudder.
- Meet new people from different cultures and walks of life whose perspectives are likely to differ from your own.

Manage Expectations

As Heraclitus once said, "The only constant is change." In today's fast-paced world, the difference between success and "failure" lies in a company's ability to adapt.

Whenever you are leading a company or team through change, managing expectations is imperative. First, provide structure by clarifying the group's direction and vision. Set clear boundaries. Define everyone's scope of work. Clearly communicate what is expected from others and learn what they expect from you. Align expectations as needed.

Make no assumptions. Avoid falling into the trap of assuming someone has the same understanding of a situation, project, deadline, or task. Providing a set of operational guidelines can empower the team to take initiative.

Next, set motivating goals that are aligned with the vision and key initiatives, as well as with the goals of employees, to help them stay on track.

Keep an open line of communication and check in periodically to see how things are progressing (or not progressing). Be open to give and receive constructive feedback.

Always aim for clear and consistent communication.

Develop an Effective Problem-Solving Approach

Problem-solving involves being able to get to the bottom of an issue, rising to a challenge, and being analytical, creative, curious, and tenacious.

The IDEAL model of problem-solving — which stands for identify, define, explore, act, learn — can be used within a range of contexts. I have modified the model to focus more on the solution rather than the problem.

1. **Identify** both the problem and the opportunity.
2. **Define** your goals. What outcome do you want?
3. **Explore** possible strategies or solutions. Compare the benefits and risks of each one. How will each option be received? Which will be most effective?
4. **Act.** Take action. Choose a strategy or solution, create an action plan, and take steps to implement it.
5. **Learn.** Look back and learn from your actions. Did they work? (If not, then go through the process again.) What will you do next time? How can the strategy be improved?

ACTION STEPS

Pause. Breathe. Choose Gratitude.

Building and sustaining a mindful gratitude practice elevates our consciousness. Take time to bring the positive to the forefront of your mind by keeping a daily gratitude journal. Take a moment to reflect on what is currently going well for you and what you appreciate regardless of your circumstances. Even on our worse days, there is always something or someone to appreciate and be grateful for. Switching to a gratitude mindset is especially helpful when you are in a negative state. Gratitude annihilates anger. You cannot be angry and grateful simultaneously. It is crucial for us to be mindful and thankful of all the treasures that exist in our lives.

The practice is simple and powerful. Here is how to get started: Pause. Breathe. Ask yourself:

- *Who or what inspired me today?*
- *What brought me happiness today?*
- *What was the best part of my day?*
- *What did I learn today?*
- *What are three specific things I am most grateful for?*

Reflect. Document. Share.

The same spirit of gratitude can find expression around the dinner table. Ask your loved ones what the best part of their day was. Another option is to choose someone to be your "gratitude buddy," and commit to a daily phone call or text message, sharing three things each of you is most grateful for. Researchers have discovered that a daily gratitude practice rewires your brain and body for improved health and joy. This is especially helpful when adapting to a stressor. Your gratitude practice builds your resilience reserve.

Be Your Own Best Friend

When something goes wrong in life, our natural instinct is to either wallow in depression or criticize ourselves. Instead, appreciate the positive and give yourself advice on how to best rectify or respond to the issue.

Imagine that you are speaking to your best friend, who is going through a similar situation. What would you do? What advice would you give? Apply that advice to your own life. While it is admirable to show compassion and understanding toward others, we too often forget to react that way with ourselves. Remember to be kind to yourself.

Approach Life as an Explorer

Perfectionism and attachment are significant sources of disappointment. Set high yet reasonable standards for yourself and for others to lessen the weight and pressure.

We tend to get caught up in a limited mindset of only focusing on how our life should be and end up missing out on opportunities that open new experiences and possibilities. This occurs when we approach life from a place of expectation instead of exploration.

Be open to exploring unexpected outcomes instead of expecting a specific outcome. Attachment to a particular outcome, even if it is reasonable, sets us up for disappointment. Focus on exploring, instead of expecting, a more fun and joyous life.

Reframe Negativity

Stress is part of life, and resilience is part of adapting. Do not let stress and negativity poison your perception of yourself, others, and the world.

Listen to your Inner Coach, who asks, *What is one good thing about this situation?* Every cloud has a silver lining, so challenge yourself to find it. Choose to be optimistic. It can ward off stress-producing negativity and keep you healthy. Studies show optimism helps people cope with disease and recover from surgery. Having a positive outlook impacts our overall health and longevity.

KEY TAKEAWAYS

- A person's ability to adapt can be likened to how a building will be affected by an earthquake. The more flexible the construction, the more likely the building will survive. If you cannot avoid or alter a situation, there is no other choice than to adapt.
- Daily pressures can be useful signs about the sources of stress in your life. Ask yourself, *What can I learn from this situation?* Such pressures are a good occasion to be mindful of the bigger picture, the map you are creating for your life.
- Resilience leads to better health, greater happiness, and more success. Upgraded habits and mindset will enable you to create a resilience reserve you can tap into in times of stress.
- The key to adapting is to reframe your outlook and perception in a positive light. When you experience seemingly unmanageable pressures in both your professional and personal life, you have the choice to let the negativity win or to maintain a positive outlook.
- Take the path of least resistance and go with the flow, as opposed to swimming against the current. Like the judo practitioner, seek to redirect an opposing force instead of fighting it head-on.
- If we maintain an opportunity mindset and remain flexible, open, and curious, we can adapt to stress and grow stronger and wiser as a result. Go beyond resilience and seek to bounce forward and thrive amid change.
- Leaders and employees who develop resilience have an advantage and are better equipped to adapt to the disruptions in today's business world of VUCA: volatility, uncertainty, complexity, and ambiguity.

CHAPTER EIGHT

ACCEPT WHAT YOU CANNOT CHANGE

THE SEVEN A's

Adopt

Allocate

Avoid

Alter

Adapt

ACCEPT

Attend

We cannot control everything. We cannot control traffic patterns, people, or the weather. We cannot control the stock market, taxes, or the loss of a loved one. In fact, we cannot control most things in the world, no matter how much we try. Moreover, we cannot control nor accurately predict the future.

Every minute that we attempt to control the uncontrollable is a minute wasted.

Learning to accept what we cannot change is a step toward gaining peace of mind. Let us not waste even a minute stewing in frustration and anxiety over what is unavoidable.

There are times, both in our business and personal lives, when things are simply out of our hands. What if the part of your business that you love most just happens to be the least profitable or is losing money? You must let go of the unprofitable parts of your business and pivot. Doing so is understandably a difficult task, particularly when you let go of things that bring you pride and joy. However, it is necessary.

Arguably one of the biggest challenges I see with my clients is the inability to let go. Even when they recognize a situation is out of their control, they do not want to accept that it is time to find a new solution or compromise.

When you work with the Seven A's, you first try to avoid, alter, and adapt to a stressful situation. When these three approaches do not work, the next best option is to accept what you cannot change. This helps you focus on and be present for what you *can* control.

Most leaders are competitive in nature, sometimes at the cost of thinking they can be in control at all times. They can become agitated, frustrated, and angry when a situation is out of their control. When this happens, it is essential to make a mindset shift and accept what cannot be changed.

For instance, when stranded in traffic, you cannot magically honk your way through other cars to be on time to your meeting. Many New Yorkers try and usually find this out the hard way. You can, however, control how you spend your energy. You can look for the upside and work with circumstances rather than against them. Stuck in traffic, doomed to be late, you can choose to remain calm so you do not arrive upset (letting stress get the better of you), or even use the time constructively, by calling a friend or listening to a podcast or audiobook.

This simple positive shift in mindset is not always easy (as I know firsthand). It is even more critical, though, when we feel the urge to control other people. During conflicts, our first instinct is to try to convince the other person to agree with us. This usually results in nothing but a tug-of-war and wasted time.

We cannot control how *others* react. We can only control how we respond. Further, no matter what has happened, we cannot rewind time and undo the past. Acceptance is not about liking what we do not like, agreeing with what we do not agree with, condoning bad behavior, or giving up.

Acceptance is recognizing what has occurred and then responding appropriately.

Forgiveness Is Freedom

Forgiveness does not mean sacrificing our beliefs. If someone we trust betrays us, or if the reality rug is ripped out from under us — say, someone lies or cheats in a relationship — we cannot change what another person has done.

Forgiveness simply means accepting what has happened, acknowledging that we do not like it or do not approve, and then letting go of the negative energy — the anger and resentment — that comes with holding grudges. Forgiveness does not mean forgetting, nor does it mean condoning or excusing an offense. Rather, we adjust our reaction to the offense so it is no longer emotionally charged for us.

This goes both ways, of course. If we harm someone, intentionally or not, we should acknowledge what we have done, admit it was harmful, and apply forgiveness to ourselves.

A Buddhist teaching that has made a strong impression on me compares holding on to anger like grasping a hot coal with the intent of throwing it at someone else. *You* are the one who gets burned when you hold on to anger. Instead, accept and forgive. This may take time, but it fosters your own peace of mind.

In due course, the most difficult but healthiest way to respond after someone has wronged us is through forgiveness. I know how hard forgiveness can be, but I also know how much better it is in the long-term.

Keep in mind that forgiveness is not about giving up our beliefs or letting someone else off the hook. Forgiveness is freedom from our own anger or pain. It is about letting go of our attachment to the past so that we are free to be engaged in the present.

Once we truly acknowledge and accept that something is out of our control, we can move on, stop wasting energy trying to change it, and free ourselves of unnecessary stress and anxiety. If someone has hurt us, what we can control is creating boundaries to manage future situations or interactions with that person. We can choose how emotionally invested or present, if at all, we want to be with that person moving forward.

The more experience you have accepting difficult situations or difficult people, the stronger that muscle becomes. It will then be easier to pivot toward the productive and healthy path that helps us let go, make the best of an unwanted situation, and forge ahead.

Trying to Control the Uncontrollable

During the 2016 presidential campaign, I helped staffers at Hillary Clinton's headquarters in Brooklyn manage their stress through workshops and one-on-one coaching. This was a welcome relief for many of them, given the heavy pressure they were under and the gravity of their work.

On the way to one of these workshops, I was able to put my mindfulness teaching into practice in my own life. Knowing I needed some time to set up in advance, I checked ahead for any obstacles that would prevent me from arriving on time. I made sure to check the distance, subway delays, and weather conditions. I decided to leave early to give myself ample time.

It was rush hour, so I resolved to take the subway instead of Uber. The train made all of the usual stops with no unexpected delays. Everything was going according to plan. However, as we approached my stop, and I readied myself to get off, the train flew right past the platform! Several other passengers looked as confused as I was. I could tell the same thought was flashing in our minds: *What the heck is going on? This isn't the express train!*

The train ran past two more stations before finally screeching to a stop. I was finally able to get off. Feeling lost and on edge, I ascended the stairs to the street and got caught in an unexpected downpour. I tried to alter my situation by finding a taxi or an Uber, but to no avail. The traffic was terrible.

This was exactly what I had been trying to avoid by planning every detail ahead of time and preparing myself, but no luck. So I descended back into the subway station, knowing time was ticking. When the correct train arrived and I finally jumped on board, it was 7:28. I had planned to arrive at the workshop at 7:20 in advance of the 7:30 start time.

Sitting on the subway car, wet and shivering from the cold, tapping my feet out of anxiety, I took a deep breath. I began practicing what I teach. I closed my eyes, uncrossed my legs, and sat back in my seat. My breathing had become shallow, so I took a deep inhale and a deep exhale to slow it down. As I tried to gain control of my thoughts, here is what ran through my mind:

- I had done what I could to arrive early and prepared.
- I was not successful, but that was due to circumstances beyond my control.

- I was at the mercy of the subway's unpredictable schedule, and all I could do was accept that fact.
- I would arrive later than planned, and the only thing I could control was how I responded to being late.
- I did not want to show up to my own stress-management workshop stressed, so I needed to address my stress head-on.

In the subway, I chose to become present and to meditate.

I slowed my breath and heart rate.

I calmed myself down just in time for my stop.

I exited the subway and climbed to the street, where rain was pouring even harder than before. Without an umbrella, I ran toward my destination two blocks away.

In the lobby, I composed myself and stepped into the elevator. My heart rate had risen once again. This was all I had: an elevator ride to make myself look presentable and to calm my nerves to deliver this presentation. Soaking wet, I gathered myself, stood in the popular power pose (feet apart, hands on hips, chin tilted upward), and meditated again. Due to my daily practice, I was able to reach a calm and confident state within the brief elevator ride.

I arrived late and started setting up for the workshop. I shared what had happened, saying, "I apologize for being late. There were subway delays, and ironically, I found myself stressed on my way to teach a stress-management workshop!" The participants smiled and laughed along with me. "I was able to use some proven methods that I'll be teaching today." As it turned out, my stressful experience helped me establish a great rapport with my audience.

Because of how I responded, my presentation turned out even better than it might have if everything had gone to plan. When things went wrong, instead of spiraling into a hole of anxiety by trying to control the uncontrollable — the New York subway, the rain — I practiced mindfulness. I adjusted my outlook and expectations, accepted the situation, and responded appropriately.

I used all of the Seven A's to help me be mindful that day:

- I tried to *avoid* the stressor by leaving early. (That did not work.)

- I tried to *avoid* inclement weather by checking the forecast (which inaccurately showed clear skies).
- I tried to *alter* the stressor by taking a taxi or Uber instead. (That also did not work.)
- I *adapted* to the stressor by returning to the subway. (I was back on the right track.)
- I *accepted* what I could not change: I was going to be late for my own talk.
- I *altered* what I could change: my mindset. I meditated on the subway.
- When running in the rain brought my stress back, I *adapted* and *accepted* again. (Never give up.)
- All of these reactions were supported by my resilience reserves, which I had built through *allocating* play and recovery time and *adopting* healthy lifestyle choices.
- Finally, once I arrived, I *attended* to my connection with myself in the elevator, and I connected with my audience in order to successfully lead the workshop. I also found meaning and purpose in my experience by using this story as an example of what I teach and practice.

Hitting the Reset Button

In other words, put simply, I chose to hit the reset button.

Similar to a mindful self-check-in (see "Mindful Self-Check-Ins: Be Present to Stress," pages 96–98), this is a tool to avoid rumination: repetitively playing a problem or regret in your mind like a film reel. Psychologists find that we are more vulnerable to stress and anxiety when we ruminate about the past or worry about the future, neither of which we can control.

I helped my client Jessica deal with situations she found overwhelming by having her visualize a reset button. As an executive for a global Fortune 500 company with a heavy travel schedule, Jessica often felt a lack of control.

Tailoring *Pause. Breathe. Choose.* for her, I had her imagine a reset button at the center of her palm with a direct connection to her brain. When she needed to quiet negative chatter, she would hold her palm in front of her and press the imaginary *Pause. Breathe. Choose.* button. At the same time, I told her to do a companion breathing exercise: She would take three breaths and visualize a colored number synchronized with each breath. First, a red 1 to stop the negative thoughts, then a blue 2 to breathe calmly and reset, and finally a green 3 to choose a better mindset.

Afterward, Jessica was able to reengage with the situation in a more mindful, positive way by accepting what she could not control and focusing productively on what she could control.

This is just one of many ways to quiet the primitive part of our brain, the amygdala, that generates a fear-based response to stress. Some call this region our "lizard" brain. It is fully developed at the age of two, and a big part of our maturation process from childhood through early adulthood is allowing the rest of our brain to catch up so that our primitive brain does not dominate our decision-making. When a person consumed by anxiety and fear starts spiraling emotionally over the smallest matter, we could describe them as acting like a toddler. It would not be far from the truth. Just as we might distract a two-year-old instead of trying to reason with them, distracting our primitive brains amid stress is often the best strategy. Once we have quieted that primitive brain, our creative intelligence can kick in and focus clearly on solutions.

When working with Jake — who would lose control of his anger when speaking with his ex-wife — I had him pause, take a deep breath, and internally repeat a mantra (*not this, not this*) to interrupt his rage in the moment. This technique helped him choose to respond calmly and rationally. Letting go of his anger allowed him to process his grief over his divorce without holding on to or ruminating about the past. Eventually, he arrived at a place of forgiveness.

Another approach is to imagine you are holding a TV remote control. When you feel fearful, angry, or frustrated, or when you start judging yourself or others, hit the pause button. Breathe. Then change the "channel" to a more accepting, curious, and open mindset. This is an effective way to switch from your Inner Critic to your Inner Coach.

Standing in the elevator, trying to compose myself before my presentation, I hit the reset button. I knew not to feed the bad dog, my Inner Critic. I knew I could not change what had already happened.

Instead, I accepted the situation I was in: wet and late. I also chose to feed the right dog, my Inner Coach. I used my Upgrade Method to improve my mindset by replacing judgment with curiosity. Rather than be self-critical — thinking, *Why did I do this wrong?* — I focused on the curious and positive thought, *What is the best thing I can do right now?*

Acceptance is at the heart of all the approaches outlined above. We cannot reset until we mindfully accept the stresses we are going through. We cannot move on in a healthful way until we accept what we are unable to control. An ongoing mindfulness practice will increase your ability to reset and move on by reducing the influence (and even the size) of your primitive brain.

Pivot and Focus on What You Can Control — Your Self

In 1985, Steve Jobs was let go from Apple. After dedicating so much time, effort, and passion, he was fired from his own company. Steve could have looked at his life's map and headed down an unhealthy route. He could have dwelled upon the fact that he had been fired, convincing himself that everything he had worked for had just gone down the drain: his purpose, dreams, goals, impact, and career. After all, people give up all the time. He would not have been the first. Or he could have chosen to be bogged down in an extended power struggle at the company he had founded.

Instead, he went back to what he loved. He wanted to create something amazing again. If Apple was not going to let him do that, he would do it without them. He accepted his new reality and moved onward to the next thing: He started the company NeXT. The name itself reflects his intention: to let go of what he could not control and to move on to something new.

Steve Jobs pivoted, and this is an essential skill today. Very few of us will remain at the same company, or even in the same career, for our entire professional lives. We need to be able to pivot, but you cannot pivot and fully commit yourself to the next endeavor without accepting what you cannot control and letting go of any attachment.

Accepting what we cannot control frees up our focus and energy. As Tony Robbins, a performance strategist says, "Where focus goes, energy flows."

Choose to focus on what you can control because that is where energy flows.

At the time, being fired from Apple must have seemed to Steve like the worst thing that could have happened. In hindsight, it proved to be a defining moment in his life. Steve focused on what he could control. He let go, pivoted, and redirected his energy to create another great company. After he created NeXT, Apple wanted Steve back full force, and he returned to eventually become Apple's CEO again.

Attempting to control the uncontrollable is a waste of energy and a waste of your life. When you cannot control something, the best thing to do is to let it go.

There is a long list of uncontrollables. We can never control the past. We have less control over the future than we think. It is usually foolhardy to try to control others. Many external situations are at least partly beyond our control.

What we can control starts with us: our mindset and our habits. We can always control how we perceive a situation. We can make a mindful choice to focus and frame our perceptions on the positive potential of the moment.

Let go of what you cannot control. Let go of attachments. Let go of resentments. Let go of fear. Let go of negative thoughts. Let go of regrets. Let go of everything that no longer serves you.

Let it go.

Forgiveness is freedom. Forgiving is remembering without anger.

When you cannot avoid, alter, or adapt, then accept, pivot, and move onward and upward.

Refocus your energy on what you can change.

Pause.

Breathe.

Choose to gain peace of mind.

Focus on What You Can Control

We have the power to change what we do not like in our workplace and in our life. As Maya Angelou said, "If you don't like something, change it. If you can't change it, change your attitude." Our stress only escalates when we try to exert control over uncontrollable things. We inevitably set ourselves up for disappointment, since many things are beyond our control. To avoid this, choose to focus on what you *can* control.

Here is a list of what you can control:

- Your mindset
- Your attitude
- Your response
- Your actions
- Your words
- Your work ethic
- Your perceptions
- Your efforts
- How you respond to your feelings
- Whether you feed the good dog or the bad dog

Refer to this list when you are trying to control things that are out of your control. Accept what you cannot change and take full advantage of what you can change. Remember to choose to focus on what you can control because that is where energy flows.

Pivot or Perish

If you are trying to drive into the future while looking in the rearview mirror, you will crash. Entrepreneurship has no shortage of common pivots — when it is time to let go of the past and move boldly into a new direction. When startup founders reach an impasse and have to accept that their company's business model is not working or gaining traction due to factors out of their control, it is time to pivot or perish.

Evaluate what needs to change: your customer, the problem you are solving, the solution, the technology, the growth strategy. The biggest mistake entrepreneurs and startup founders make is falling in love with their product or service. What they need to do is know their customers and fall in love with their ideal customer. Steve Jobs focused first on the customer experience and then worked backward with the technology. He said his strategy and vision for Apple "started with what incredible benefits can we give to the customer, where can we take the customer, not starting with let's sit down with the engineers and figure out what awesome technology we have and then how are we going to market that."

Laugh

When work or life seems out of control and you experience feeling negative emotions, change your state. The easiest and quickest way to change your state is to change your physiology. Have a good laugh. It changes your nervous system and attitude. Laughing offers an emotional shift in how we perceive the stressor and creates a physical response that relaxes us, relieving tension and stress. Watch funny videos on YouTube, share a joke with colleagues, or recall a recent funny memory and laugh the stress off all the way to your next meeting.

ACTION STEPS

Become a Curious Problem Solver

My Upgrade Method encourages you to upgrade a less-helpful or negative choice with a better, more positive one. This applies to everything, from diet to attitude, and it can improve your ability to solve problems. If you find yourself angry with someone, spiraling out of control, or full of judgment, upgrade your mindset and change the channel to curiosity. Accept the problem and become curious about it. What can you learn from the situation? How might it be used productively? Or how could you respond empathetically?

This upgraded mindset enables positive energy to flow, moving you forward toward whatever is next. Upgrading your mindset might not necessarily be easy or happen quickly. Give yourself time to employ patience and empathy, and the results will unfold.

One simple method for becoming a curious problem solver is to replace the question *why* with *how*. Asking how is more useful and productive. It focuses on the process or situation and achieving a goal. Trying to answer the question why can keep you stuck on what you cannot change and prompt defensive reactions, excuses, stories, rationalizations, and blame.

A meditation and mindfulness practice can also help you distinguish rumination (worrying about what you cannot control) from actual problem-solving.

Practice Forgiveness

The humble act of forgiveness is deeply personal. It takes strength, courage, compassion, and wisdom to forgive, whether another person or yourself. It is not easy. Yet studies have found connections between forgiveness and our personal physical, mental, and spiritual health. It also plays a vital role in the health of families, communities, and nations.

I encourage you to practice forgiveness, but it is important to remember what forgiveness is and is not. Forgiveness does not mean you give consent, condone, pardon, or excuse another person's actions. It does not mean you forget the incident happened. Forgiveness is not something you do for the other person, and the other person does not necessarily need to know they have been forgiven. Forgiveness does not mean the person should remain part of your life.

Forgiveness is freedom.

That said, forgiveness is a nonlinear process. It often takes time and requires several steps or phases. It also requires emotional awareness and processing pain mindfully (see chapter 10). Everyone will have a different experience, and every situation is different. I have distilled the process into four phases, and ultimately, someone may toggle between these phases multiple times.

PHASE 1: AWARENESS AND ACCEPTANCE

Pause. Acknowledge the reality of what occurred and how you were affected. Accept that it happened. Be aware of how it made you feel, react, or respond in the moment. Be aware of any symptoms of stress (per chapter 5). Take time to decompress and process your thoughts and feelings. Journal or share with a friend, family member, or coach.

PHASE 2: GROWTH AND GRATITUDE

Breathe. Meditate. Spend time in nature. Uncover the upside of the situation. What did you learn about yourself or about your needs and boundaries? What is one good outcome of the situation?

PHASE 3: EMPATHY AND CURIOSITY

Choose to be empathetic and curious. View the situation through the reverse lens, from the view of the person who has wronged you. See through their eyes. Feel through their heart. Walk in their shoes. Upgrade your mindset. Replace judgment with curiosity and empathy.

PHASE 4: FORGIVENESS AND LIBERATION

Write a letter to the person. You do not have to send it. Forgiveness does not require that the other person know they have been forgiven. Consider forgiveness as a gift to yourself, not a gift to someone else. Or if you prefer (and it is possible), speak with the person for closure. Then choose to let it go. Release the emotions that prevent you from moving forward and from being happy again. Revise your narrative of the incident.

Choose to Let Go

Business leaders and entrepreneurs, by nature, prefer to be in control, but the desire to impose your will on a situation has limitations. When you are stopped in your tracks, facing an uncontrollable situation, pause to become present.

Reset your brain and shift away from judgment, fear, or panic mode by acknowledging negative thought patterns. Visualize hitting the *Pause. Breathe. Choose.* reset button.

Step away from anxiety and misery.

Breathe, choose to accept what is, and respond appropriately. Let go of what no longer serves you to have peace of mind. Choose to be a problem solver, and pivot to make the best of the situation moving forward instead of pushing against something that will not budge.

KEY TAKEAWAYS

- Every minute that we attempt to control the uncontrollable is a minute wasted. Learning to accept what we cannot change is a step toward gaining peace of mind.

- Acceptance is recognizing what has occurred and then responding appropriately. We cannot control the past, the future, or other people. Accepting what we cannot change is a crucial strategy in managing stress and building resilience. It also frees our energy to be creative and productive.

- Forgiveness is freedom. It simply means accepting what has happened, acknowledging that you do not like it or approve, and then letting go of the negative energy (the anger and resentment) that comes with holding grudges. In due course, forgiveness is the most challenging but healthiest way to respond when someone has wronged you.

- When you are faced with a situation that you cannot control, use the Upgrade Method. Replace judgment with curiosity in order to understand the situation and respond effectively and productively.

- When negative thoughts and emotions take hold, hit the reset button or change the channel. Visualize an actual *Pause. Breathe. Choose.* reset button on the palm of your hand. Resetting acknowledges what is happening while choosing a more positive and productive mindset.

- Be willing to pivot and let go. If something is not working, despite your persistent efforts to make it work, pivoting to something new might be more productive. Many businesses and entrepreneurs owe their success to their ability to pivot.

- Choose to focus on what you can control because that is where energy flows.

---•---

CHAPTER NINE

ATTEND TO CONNECTION WITH SELF, OTHERS, WORLD, AND UNIVERSE

---•---

THE SEVEN A's

Adopt

Allocate

Avoid

Alter

Adapt

Accept

ATTEND

There is a disconnection between our hearts and our minds that often results from overconnection with our electronic devices and busy schedules. It is essential to disconnect from these mind-numbing distractions in order to reconnect with our true Self.

Disconnect to reconnect.

A mind removed from endless distraction seeks to create its own stimulation. In fact, studies have found that boredom holds creativity-boosting power because a "restless mind hungers for stimulation."

These studies remind me of something Steve Jobs said. He believed that we should not overschedule our children, allowing them instead to "get bored" so that they can discover who they are and what they like.

The next time you have a gap of time in your day, refrain from filling it. Resist picking up your phone or other electronic devices, which could temporarily entertain you with something diverting like your never-ending social media feed.

All of the Seven A's represent choices that can lead us toward greater fulfillment — such as adopting a healthy lifestyle, allocating play and recovery time, avoiding chronic stress and fostering helpful eustress, altering and adapting to negative situations, and accepting what we cannot change.

However, these choices will make little difference if we cannot truly take what we learn and apply it holistically to our lives. Beyond the Action Steps at the end of each chapter, which involve various changes that can positively improve our lives, we need to acknowledge the significance of *connection*.

Attending to our various connections is about taking the time to pause, breathe, and choose to become more aware of our place in the world. This realization starts with our Self and moves outward. In seeking deeper fulfillment, we need to connect with Self, others, world, and universe.

Failing to establish any of these connections will diminish our quality of life. We will ultimately lack authenticity, inner peace, inspiration, and fulfillment.

If we want to see change in the world, we must start with our Self.

Without being connected to our authentic Self, our thoughts and feelings, our body, and our environment, it is impossible to be aware and connected when we move outward to others, world, and universe.

Attending to all of these connections brings color into our life and, by extension, light and vibrancy into everything around us. For instance, you cannot love another person if you do not fully and truly love yourself. You cannot understand another person if you do not understand yourself. You cannot add meaning to the life of another person if you are not living an authentic life yourself. Doing so starts from within.

When you attend to connection with Self, others, world, and universe, you can truly *become the CEO of your well-being*. This is essential to be an influential leader, a supportive and compassionate parent and spouse, and an overall good person. Attending to your connections will lead to an improved quality of life, fulfillment, and awareness.

Self: Morning Ritual

Attending to the connection with our Self is the most intimate and fundamental part of our journey. My personal method of attending to my connection with Self is through the daily practice of Transcendental Meditation (TM). Every morning as soon as I wake up, I use my RPM Method (rise, pee, meditate; see "Explore the RPM Method," page 45).

After waking up, I make a quick trip to the bathroom, and then I sit still and quiet for twenty minutes. While I sit and meditate, I do not attempt to banish thoughts from my mind. Thinking is natural and even part of this kind of meditation. Many of my clients say, "I can't meditate because I think too much." This is not an issue in TM, in which thinking is a byproduct of the meditation doing its work, relieving stress and anxiety.

To better understand Transcendental Meditation, imagine your mind is an ocean. The more active the ocean's waves, the more active your conscious thoughts, the more stress you have. The less active the waves, the less you have to worry about.

While practicing TM, *watch* the waves of your mind, instead of trying to control them, while repeating a given mantra. As you dive deeper into the ocean that is your mind, notice a growing sense of calm and peace.

Even though the waves around you are in constant upheaval and motion, the deeper you go, the calmer it seems. The waves are only crashing on the surface. As you continue to transcend into a deep state of profound relaxation and peace, at some point you can no longer hear the waves, and your conscious thoughts calm and quiet themselves.

TM is effortless and straightforward. After twenty minutes of "me time," I feel genuinely connected with my Self, and I am ready to hit the ground running — and conquer the world.

During jam-packed days, I still find a way to squeeze in a few minutes of meditation first thing in the morning. In fact, those are the days I need meditation the most and cannot afford to skip it.

I gain inner peace, greater energy, clarity of mind, creativity, and awareness from my morning meditation. Who would not want to start the day tapping into their own highest potential?

Our minds may continuously be in "go" mode, like the endless thrashing on the surface of the ocean, inundated with decisions to make, to-do lists, tasks, and all the stresses of our day-to-day lives. Yet within all of us is an ever-present calm, which we can access if we dive deep enough. Although this calm is always there for us, we lose touch with it when we are stuck at the surface of our minds.

TM helps me dive deeper into the calm below the surface. This is how I am able to connect with my higher Self. As Rumi wrote, "The quieter you become, the more you are able to hear."

We spend our lives entrenched in thoughts, processes, and visions. When we live mostly in our heads, it becomes more difficult to quiet our minds and dive deeper, where there is less chaos.

By practicing a mindfulness ritual like TM, you essentially awaken your heart and create a stronger connection between your heart and your mind.

Perhaps your version of "me time" is going for a walk or a run, spending time in nature, or practicing yoga. These types of moving mindfulness practices can be just as effective as seated ones, like Transcendental Meditation. Whatever your practice or ritual is, revel in your own company. Commit to creating a mindful habit to attend to this connection with your Self. As a result, you will experience a ripple effect of beneficial impacts across all areas of your life.

Others: Cultivate Meaningful Relationships

After attending to our Self, it is vital to work on our connection with others. Strengthening our connections with others can help us tap into the useful energy of eustress.

One of my clients, Carolina, is a single working mother who felt she was not living up to her full potential. Her days were filled to the brim with the bustle of being an executive at a Fortune 500 company and tending to her two children. Yet she felt something was missing. I asked her, "What do you crave most?" She answered, "Socializing with other people. Getting out. Connection." She felt a sense of emptiness and believed that a lack of meaningful relationships impacted her work.

First, we worked on personal values and mission exercises to uncover what was most important to her, so she could implement actions that supported her values and goals. It is far easier to be motivated to make changes when you are in touch with a sense of purpose (see chapter 12).

We then moved to small action steps to restore her connections with others, including a "date night" with her friends once a month. She committed to making it on the same day and time: a nonnegotiable part of her schedule. She also joined a book club and prioritized finding a reliable and trustworthy babysitter, so she could pursue such activities.

As a result, Carolina began living better by diving deeper into the aligned desires of her mind and heart. She realized exactly what she was missing, a disconnection from others, and uncovered ways to repair that, all of which stemmed from her willingness to dig deep within and take empowered action.

As I do with all of my clients, I also worked with Carolina to deepen her professional relationships in the workplace. This was also important for my client Jake, who was going through a difficult divorce (see "More Than Talk: Strong Communication and Culture," pages 114–15). Jake chose not to share his private life with his colleagues, but he also recognized that his personal difficulties were affecting his team dynamics and his relationships with his coworkers.

To help Jake reconnect with his team, I recommended he implement weekly one-on-one meetings instead of team meetings. I suggested he start off each meeting with the intention to listen more than he spoke and to ask a series of questions similar to what I do in my coaching sessions: "What's new and good? What challenges are you facing? How are you going to approach them and find a solution? Where do you need help? How can I support you?" He took these meetings seriously and did not cancel them except for a dire need, and they worked. His team reported feeling supported and valued in their roles, and they found their one-on-one meetings helpful.

It is common in the workplace to come across individuals who are disconnected from their Self. This, in turn, seeps into their professional lives, and it affects their relationships with other people. Restoring connection with Self and others leads to more engaged employees and teams, and it translates into improved business outcomes.

Disconnected people tend to lack emotional intelligence and focus narrowly on the task at hand; they often do not factor in the feelings and thoughts of others. They rarely upgrade their mindset (by replacing judgment with curiosity) or try to see the world through another person's perspective.

Successful leaders first foster a healthy relationship with their Self and then with others in all parts of their life. They have high emotional intelligence. Most mistakes or conflicts that occur in the workplace result from disconnectedness, which consequently results in miscommunication.

Miscommunication is aggravated by assumptions and vagueness. Disconnected individuals can be quick to assume that others understand the meaning and message they are trying to convey when this is not always the case.

For example, imagine a vice president who announces that, following a merger with another company, his department will undergo changes, but he does not disclose any details. Since the vice president was privy to the merger negotiations, he knows the changes will increase productivity and will not include any job losses, but his team does not know this. It is natural for the employees to be concerned and to worry whether they will keep their jobs, but the vice president assumes that, since he is not worried, no one else will be worried. Or perhaps the vice president himself is anxious about the changes, and he knows not everyone will be happy, so he chooses to avoid difficult conversations with his team, keeping them in the dark.

This lack of communication creates unnecessary stress and strain for everyone that could be avoided if the vice president attended first to his connection with Self and others, or the members of his team. The strength (or weakness) of our various connections creates a ripple effect throughout our lives. Just as upgrading a habit or mindset in one area of our lives will have a positive influence in other areas, deepening one connection will likely deepen others as well. Research indicates that improved relationships in the workplace increase well-being and engagement.

Connection is a kind of energy. It is contagious and expansive. When we nurture the connection between our heart and mind, our own vital energy or prana is free to flow without obstruction. Mindfully restoring our connection with others has this same effect. Attending to these connections is, in a sense, its own kind of mindfulness practice, one that begins with deep listening, first to yourself and then to others.

When Stressed, Connect!

It is vital to attend to our connection with others regularly. This is especially crucial during times of stress, when our first reaction — our fight-or-flight response — can lead us to either become defensive or retreat, both of which cause disconnection. However, if we make a mindful intention to reach out and connect, our body's own chemistry will work in our favor and help us overcome these responses.

As part of our response to acute stress, our brains are flooded with a cocktail of hormones and other chemicals (see "Make Stress Your Friend," pages 94–96). If we have a positive mindset about stress, many of these chemicals are beneficial and keep us energized, focused, and on top of our game.

One of those chemicals, oxytocin, can also help us connect more deeply with others. Called the "love" or "cuddle hormone," oxytocin in fact plays a more complex role in sharpening our social instincts.

As health psychologist and lecturer at Stanford University Kelly McGonigal writes in *The Upside of Stress*: "When oxytocin is released as part of the stress response, it's encouraging you to connect with your support network. It also strengthens your most important relationships by making you more responsive to others. Scientists refer to this as the *tend-and-befriend response*. Unlike the fight-or-flight response, which is primarily about self-survival, the tend-and-befriend response motivates you to protect the people and communities you care about." While the tend-and-befriend response appears to be stronger in women than in men, biology is not destiny. Our brains and how we use them are fluid and evolving, not fixed.

Clearly, connections are essential in the midst of stressful situations, and those situations actually serve to deepen our relationships. Beyond that, they are a critical part of our overall well-being. Attending to our connections with others is a long-term investment in health that protects the mind and body from stress and aging.

Robert J. Waldinger, a psychiatrist and Harvard professor, oversees the Harvard Study of Adult Development, the world's longest longitudinal study on happiness, which began in 1938 and is still running strong. He sums up the study's biggest lessons in a popular TED Talk: "Good relationships keep us happier and healthier. Period." Loneliness, he says, is "toxic. People who are more isolated than they want to be from others find that they are less happy, their health declines earlier in midlife, their brain functioning declines sooner, and they live shorter lives than people who are not lonely. And the sad fact is that at any given time, more than one in five Americans will report that they are lonely."

The study finds that it is the quality of our close relationships that matter most, not the number of our friends or if we are in a committed relationship. "Good relationships don't just protect our bodies," Waldinger says, "they protect our brains." Being in a securely attached relationship to another person in your eighties protects and preserves mental health. Physical pain does not affect our moods as much, and our memory stays sharper longer.

The shifting focus of the Harvard study reflects an evolving understanding of how critical connection to others is to our health. "When the study began, nobody cared about empathy or attachment," said a previous director of the study. "But the key to healthy aging is relationships, relationships, relationships."

Reconnect and Reboot

I have been fortunate to witness firsthand the power of reconnecting with others and Self while working for several years at the Omega Institute in New York. I was a coach for Joe Cross's Camp Reboot, a five-day camp where attendees in varying degrees of health come together to drink juice, detox, and learn new healthy habits. Joe Cross is known for his 2011 documentary *Fat, Sick & Nearly Dead*, and my job at camp was to help create an inclusive community and to inspire and assist in the attendees' transformations.

During our time together, participants often related that they have been too embarrassed by their appearance to bring themselves to go to the gym, which had led to an unhealthy cycle that subsequently sent them spiraling downward. But at Camp Reboot, they formed new and healthier habits in a safe environment that made them feel comfortable to open up to others and work through their vulnerabilities.

The first day of the five-day camp was intense. After a day full of lectures, three hundred people were split into groups of twenty and paired with a coach, before ending the day with a smaller group session. I was one of the coaches leading the daily group sessions.

Within the smaller group sessions, I encouraged people to open up, sharing their personal, heartfelt stories and delving deep into where they are now and where they want to go. Invariably, as participants express their vulnerabilities, they are met with tears, hugs, and laughter, and most importantly, breakthroughs and transformations are shared.

Would I be able to help these people if I were not connected with my Self? Would they truly open up and connect if they were merely listening to reply, rather than listening to understand?

After attending to your Self, attend to your connection with others. This means listening with the intention of understanding, not just listening with the intention of replying. This means acknowledging others with curiosity and empathy instead of judgment. Attending to your connection with others is how you expand your connection to the world and universe, and how you experience fulfillment every day.

Think quality over quantity. We do not need a hundred friends. We need a few closely connected friends, people with whom we can build authentic and lasting relationships.

As a coach at Camp Reboot, I found it extremely fulfilling to guide people through their transformations. Every year, I was inspired by the individuals who found the courage to show up and participate. People came to us with a deeply rooted fear of judgment, but they nonetheless had the conviction to persevere. Their courage and perseverance enabled both their transformation and their connection with themselves and others.

Making genuine connections with others is about first tapping into our true Self, and then connecting to others with an open mind and an open heart.

When we come from the same place, from the awareness and practice of authentic connection, the result of that interaction is more meaningful and enriching. It lends itself to greater expansion of the heart and mind, enabling everyone to both receive more and give more.

World: Rise2Shine

What about others who are not in your immediate circle? Attending to your connection to the world is the next step in the process of moving outward from Self to the universe.

In 2009, I was sitting at the W Hotel bar in Atlanta with a few friends, talking about how we wanted to make a difference in the world. We were all working jobs that left us feeling unfulfilled and were seeking to serve some higher purpose.

We agreed that the best course of action would be to do something for children, as they are the most vulnerable members of society and the least able to help themselves. After some discussion, we were drawn to Haiti, the poorest country in the Western Hemisphere and with the highest infant mortality rate.

In 2010, shortly after we made this joint commitment, a devastating 7.0-magnitude earthquake hit the small island, making a bad situation worse. We took this as an urgent sign, and after some research, we found a place in Fond Parisien, Haiti, to open a local school, which we named Rise2Shine.

In that area of Haiti, the most elaborate homes consisted of only four cement walls and a tarp covering a small surface area of the bare dirt floor. More often, makeshift homes were built out of brush and cardboard. These small spaces would house families of up to eighteen people.

Mothers walked their children to school one to two hours each way in scorching heat. Many women had children from multiple fathers, all of whom had disappeared, leaving them to parent alone. I met one nineteen-year-old woman who had three children, all due to rape, which tragically is a common occurrence.

Just as heartbreaking, these single mothers often did not even know their own age, let alone the ages of their children or the current date. It truly meant the world to us that we could make a tangible difference in some of their lives.

Just over a year later, the school's opening ribbon-cutting ceremony was scheduled, and we went to witness this momentous day in the lives of some of the forgotten children and families of Haiti.

Our opening event was pushed back at the last moment due to delays on behalf of a board member and the town's mayor. The ceremony, which had been scheduled for November 9, 2011, was spontaneously rescheduled to take place two days later, at the meaningful time of 11:11 AM on 11/11/11.

When the doors of Rise2Shine officially opened that morning, I experienced one of my most gratifying moments. It was life-changing to witness the countless smiles on the faces of mothers and children at our opening ceremony, knowing their lives would be significantly improved. I will never forget that day.

Seeking a connection with the world, my friends and I built an institution that will make real and lasting change for years and generations to come. I knew our work could be meaningful to the children we serve in Haiti, but I did not realize how much it would help me in return. Rise2-Shine gave me a far greater perspective of my Self in relation to the world.

Today, Rise2Shine continues to grow, fulfilling its mission of feeding and educating children who otherwise would have a meager chance of survival. There are now over seventy kids enrolled. My cofounders and I return annually at the start of the school year to interview children and their families as they line up, hoping to be accepted into the school. We choose the kids who come from the most abject poverty. This is not easy because they all share similar conditions. The trip is always bittersweet. We welcome a new class and give hope and future to some, but at the same time know that, due to limited resources, we cannot accept everyone.

Rise2Shine is a profoundly fulfilling part of my life and a connection to the world that I learned I need. After coming home from our initial trip for the school's opening, I knew I had changed; it showed in my daily life.

Today, as I walk into my kitchen for a glass of water, or take a shower or open the refrigerator, I remember the Haitians who trek for hours barefoot in tattered clothing to retrieve buckets of fresh water, carried on their heads in blazing-hot conditions. This new level of mindfulness makes me grateful for each drop of water and the roof over my head.

Connecting to the world broadens our perspectives and helps us realize our sense of responsibility and purpose. It makes us think about things that would not usually cross our mind or directly impact us. We must expose ourselves to this kind of connection to gain this critical awareness. Indeed, the world, with all its beauty and all its pain, needs us and is not something that should ever be dismissed or taken for granted.

Universe: Pieces of the Puzzle

Connecting to the universe is the hardest piece of the puzzle. To me, this means trusting that your higher Self is part of a greater plan and that you are where you should be in this moment.

This belief in a greater plan does not have to be rooted in religion; it is not about karma or past lives. In my case, I am a nonpracticing Muslim, born in a primarily Muslim country, but now living according to my own spirituality, values, and cultural traditions.

Those who are religious can understand "universe" to mean "God" or "gods" or whatever terms are most meaningful. Those who are agnostic or atheist can understand "universe" to mean being part of the larger scheme of nature and all things. Those who are spiritual but not religious can understand "universe" to be meaningful interconnectedness with everything.

However, to me it is important to feel connected to a higher being, a higher power, or a higher purpose that gives our life deeper meaning. That higher being can also be our higher Self. This connection enables us to align our personal goals with this higher purpose, even if we do not know where our life will lead. At root, this is belief in a powerful universe, one that has a place and a plan for each of us.

To look at it another way, "prayer" is often associated with *asking* for something. Connecting with the universe, on the other hand, is about *listening* — with our heart and mind — and tapping into our senses for the answers. It is about choosing to strengthen our intuition. We might not see, hear, feel, or even understand the signs that come our way until we are in alignment with our greater plan, flowing with the current instead of fighting against it.

When we connect with our higher Self, to others, and to the world, we no longer live on autopilot. We awaken and connect with the universe. We often see the world through a lens clouded by ego, stress, and fear, and this affects our actions and decisions. Connecting to the universe defogs the lens, and this clarity of vision helps us find peace. We unite our gut feelings and natural intuition with our thoughts, our heart with our mind. We stop making decisions based on fear and judgment and instead make them from love and clarity.

We need to trust that there is a greater power and to allow our Self to tap into its energy. I experienced this realization in my own life as a result of a series of providential events.

In 2014, not long after returning home to San Francisco after coaching at Camp Reboot in Rhinebeck, New York, I entertained the thought: *It would be great to temporarily move to New York City for a new experience.* At the time, I could barely make the decision to buy a pair of shoes on a whim, so spontaneous thoughts were unusual.

However, only hours after this idea popped into my head, I received an email from a vice president at JPMorgan Chase, whom I had just met at Camp Reboot. She invited me to do a wellness training for her leadership team in New York City.

I took the job, and soon after, I received a text from a friend in Manhattan: He was going on vacation at the same time I was going to be in the city, and he needed someone to house-sit and take care of his dogs. It was meant to be. My idea, timing, place, intention, and purpose were all in alignment.

I had such a great time working and playing in Manhattan that, at the end of the training, I could not bear the thought of leaving, so I stayed for another month.

I fell even more in love with the city. I decided that if I could find an apartment in this particular three-block radius in Soho, I would move across the country. This was a decision that was completely out of character for me — as many of my loved ones will attest.

Fortuitously, I had already planned to meet my cousin Bahar for lunch the following day. She happens to be a savvy Manhattan realtor, and we used our time to view a few apartments. By the end of the week, I had seen two viable apartments, though my heart was set on one.

I knew I had to act quickly, but before I could, I received a call that instantly burst my bubble. Someone else who had seen my first-choice place right before me had taken the apartment that very same day.

By this point, I was already excited yet nervous about relocating — even though all my friends and family were on the West Coast — and I was determined to make it work. I chose not to get discouraged. I contacted the agent for my second-choice apartment, who said it could be mine if I wanted it, but I needed to be at the lease signing within the hour and have a cashier's check made out to the owner. I hustled, got the cashier's check, and showed up on time, but the agent said the cashier's check was made out to the incorrect name and was not acceptable.

I grew frustrated. The check was made out to the name they had given me, and it was late on a Friday afternoon. I was leaving New York on Monday morning, so this was the only time I could sign the lease. Unconcerned, they told me there was nothing they could do without a cashier's check. I sprinted back to the bank, entering the doors just as they were closing.

As I stood in front of the teller window, about to have them issue a new cashier's check, I received a call. The offer on my first-choice apartment had fallen through, and it was now available again.

"You're kidding me," I blurted into the phone. "I almost signed for another place!" I quickly left the bank and went to sign the lease for my first-choice apartment.

Was this coincidence or providence? I choose the latter. Whatever you call it, I was thrilled. Somehow, the impossible had become possible: I had gotten my first-choice apartment in the neighborhood I wanted only days before I had to return to San Francisco.

That Friday afternoon, after running around like a headless chicken, I decided to take a break for a massage. I had a deep ache in my neck and shoulders, where I tend to hold stress. I was wearing a *rudraksha mala* beaded bracelet I had gotten in Rishikesh. This bracelet is meant to be worn when you need guidance and enlightenment. When you no longer need it, the story goes, it will fall or break off. I had worn it every day since I had been in India, three years prior. Before the massage, the masseuse asked me to remove it, and while trying to take it off, it snapped and fell to the floor.

This bracelet broke at the moment it was supposed to. I had finally awakened to the possibility that the universe was trying to tell me something. *I was here.* I did not need the bracelet anymore. I was okay.

After the massage, I took a relaxed walk back to my new apartment and passed by a jewelry store with three necklaces in the window. I happened to glance at the center one, upon which the engraving read: *You are meant to be here.*

These were all my signs: the idea, the job, the dog-sitting apartment, the check, the lease, the new apartment, the bracelet, and the meaningful message. I felt no doubt that there was a greater meaning to my move to New York City, something I was only able to acknowledge by being awake and present to the synchronicity that occurred. We can ask, wonder, and pray, but it will all be in vain if we are not awake to receive the answer.

Ralph Waldo Emerson said, "Once you make a decision, the universe conspires to make it happen."

You are meant to be here.

One could easily brush off the greater meaning of this chain of events as magical, mystical, or even silly. To me, it represents what can happen when, through connecting to our Self, we connect to the universe. It represents trusting that there is a higher plan and our lives have purpose, which both reveal themselves through the different signs and pieces of the puzzle.

For me, this providential sequence was like the pieces of a puzzle coming together. I had spent almost my entire life, since I was two years old, living in the Bay Area. Moving to New York City was a big transition outside of my comfort zone. Yet at that time, I knew I needed to shake my life up, and having so many things come together in such a short and timely manner was a confirmation that I was on the right track. My decision to move to New York City opened up numerous possibilities for me, both personally and professionally. I expanded my business from coast to coast and worked with other wellness companies to help revolutionize the corporate wellness industry. My future husband also relocated to New York City from San Francisco, and today we are both thriving. Clearly, my "spontaneous" impulse was the right thing to do.

Have you experienced multiple signs that focus your attention on a specific path or intention you have set for yourself? Sometimes we cannot see the whole picture of what the puzzle is supposed to look like, but we can tell as pieces fall into place and fit together seamlessly that something beautiful is being created. Similarly, the pieces of your career or life can come together in a meaningful and timely way for your highest good.

Has something stressful in your life suddenly worked itself out? Or perhaps, something you had been struggling with one day required less energy and worry? This is your plan unfolding.

Synchronicity happens. There are no coincidences when you are awake to the meaningful signs. Pause. Breathe. Choose to open your eyes and heart and be mindful of what is going on within you and around you. There is an energy or being that is more powerful than anything or anyone.

Connecting to the universe is about being awake in order to connect the dots, to understand, and to trust that, somehow, life will make sense, even if only in hindsight. There is a higher purpose, even when we cannot see it.

Trusting this is even more important in the face of the divisions and distressing events that fill news headlines. Racism, war, disease, climate change, and politics divide us as human beings. When we witness inhumanity, it can become difficult to feel like we are all connected, that we are one.

Nurturing that connection starts with each of us as individuals. We must not be swept away by acts of terror and discrimination. We must instead tear down the walls that divide us.

Open your heart, connect with your Self, and connect with those around you, so that we can connect as a world.

The world would be a more wholesome place, a much smaller, more connected place, if we dissolved the separations that arise because of our egos, pains, adversities, regrets, and problems. We would be open to limitless possibilities and discover creative ways to overcome the issues that divide us. Our relationships would be more meaningful.

Imagine what it would be like if we were all living the best version of our Self.

We could all be connected.

We could be one.

BUSINESS HACKS

Cultivate Strong Relationships

Developing strong connections in the workplace is just as important as those we build with friends, family, and other communities. In your workplace, whatever your job, foster a culture that prioritizes the relationships between you and your colleagues. Leaders can do this by holding friendly competitions or having two unlikely departments come together for a project.

We are far more likely to experience joy when we have a friend in our workspace. A LinkedIn study found that 46 percent of business professionals worldwide say their friendships at work contribute significantly to their overall happiness.

Emotional support helps ease depression, anxiety, and illness. Colleagues who are engaged with and support one another are likely to be better employees, driving the company in a positive direction through improved teamwork, overall morale, and higher productivity. A *Harvard Business Review* study found that "reducing isolation at work is good for business."

The well-being of employees, our company, and our Self could very well depend upon the connections we make and encourage among everyone. Ensure this by operating with appreciation, inclusion, and mutual respect, which builds trust. Help others achieve their goals and show genuine care for their overall well-being.

Make People Feel Important

What defines a great leader is their ability to make every individual feel valuable and indispensable by acknowledging and engaging them in authentic conversation. If we help colleagues and employees feel empowered and essential to the operation, everyone's well-being, along with the business's well-being, will prosper. Make your praise sincere by being specific and talking to people one-on-one while making eye contact. Appreciation and recognition go a long way. Maya Angelou once said, "People will forget what you said, people will forget what you did, but people will never forget how you made them feel."

Be a Connector

When it comes to success, an important component can be who you know. Be at the center of your network, and connect people with one another as often as possible, to form new relationships, make unlikely connections, and expand your horizons through genuine networking.

Contribute to the Community

Volunteer work is incredibly fulfilling and provides unique perspectives on the world. Choose to incorporate service into your life and your company and make a difference in the lives of those less fortunate. Not only will you improve the lives of others, but your life will also become significantly more meaningful as a result.

By volunteering, we serve, learn, grow, and connect with the world of which we are an inextricable part. To gain a fresh perspective, intentionally put yourself in foreign places and see the world through eyes other than your own. Your world at home is not all there is, and conveniences you take for granted every day may represent hardships for someone else.

Then, encourage colleagues and your company to get involved with the community. Executives can allow employees to contribute a certain number of hours or days every year to pay it forward at local organizations; offer flexibility to accommodate those organizations. Companies such as Salesforce, Deloitte, Cisco, Genentech, PricewaterhouseCoopers, American Express, Etsy, and Autodesk allow for at least five days off annually for volunteerism. Encourage others to step out of their comfort zones and volunteer in a space that feels foreign to them. Research shows that acts of generosity or charity result in beneficial health and well-being outcomes.

ACTION STEPS

Find Peace in Solitude

In the ocean of your mind, you can continuously feel the swell and crash of the waves. They rise and fall around you, clamorous on the surface. The deeper you dive, the calmer the water becomes.

Our minds tend to be stuck on the surface, tossed and battered by the waves because we do not make an effort to dive deeper. There is always a portion of the mind that is already calm: that gives you creativity, clarity, focus, and fulfillment. You just need to dive down to access it.

Pause. Breathe. Choose to meditate. Play. Connect with nature. Whatever it is that makes you feel at ease and at peace with your Self, do it. Find your happy place in solitude.

Spend some time in a park with a cup of coffee or a good book. Sit silently. Take an urban or mountain hike. Journal a stream of your thoughts, feelings, emotions, and ideas, void of any filters. Move your body. Create art. Listen to your favorite music. Stay in the shower a little longer. Do whatever it takes to cultivate a peaceful state.

Quiet your mind and connect with your Self in order to be present every day. Develop a morning ritual that fosters and prioritizes this connection before being caught up in the busyness of the day.

Choose the People You Surround Yourself with Wisely

Be aware that who you surround yourself with easily becomes who you are, as we tend to take on the traits of those we spend the most time with. Choose to surround yourself with inspiring people and breed positive thoughts and big ideas.

Listen without Judgment

How can we connect with others if we do not listen to them without judgment? This is the only way to gain a clear picture of what is happening in our relationships, our home, and our company. Practice being present and actively listening. If judgment arises, replace it with curiosity using the Upgrade Method.

Listen to truly understand, not to respond. Listen consciously and with an open heart. We are so attached to efficiency that we often look down at our phone while having a conversation instead of maintaining eye contact, blocking the possibility of a deeper connection.

Take "Busy" Out of Your Vocabulary

When most people are asked, "How are you? What have you been up to?" they generally reply, "Oh, I've been really busy."

Saying "busy" is like shutting the door in someone's face, forfeiting the connection we might have made. Practice taking "busy" out of your vocabulary; challenge yourself to do this for a week.

The next time someone asks how you are, share with them how you truly are and what you have actually been doing. Otherwise, you are dismissing the question and the opportunity to connect on a deeper level.

Allow yourself to be open. Allow yourself to authentically connect with others. Share more. Be vulnerable. Vulnerability opens up connection. This helps you connect deeper with employees and colleagues. It also helps others better understand you. If you refuse to take on a task because you are "too busy," this dismissal could lead to resentment and misunderstanding. However, if you explain your situation and strategize ways to help the other person — perhaps by reprioritizing tasks — this honest communication can strengthen your relationship.

Many people use lack of time as an excuse not to connect. They say, "I don't have time to see my friends," or "I don't have time to sit and meditate or go for a run." They go through the motions each day like a robot, feeling very disconnected.

One of the things that I have learned from working with so many executives is that it is lonely at the top. Steve Jobs felt this. But loneliness affects anyone and everyone. Do not let your own busyness keep you from connecting with Self, others, world, and universe.

If you choose to prioritize connection, you can always find the time. Remember, attending to your connections does not take away from your life; it is your life. Connection revives us and gives us meaning and joy.

Acknowledge the Daily Signs

Visualize exactly what you want in as much detail as you can. Create a vision board with pictures or write your ideas and vision down. Make sure you visit your vision daily, perhaps in the morning before you start your day, so you can prepare and train your brain to be on the lookout for signs of validation.

Acknowledge all the signs — or what you may think are coincidences — that occur in your day. Be prepared for signs to surface in the most bizarre and unpredictable ways and places, like overhearing a conversation at a coffee shop or having a seemingly inexplicable urge to do or not do something.

Unexplained feelings can help guide you toward the right answer without really knowing how or why you got there. A higher power is out there, guiding you. Whatever you call this higher energy, acknowledge it, open yourself up to it, listen and watch for it, and connect with the universe.

Finally, reflect nightly on the meaningful signs that were brought to your awareness, and connect the dots.

KEY TAKEAWAYS

- In order to live an authentic life and to see change in the world, you must attend to your connections with your higher, true Self first. Then, move outward to others, the world, and the universe. Expand your mind and your heart by attending to these connections in order to improve the quality of your life.
- Attending to the connection with your Self is the most intimate and fundamental part of your journey. Revel in your own company. Choose to commit to a mindful daily practice to nurture your connection with your Self so that your vital energy or prana can flow freely. As a result, you will experience a ripple effect of beneficial impacts across all areas of your life.
- Connecting with others means listening with the intention of understanding, not just replying. It is about acknowledging others with curiosity and empathy to cultivate meaningful relationships. This is how fulfillment is brought into your everyday life and into your relationships. "Good relationships keep us happier and healthier. Period."
- Connecting to the world broadens our perspectives and helps us realize our sense of responsibility and purpose. It makes us think about things that would not usually cross our mind or directly impact us. If we do not expose ourselves to this kind of connection, we will lack critical awareness.
- Connecting with the universe depends on trust that our higher Self is part of a greater plan and that we are where we should be in this moment. It is about listening with our heart and mind and tapping into our senses for the answers. It is about choosing to strengthen our intuition.

PART III

Promote Your Self
to the CEO
of Your Well-Being

THE THREE P's

• THE THREE P's •

PAIN, our greatest teacher for growth

PRANA, our energy to be fully engaged at work and in life

PURPOSE, our drive for meaning

In this book, part I explores how mindfulness is the bedrock of well-being, and part II presents the Seven A's, which are tools and strategies for making mindful choices to manage stress, build resilience, and live a healthy, happy, connected life. Part III delves deeper into purposeful growth and introduces the Three P's: pain, prana, and purpose. These represent powerful dynamics that can lead you to achieve your fullest potential and evolve into the best version of your Self.

Strewn across the map of life are experiences of pain. Pain can be physical or emotional, and it can stem from both personal and professional life. A business or organization can experience pain as well. Pain is a universal experience but suffering is a choice. If we choose to reframe our pain, it can serve as our greatest teacher and as a catalyst for growth. We can take pain and turn it into drive, and then use that drive to change our life (or our business) for the better.

The pain of growth leads us to realize the significance of life, breath, our vital energy, and flowing prana. When we tap into our vital energy, our prana, we can tackle the pain of growth and emerge from challenging situations stronger than before. The mindful choices represented by the Seven A's help unblock our prana, which promotes healing. Our goal is to achieve a *prana flow state* that enables us to attain and sustain peak performance.

Then, when this vital energy is aligned with a higher purpose, it animates our life and gives it meaning. We experience the best version of our Self. When we realize our purpose, we have more than a job, more than a career. We have a mission in life.

Ultimately, when we put everything together, we become what I call a *Mindful MAP Maker*. The acronym MAP stands for *master mindfulness*, *apply the Seven A's*, and *promote your Self to the CEO of your well-being*, and it represents adopting a holistic approach to life. In practice, this means we see the big picture and take empowered and aligned action to create the life we desire. Charting a life purpose is akin to mapmaking: We connect the dots of the past to lead to our desired future, creating a coherent and meaningful narrative that shapes our story and destiny. A Mindful MAP Maker designs and pursues a life of purpose.

This begins by asking, What is important to you? Is it to lead by example? To have a competitive edge? To be respected? To love and be loved? To be happy? To have a sense of belonging? To make a dent in the universe? To make the best decisions for your family, friends, colleagues, and employees?

You can only work toward your goals effectively if you are the CEO of your well-being.

In order to promote your Self to CEO of your well-being, you must allow pain to teach you, optimize your prana to a higher purpose, and become a Mindful MAP Maker. I use the word *promote* intentionally. Think of it as the Big P. When we settle for something less than the best version of our Self, we are like a middle manager — competent perhaps, maybe successful and reliable, but with the potential to be much more. A CEO is a visionary like Steve Jobs. They name the destination, and as captain of the ship, they lead the way, guide and inspire others, and navigate through inevitable rough and stormy seas while protecting everyone on board. This is true on every level and in every role, personal and professional, whether you are a literal CEO, a manager, a clerk, a parent, a partner, a son, a daughter, or a friend.

Through the journey in this book, you can learn to live a healthy and successful life that does not sacrifice self-care or connection with family and friends. Your life is an integrated whole, a single ecosystem. You *can* have it all!

Are you ready to take the next step and give yourself the ultimate promotion?

CHAPTER TEN

PAIN, OUR GREATEST TEACHER FOR GROWTH

THE THREE P's

PAIN

Prana

Purpose

Pain can be an invasive, paralyzing part of life. Emotional pain, physical pain, pain caused by stress or disruptions in our career — we experience different types of pain for many reasons. Pain can lead to chronic stress and foster disease if our resilience reserve becomes depleted. Pain can be a shock to the system that jars us from the familiar and sends us hurtling into the unknown.

A client of mine shared a story about his friend, the CEO of a company in England. One day, his friend's company imploded and went bankrupt. The day after, the CEO's wife found him in their home, dead by suicide.

No tragedy, no matter how painful, means the end of life. When pain is so bad we cannot imagine continuing, we must pause, breathe, and simply choose to continue breathing. In the moment, pain can feel overwhelming, but pain will pass. As difficult as it may be, our job is to see pain as a teacher. To approach it as an opportunity for growth. Sometimes, that can be the only choice we have, and our life depends on making it.

Pain can turn our world and our internal compass upside down and shove us into darkness. Simultaneously, however, pain can shock us or catapult us out of everyday autopilot.

Everyone has experienced emotional and physical pain, whether that involves abuse, betrayal, abandonment, grief, shame, rejection, loneliness, chronic physical pain, disease, or countless other things. Yet everyone's experience of pain differs. Further, what causes pain can differ. What drives one person to feel tremendous grief might not affect someone else in the same way. This is why it is impossible to evaluate, judge, or compare experiences of pain. What really matters, and what this chapter focuses on, is acknowledging pain when it exists, learning to cope with it, and growing from it as a result.

Acknowledging pain is rarely easy. We spend our lives trying to avoid pain, and when it arrives, we often try to deny or minimize it. However, the moment we feel pain is when we must pay attention to our thoughts, feelings, and actions. This fosters the understanding that helps us manage what hurts, persevere, resolve the problem (if possible), and better equip ourselves to handle pain the next time. Further, we can prepare ourselves ahead for life's adversities by practicing the Seven A's, building our resilience reserves, and actively tending to our well-being.

We must recognize pain for what it truly is. At its worst, pain invades and paralyzes us, making us vulnerable to chronic stress and disease. At its best, pain is a catalyst and our greatest teacher. It can prompt new growth and make us more resilient. It presents challenges that, if we embrace them as opportunities, can make us stronger and better able to withstand or recover swiftly from difficult conditions. Pain is a tool in promoting our Self from one level to the next, in letting go and moving forward.

Everyone falls down. What matters is how we respond to the stumble and choosing to get back up.

The Ugly C-Word

On the day that Steve Jobs died of cancer, I was immobilized with shock. The pain was so great that I did something out of character for me: I expressed myself through writing. I pulled out an unused journal and began to write about Steve. This urge to express my pain and how Steve impacted my life eventually gave birth to this book.

The day of Steve's death, October 5, 2011, is ingrained in my mind as if it were yesterday. That morning, a breaking news alert on my phone displayed the terrible news. I was in pharmaceutical sales and had a lunch meeting scheduled in downtown San Francisco with a handful of doctors. From the window of the doctor's office, I saw a crowd surrounding the Apple Store in Union Square. After the meeting, I went down and immersed myself into the crowd of sobbing strangers, who plastered the glass storefront with photos, quotes, and messages, and who laid bouquets of flowers on the sidewalk.

In another out-of-character action, I became emotional in public. Steve was my greatest mentor and had played a significant role in my life. He was also the most impactful and iconic visionary of our time, the quintessential tech founder and leader.

Here I was, among hundreds of people who had likely never known Steve personally, yet who were crying alongside me in their loss. I was overcome with a feeling of immense gratitude for the opportunity I had been given, to have personally known and interacted with him daily. He is an inspiration for the life I live today.

Before I worked with Steve, my parents had been my greatest mentors and supporters. They have never faltered in encouraging me to be myself. They are proud of the person I am and have always placed complete trust in me. Whenever I go to them for advice, the conversation always ends with: "We trust you; you know best," or "Just be yourself." These were the last words I heard before going in for my interview with Steve. I know I always have their support.

When I was living in San Francisco after college, my mother was diagnosed with the ugly C-word, stage-three breast cancer. It was time for my mother and me to reverse roles. My father, nine years older than my mother and a prostate cancer survivor, could relate to what she was going through and provided her with emotional support. I became her primary caretaker and her rock as she fought through the cancer. It was one of the hardest things I have ever done, and I altered my world to be with my parents as my mother fought for her life.

Her surgery for a full bilateral mastectomy lasted seven hours longer than scheduled. The minutes and hours dragged on, and time lost all meaning in the hospital waiting room. I was full of anxiety, waiting, pacing up and down the halls anticipating the outcome. When she finally came out of surgery, and my father, brother, and I were permitted to see her, I saw a different version of my mother lying on the crisp white sheets of the hospital bed. Her eyes were closed, her face pale and bloated.

My mother looked dead. This woman on the bed did not look like my mother.

I thought, *Where is she? That's not my mother. My mother is gone. Where is she?* My eyes filled with tears as I was overcome with emotion. I ran out of the room before she could open her eyes. I did not want her to see me upset. I composed myself and returned by the time she woke up. The outcome could have been different. It could have been fatal. Now, both of my parents have survived cancer, and I am incredibly grateful each day to still have both of them in my life.

In a strange way, I am also grateful for the emotional pain I experienced as her caretaker. That pain deepened our connection and sealed our bond. I was there for her as she had always been for me. A few years later, she would do the same for my cousin and aunt. We feel pain for the things we care most about, which is why pain can be such a great teacher, and why we must always be mindful of it.

Later, when I was in India, I had conversations with three different swamis (Hindu ascetics), and I asked each of them separately about my mother's experience with cancer. I asked, "Why do bad things happen to good people?" To my surprise, each of these three holy men had a nearly identical response:

"Good and bad do not exist. They are simple concepts that we, as human beings, decide to place a label on."

In retrospect, they were telling me that every experience is an opportunity to learn if we choose to see it as such. The pain we experience today can provide comfort and support to someone else tomorrow, just as my father and I did for my mother, and my mother did for my cousin and aunt while battling cancer.

We can look at painful experiences as roadblocks, but that reflects a limited mindset. Even the most painful experiences can be our greatest teachers, instilling in us a growth mindset, enabling us to experience miracles. Just as a positive mindset can empower us to harness stress, pain can be a catalyst for growth if we embrace it as a teacher.

Throughout our lives, we are always trying to get from point A to point B. But sometimes, instead of experiencing detours and delays, the plane crashes. Great pain occurs, disrupting our entire life and identity.

A life-threatening disease can be the ultimate upheaval. It does not matter what you were doing right before cancer or the plane crash: whether finishing your life's biggest project, launching a product, or raising capital. That all becomes inconsequential. All that matters going forward is survival and what your life will be like from that point onward.

One minute you are walking into a doctor's office, worrying about an upcoming board meeting. The next minute you are walking out and no longer recognize the world around you. Everything (priorities, perspectives, thought processes) changes as you think: *What is my life going to be like?*

Your being is suddenly split into prediagnosis and postdiagnosis, and for a time, you are left feeling hopeless and helpless. You can do your best with what you can control by managing your stress and building resilience, adopting a healthy lifestyle, and helping prevent disease. In the end, death is not something we control. This is why we must not take life for granted. We must live our best life with purpose and passion.

Unexpected cancer-like events can also infect a business, leaving us trying to figure out how we are going to revive and survive in the face of uncertainty and upheaval. Companies run out of money. People make bad decisions. Someone might drive the company over the cliff. Board members could turn against us, as in Steve Jobs's case.

How on earth do we turn this around? How do we turn an obstacle into an opportunity?

Pause. Breathe. Choose to be curious. Ask yourself, *What is the upside of this situation that I don't see at the moment?* If you cannot see anything positive — which is natural in the darkest of times — take a wild guess. Or ask yourself, *What is the lesson I'm supposed to learn?* Remove the phrase *I don't know* from your vocabulary. This constraint can prompt you to reframe the situation and to use pain as a guide leading you toward an unexpected answer.

Startup "Failure"

Prior to his return as CEO of Apple, Steve Jobs experienced the greatest "failure" an entrepreneur can ever go through. He had built a company from the ground up, one that changed the world as we know it, only to be fired from it.

He could have chosen to frame this as a "failure" and quit innovating. But just because he was no longer the CEO of Apple did not mean he was no longer the CEO of his well-being. He embraced this painful circumstance as an opportunity to start another company.

"I didn't see it then, but it turned out that getting fired from Apple was the best thing that could have ever happened to me," he later reflected. "The heaviness of being successful was replaced by the lightness of being a beginner again, less sure about everything. It freed me to enter one of the most creative periods of my life."

In business and in every aspect of life, the possibility of "failure" is always present. A company could lose money or never take off. An expensive prototype might not receive a patent or succeed in beating its competition. We all have an Inner Critic yapping in our ear with one negative thought after another.

- *I didn't make the right decision.*
- *I could've done better.*
- *I screwed this one up.*
- *I'm a failure.*

I choose to believe that *there is no such thing as "failure." There is only experience that provides us with the feedback, insight, and wisdom to steer us back on course and evolve.*

Steve was not fired because he "failed." He received feedback from the members of his board, and he used that feedback to evolve. This hurt, but he used that experience of pain to grow. Pain became his teacher.

Some of our decisions will be wrong. We will make a bad choice, be outsmarted, or find circumstances conspiring against us. What do we do as pressure mounts, insecurity runs wild, and the voice in our ear whispers *failure, failure*? When we are in pain, we cannot see the light at the end of the tunnel.

We need to do what Steve did. We need to reframe pain as a tool for growth, learn from it, and discover the hidden opportunity. Again, there is no such thing as "failure," only initial disappointment. Instead of perceiving failure as a *lack* of success, see it as an opportunity to *gain* insight and grow. In other words: Pain + Reflection = Growth.

Unexpected Death: Physical and Emotional Loss

The loss of someone close to us can quickly turn our world into an unfamiliar place filled with dark, sinking, relentless pain. There are many forms of loss a person can experience, and each comes with its own kind of grief. Everyone's grief is personalized, and the grief process is nonlinear, with no order or schedule.

As we know, the most common form of loss is death. The loss of a loved one will always be tragic, but even more so when it is unexpected. It can be life's most stressful event and cause significant upheaval. We experience bereavement, which literally means "to be deprived by death." Different kinds of relationships lead to varying types of grieving. The pain felt from the loss of a spouse is different from the pain felt from the loss of a parent or child. Different hopes and expectations are shattered.

The end of a relationship is an entirely different type of loss. We face such losses in both our personal and professional lives. We have all experienced friendships or romantic relationships come to an end. At work, someone close to us might resign or be fired; they move on and leave the company, and this might end or fundamentally alter our relationship. These relationship losses and transitions challenge us. We wonder what we will do without the deep connection we once experienced with someone.

How can we manage our pain so that we can still salvage the relationship? How do we retain integrity when ending a partnership? With mindfulness. We need to fully feel and begin to process the pain before considering what is next. This is particularly important when a romantic relationship ends or we feel anger at someone. Breaking down or blowing up at someone can wreak havoc and ruin any chance of creating a new relationship on different terms. Being present to our pain is both healing and pragmatic.

The most important thing to do when suffering a loss is to be gentle with yourself. Do not judge yourself for your emotions or for events and people out of your control. Your feelings are valid, however intense they are. Give yourself as much time as you need to feel the pain and recover. Do not expect healing to follow a timeline, and do not hesitate to ask for help.

I know firsthand that we cannot predict when pain will come or how we will react, but if we choose to be gentle and kind with ourselves and respond mindfully, we can recover and move on.

Seven months after I ended a four-year relationship — and while I was still recovering from this loss — I received an email from a "friend" who shared with me new revelations about her and my ex-boyfriend that shocked and paralyzed me. Without going into details, what she told me involved horrifying actions that had been disguised from everyone who knew them for years. I had once considered my ex-boyfriend to be Prince Charming, but these revelations turned him into a villain in my mind, and my (former) friend was his accomplice. This plot twist completely crushed my perception of our romantic love story. Not only did I feel completely shattered, outraged, and appalled, but I questioned everything in my life up to then. I was rocked to my core.

After the initial shock of her email, I first blamed myself. I was angry and disillusioned for not seeing their elaborate lies and deception. Feelings of betrayal pinned me down. Getting through each minute, each hour seemed unbearable. And since my mind could not process the pain, my body manifested it physically. I became pale and constantly felt sick to my stomach. I was too nauseated to eat and rapidly lost fifteen pounds. I looked and felt like death. At some point, I curled up into the fetal position in my bedroom, unable to move. I succumbed to pain and emptiness and could not get out of bed. I felt I had no meaning or purpose. I felt shattered beyond repair.

In these moments, we have a choice. We can give in to hopelessness and despair, knowing that this is a self-destructive path, or we can face what is happening and be fully present, no matter how uncomfortable that might be. We can pause, breathe, and simply choose to keep breathing. In time, and sooner than we might think, hope, determination, and self-worth will return.

I had done nothing wrong. This person was not worth ruining my life. Despite feeling lost in a void, I paused. I took a breath. I made a choice to stand up. Since I could not think of how to move forward or move past what had happened, I thought about what I could do in that moment.

I chose not to lash out. I chose not to hysterically call my friends and family. I decided I needed time alone to process the situation. I took charge of my own healing on my own terms. I meditated and went to yoga daily, doing everything I could to become stronger. For six months, I processed this deep emotional pain. My closest friends and family knew something was wrong, but I was not ready to share.

During this particularly vulnerable time, I felt that if I went straight to those around me, they might influence my decisions, my thought processes, and by extension, my ability to cope and fully heal.

After I took the time to process the events, I decided to confront the pain directly. Gathering as much composure and integrity as possible, I reached out to my ex-boyfriend, hoping for clarity and truth. When he refused to provide that, I chose to terminate our relationship and completely cut him out of my life. I chose to put this pain to rest and no longer have it be a part of my life. Only then did I reveal the truth to my close friends and family, to explain why I had been reclusive for six months. In time, my grief would stop, and I moved onward and upward.

Everyone is different, and there are many ways to process pain. While in this instance I chose to be alone as I processed my pain and grief, it is often helpful to seek the support of others. Whatever you choose, it is critical to give yourself time. Let yourself feel the pain, and once you have done so, accept it.

Reflect, forgive, and let go in order to truly move forward and grow as a result of pain.

How Trauma Gives Birth to Growth

In time, I was able to flip pain on its head. For me, I turned it into a drive to change lives (starting with myself) and make things better. After this experience, I went back to school for holistic health coaching, and shortly after that, I traveled to India, the birthplace of yoga. All of the pain, all of the tears and destructive thoughts, I experienced during that time helped empower me to evolve.

Pain became my teacher, setting me on my path to becoming the CEO of my well-being.

Trauma can produce gains that outlast its initial deleterious effects. Survivors of traumatic events often report positive changes in their lives as a consequence of the trauma. This effect is called *posttraumatic growth*, and it can take a variety of forms. This growth can include the following:

- Greater awareness and appreciation for life
- The realization of the need to make more meaningful connections with others

- A deeper sense of self
- Stronger spirituality (whatever that means for you)

Posttraumatic growth transforms you into a stronger, wiser version of yourself and raises your emotional intelligence. Emotional intelligence — the ability to identify and manage emotions, both your own and those of others — is a vital trait to possess and cultivate. It involves using social skills to foster rapport and trust with others. Emotionally intelligent leaders seek to understand, better communicate, and connect emotionally with colleagues and teams. Psychologists have found that traumatic events often lead to increased empathy and altruism. Pain teaches us lessons that can be used to ultimately live better lives and create better businesses.

We become stronger in our mind and our heart when we turn our pain into growth. I do not have any regrets about any of my emotionally painful experiences. They have been stepping-stones that have led me to live my purpose and my passion, and to do so with the love of my life, my husband. They are an important part of my journey.

In business and the workplace, with so much to do and accomplish, you may not think that you have the luxury to process your personal pain, but it is imperative that you do. You can only ignore or run from your emotions for so long before they resurface. For instance, recall my client Jake: He initially chose to bottle up the pain he was experiencing due to his divorce, but this damaged his relationship with his team and his effectiveness on the job. Once he started processing that pain directly and intentionally, his relationships at work improved.

No matter what is causing pain, those feelings will bleed into other areas of your life and affect how you relate to or function with others. Pain at home can affect job performance, and discord within an organization can be brought home, or a sudden setback in one part of the company can cause strain and conflict in others. Any combination is possible, and no part of life can be completely compartmentalized.

This is why, in business, it is important to adopt a "learning organization" mindset (see "Play and Learn at Work," pages 77–78) and to foster resilience among individuals and teams in the workplace. The two are intimately connected. A resilient organization with a learning mindset approaches painful setbacks or internal conflict as a learning opportunity and with a curious and nonjudgmental attitude. It has a strong culture built on principles of organizational empowerment, purpose, trust, and accountability.

Mindfulness, in turn, will enhance an organization's ability to learn, adapt, and be resilient. A wellness program with a strong mindfulness component enables employees and teams — when faced with a potential crisis — to step back, evaluate options, and adjust course. These tools also increase the capacity to adapt to stressors (as explored in chapter 7). Equipped with the right mindfulness and communication tools, organizations can experience posttraumatic growth as well.

In the absence of such tools, however, individuals and companies can fall into victimhood because that is often easier than dealing honestly with pain and the challenges it presents. We can blame others or ourselves, and then wonder how everything went wrong. Victimhood is counterproductive because the goal is often to avoid examining and learning from a situation, which prevents resolving painful feelings. When succumbing to victimhood is our response to pain, it does not become a teacher. It becomes heavy baggage that weighs us down and weakens our resilience.

Pain can indeed make you stronger, and posttraumatic growth can be powerful in teaching compassion, strength, and patience. Instead of allowing yourself to sink deeper, allow yourself to fully feel pain, recognize pain as a tool for growth, and rise up.

What matters is how you choose to respond to a painful experience. As Charles Swindoll put it, "Life is 10 percent what happens to you and 90 percent how you react to it." It is up to you to choose how you would like your life to be.

What You Resist Persists

In times of distress and pain, even when it seems like your world is crumbling and your life is in shambles, pause. Breathe. Choose to observe your emotions instead of resisting them. Experience your pain as a wave that comes and goes. Whether you are experiencing doubt, fear, pressure, grief, loss, or any other pain, if you push these feelings away or deny them, they will persist. As an individual or as part of a work team, be present to pain, learn from it, and grow from it.

Practice loving your emotions, even if it is difficult. Your darkness and shadows make it possible for light to shine back into your life. You must appreciate both sides by being able to *feel, accept, forgive, let go, and move forward.*

You may think you have your life mapped out. You may know who you want to be and how you want to live your life. You may know what goals you want to accomplish. You might even have the next fifty years planned out. However, all of that can be swept out from under you in a blink of an eye.

Your map can be torn to shreds, leaving you feeling utterly lost, hurt, and empty, by emotional or physical pain, the ugly C-word or business "failure." Whatever the cause, these events are signs that the universe has different plans for you than you expected. This truth can be challenging to accept.

If you doubt this, turn on the news: Something tragic is always occurring somewhere — another mass shooting, bombings, a plane crash, war, disease pandemics, earthquakes, hurricanes. Devastations are endless.

Every day we wake up not knowing what is going to happen. We turn off our alarm and brush our teeth, not thinking about whether or not these are our final hours or the last day of a loved one. We wake up and think, *Time to get ready for work and get the kids to school.* We are always working toward something, until we are not.

Life can be taken from us in an instant, which is why it is critical to mindfully live your best life *now*, not tomorrow or when you retire.

Similar to stress, pain is inevitable. Living your best life is choosing how to use pain to move forward every day, especially in moments when moving forward, or moving at all, seems impossible.

It is *your* choice.

Will you choose to let pain destroy you? Or will you, as Oprah Winfrey said, "turn your wounds into wisdom," choosing to let your pain make you stronger and wiser?

Pause.

Breathe.

Choose to make pain your greatest teacher.

BUSINESS HACKS

Create a Workplace Culture That Supports Mental Health

As a leader, make sure your company has initiatives and programs in place for employees that provide education, support, and resources for mental health. Additionally, provide trainings for managers so they are better equipped to support employees who are dealing with mental health issues.

All employees want to feel they are given appropriate support and recognition. As a leader it is your job to ensure employees feel supported, not just during tough times, but in their everyday job. Acknowledge them for their efforts and a job well done. This motivates them to continue to do good work and makes them feel good.

Address Your Customers' Pain Points

Typically, people spend money to either battle pain or pursue pleasure. The more painful the problem, the more willing people are to pay for a solution. Therefore, it behooves entrepreneurs, business leaders, and employees to focus on customers' pain points and to come up with a solution to alleviate or heal their pain.

For entrepreneurs, startup founders, and leaders, how do we figure out if our new idea, product, or solution truly addresses a customer's pain? It boils down to two questions. Can you readily describe the pain your company solves in just a few words? Using this simple explanation, can you influence a prospective customer to purchase your product and not have buyer's remorse?

If you can answer yes to both of these questions, congratulations! If not, keep at it. It can eventually be fatal for your business if you cannot articulate a compelling customer pain point and deliver a viable solution.

Practice the Feedback Sandwich Model

When communicating a concern, critiquing, or providing constructive feedback to colleagues and employees, you can minimize the pain someone may feel by sandwiching your comments between compliments:

1. First, praise the person with a positive: "I like how you..." or "I appreciate that you..."
2. Then state your concerns: "I have some ideas for improving..."; "I have some concerns about..."; or "I'd like to see more of..."
3. Finish with a positive statement: "Overall, I really appreciate your efforts to..."

This approach uses the neuro-linguistic programming (NLP) model I learned in my training. Positioning your concern within positive feedback helps someone hear your concern without feeling defensive.

ACTION STEPS

Process Pain Mindfully

In a time of intense pain, we might think that life cannot get any worse and that we will always feel this bad. This sense of hopelessness is what drives some people to turn to suicide as an escape.

Processing pain, however, requires taking the time to feel and mindfully reflect on our experience. We acknowledge and accept what happened and our feelings, gain self-awareness, and finally let go and move on.

When we use pain to teach us and help us grow, when we allow a painful experience to shape us into a better, stronger person, we will eventually look back without regret, since pain will have made us who we are today.

Pain is always very individualized. There is no one correct way of understanding or responding to it. Processing pain also takes time and happens in phases. We cannot expect to just pause, breathe, and choose to say, "Okay, I'm over it!" We make progress in stages, and we should expect pain to return at times, while trying to avoid falling into a pit of chronic stress, which can lead to disease. The intention is not to merely endure pain, but by pursuing growth and happiness, to use pain to learn and improve ourselves.

Try the following approach to process pain (and modify it as needed):

1. **Acknowledge what happened:** When a sudden powerful disturbance rocks your world, acknowledge it. This is step one. We often react with shock, followed by disbelief and denial: *This isn't happening*, or *This can't happen to me*. This defense mechanism buffers the immediate shock, but recognize and acknowledge this defensive reaction so you can move on to the next step.

2. **Feel, process, and accept the pain:** Breathe, listen to your heart, and observe your emotions (see "Practice an Emotional Self-Check-In" below). Do not push them away or ignore them because what you resist persists. Experience your emotions as a wave, coming and going, and remind yourself that *this too shall pass*. Do not judge your emotions; let them be what they are, neither good nor bad. Try not to intensify your emotions, and remember that you do not necessarily

have to act on your emotions. Practice loving your emotions by embracing, acknowledging, and accepting them.

3. **Reflect on and learn from your pain:** Step back and remember that you are not your thoughts or your emotions. Find the meaning and the lesson in the experience and in your reaction (that is, attend to your connections). Choose to be curious. Ask: *What is the lesson in this?* If it is not clear, pause, breathe, and ask: *What is the upside of this situation that I don't see at the moment?* Remove the phrase *I don't know* from your vocabulary, and keep reflecting until you discover the lessons. This often takes time, so continue your mindful self-check-ins and ask: *What am I learning from this? What's one thing I can do today to help myself?*

4. **Forgive:** Consider forgiveness of someone else to be a gift to yourself, authorizing freedom. Through forgiveness, you choose to no longer carry the weight of ill feelings, whether toward others or toward yourself. Forgiving is often easier when we consider how much we have grown from a difficult situation and how much lighter and freer we will feel once we forgive.

5. **Let go and move forward:** As you learn the lessons of pain, forgive, put down your heavy baggage of the past, let go, and move forward. Do not look back. Let go of the pain and adapt to the new, wiser version of yourself. Rewrite your story as the stronger and enlightened person you are becoming. Celebrate your own growth and evolution.

Practice an Emotional Self-Check-In

Whether as a way to help process a painful experience or as a separate awareness exercise, practice this emotional self-check-in. Ask yourself the following questions and journal your findings to help become more aware of your emotions:

- Where does this particular emotion arise?
- Where was the emotion the moment before I observed it?
- Where does the emotion go when I no longer feel it?
- Have I stored unprocessed emotions in my body?

- What happens when I repress an emotion?
- How do I feel when I judge my emotions?
- How do I let an emotion go?
- What is the relationship between myself and my emotions?
- What would happen if I acted on my emotions as I was feeling them?
- What would happen if I didn't act on my emotions as I was feeling them?

- Pain, at its worst, invades and paralyzes us, making us vulnerable to chronic stress and disease. At its best, pain is our greatest teacher and prompts growth and resilience. Pain is a tool in promoting our Self and bringing us closer to becoming the CEO of our well-being.

- Turn an obstacle into an opportunity by being curious and uncovering the upside of the situation. There is no such thing as "failure," only experience that provides us with the feedback, insight, and wisdom to steer us back on course and evolve. Instead of perceiving failure as a lack of success, see it as an opportunity to gain insight and grow.

- People experience many forms of loss, and everyone's experience of pain and grief differs. Grieving is a nonlinear process that follows no timetable or schedule and is unique to every person and situation.

- Posttraumatic growth transforms you into a stronger, wiser version of yourself. This can take a variety of forms: greater awareness and appreciation for life, realization of the need to make more meaningful connections with others, a deeper sense of self, and a stronger spirituality (whatever that means for you).

- Pain can be a teacher for both individuals and organizations. Organizations that embrace learning, wellness, and compassion will have greater resilience when facing a painful crisis or challenge. They will be able to respond to such situations creatively and with emotional intelligence. They will collectively experience their own posttraumatic growth.

- In times of distress and pain, pause, breathe, and choose to observe your emotions. Experience your pain as a wave that comes and goes. Practice loving your emotions because your darkness and shadows are what make it possible for light to shine back into your life. You must appreciate both sides by being able to feel, accept, forgive, let go, and move forward.

- The quality of our lives depends on the quality of the choices we make, so choose to make pain your greatest teacher. Acknowledge that we all endure different forms of pain and that we have the power to make it meaningful, to grow from it in order to live our best lives. We become stronger in heart and mind when we turn our pain into growth.

CHAPTER ELEVEN

---•---

PRANA, OUR ENERGY TO BE FULLY ENGAGED AT WORK AND IN LIFE

---•---

THE THREE P's

Pain

PRANA

Purpose

Are you on the path of burnout or the path of vital energy?

Prana is the vehicle to get you from pain to purpose. Free-flowing prana promotes healing and empowers you to process pain and grow from it, propelling you toward purpose. It drives your evolution, and it allows you to let go of and move beyond that pain.

Prana is the Sanskrit word for breath and life force. It is the universal principle of vital energy and defines our lives and well-being. It is the very essence that keeps us alive and thriving.

Employee engagement and cash flow are to a business what prana is to our body. Employees, and their ability to thrive and be productive, are a company's prana. Businesses cannot exist without them. As a human being, we cannot exist without prana.

When prana flows freely, it gives us the energy to be fully engaged at work and in life. Sometimes it can become blocked by fears, fatigue, pain, uncertainties, and chronic stress. The easiest way to experience unblocked prana is within, and someone with free-flowing prana is easy to differentiate from someone with blocked prana.

Similar to a kink in a garden hose obstructing the flow of water, some yoga poses can contort your body to the point that it becomes difficult to breathe. When your breath is constricted or stops entirely, your prana is blocked. It is a sign that you need to relax into the pose and breathe deeply. Your energizing conscious breath travels through your body, helping you ease into the pose and unblock your prana. This can be achieved only when you are mindful of your breath to begin with.

Life's challenges contort us and throw obstacles in our way. We internalize this stress, and our prana becomes obstructed, decreasing our vital energy. This chapter will demonstrate how to recognize and release the obstruction and to let breath and energy flow again.

Prana is within every living thing, much like water. Visualize optimal prana as clean water flowing down a pristine river.

If a tree falls into the river, it partially obstructs the flow of water.

If a dam is built, it stops the flow of water almost entirely.

If there is snowmelt or rainfall, it enhances the flow of water.

This analogy directly relates to the ACE Method of dealing with stress (see "ACE Stress Using the ACE Method," pages 86–89).

The fallen tree is akin to acute stress. We cannot anticipate when a tree might fall or prepare for the specific consequences. But if we immediately recognize when this happens, we can alter, adapt to, and accept the situation, and respond to the stressor accordingly.

The blockage of a dam is comparable to chronic stress. This stress almost completely blocks our free-flowing prana, which like water from a river backs up behind the dam, eventually stagnating and growing toxic. Real dams weigh heavily on the well-being of an ecosystem, and the dam of chronic stress does the same for our personal well-being.

Eustress is like snowmelt, a mountain spring, or rainfall, swelling rivers with clean water, feeding underground aquifers (our resilience resources), and rolling down freely toward the ocean.

This river analogy also applies to the Seven A's, which represent how to keep the river of energy flowing through you:

- **Adopt** clarity, purity, and flow of your prana.
- **Allocate** time for nature to take its course, without trying to control the ebb and flow of prana's river.
- **Avoid** contamination and stagnation.
- **Alter** the situation by removing the dam, opening the dam's floodgates, or building a new channel around the dam.
- **Adapt** by flowing around a fallen tree in the river.
- **Accept** that you cannot control nature and allow it to take its natural course.
- **Attend** to your connections with a healthy ecosystem.

Prana will wash away impurities within fatigue, stress, negativity, and pain.

How can you effortlessly flow with the current, instead of battling upstream against it?

Energy, Eustress, and Ecstasy

Ch'i has its roots in traditional Chinese medicine, and prana in Hindu culture. Most ancient cultures have a comparable term: *ki* in Japan, *ruach* in Hebrew, *baraka* in Islam, and so on. In recent years, ch'i has attracted the attention of Western medicine. Studies have explored the health benefits of tai chi, a gentle, flowing martial art that has some similarities to yoga. Harvard Medical School and Brigham and Women's Hospital have collaborated on a Mind/Body/Movement Laboratory that documents measurable health benefits of tai chi and integrative therapies incorporating non-Western approaches.

A growing body of research demonstrates the health benefits of yoga and pranayama, or yogic breathing practices. A regular yoga or breathwork practice has been found to improve quality of life and cardiovascular health, decrease stress and anxiety, promote restorative sleep, curb chronic pain and inflammation, and improve flexibility, focus, balance, and strength.

These practices are one way we turn chronic stress and acute stress into the beneficial energy of eustress. As I have said, acute stress can be harnessed productively, but that energy is not sustainable. Eustress, on the other hand, is the in-the-zone or in-the-flow state of free-flowing energy that can fuel prolonged periods of peak performance. It is a deep reservoir we can tap into when our prana and purpose are aligned.

Interestingly, people from all walks of life and all professions have described this in-the-flow state. Leaders, innovators, athletes, musicians, artists, surgeons, and everyday folks have all described experiencing a kind of ecstasy where time slows down for some and speeds up for others. I call this the *prana flow state*, unleashing a flow of limitless possibility. When we tap into that deep energy, we effortlessly achieve peak performance and access our highest potential, especially when we are working in service of a higher purpose.

Focus, Flow, and Fulfillment

The topic of flow, in the metaphorical and energetic sense I use the term, has been a subject of serious inquiry for decades. Psychologist Mihaly Csikszentmihalyi has been writing about flow since 1975, and his book *Good Business: Leadership, Flow, and the Making of Meaning* profiles prominent CEOs who have created corporate cultures conducive to flow.

This is what I experienced when I had my powerful, transformative encounter with a silent monk in India (see "Meditating in a Cave with a Silent Monk," pages 21–24). This experience bridged the gap between my head and my heart and brought them into alignment. For me, this was a spiritual experience, but there is also a scientific way to look at the cost of living in our heads. Neuroscientists are finding that our creative flow is blocked when our prefrontal cortex — the home of our brain's executive function, our Inner Critic — is overly dominant. We become prone to paralysis by analysis.

However, when our cerebellum (home to our muscle memory) is also engaged, our creative potential is unleashed. In other words, cultivating a unity of mind and body, and of heart and head, unblocks our prana and allows us to more consistently ride the wave of a prana flow state. In essence, all of the advice, Business Hacks, and Action Steps in this book — such as quieting your Inner Critic, promoting clarity, taking breaks, incorporating daily physical activity, allocating adequate play and recovery time, and so on — contribute toward enabling your prana flow state.

We have to guard against getting stuck in our heads. Yet we also need to focus. We will not be able to enter a prana flow state if our minds are scattered and distracted. We have to be engaged in the kind of sustained and mindful attention to a meaningful task that Georgetown University professor Cal Newport calls "deep work." This means moving away from multitasking, which generally does not work, and toward monotasking or single tasking.

If yoga is mindful movement, monotasking is mindful work; being fully present in the moment. In this way, focus and flow work hand in hand to free up our prana and enable us to live energetic and fulfilled lives.

Peak Performance through Prana

In my first session with new clients, I ask them, "What would you like?" Then we identify what challenges, dissatisfactions, and limiting beliefs they are experiencing. My intention is to restore flow, and this allows me to pinpoint their blocked prana and what might have put them on the path toward burnout.

When prana is blocked, we can be busy, but we may not be performing at our best. While we are lying in bed, we are not experiencing restorative sleep. We burn out trying to do everything, instead of being energized and engaged.

Though we might check off all of our to-do boxes every day, we can still be left feeling unfulfilled. Almost as if our entire day was meaningless, despite the various accomplishments we may have achieved.

Imagine a man hunched over the coffee machine in a disheveled suit, loose askew tie stained with coffee, messy hair, and bloodshot eyes with dark circles underneath. He feels lethargic, dispassionate, and depressed. He is experiencing a depletion of life force, prana, as he goes about his day, which is full of challenges he is unable to effectively deal with. This is a picture of a man with blocked prana.

Now, imagine the same man with his prana unblocked: He is happy, well-put-together, energized, with bright eyes, a sharp suit, and a spring in his step. He works in a prana flow state, and everything seems effortless. He is truly engaged. This man's prana is on point and flowing without obstruction like water down a pristine river.

What if a company's entire workforce displayed similarly unblocked prana? Employees are the most significant contributors to any company's success. Employees *are* the life force and energy of a company; they are the company's prana. When they show up to work every day feeling energized and engaged, they are experiencing free-flowing prana.

While prana may seem intangible, when a company improves and optimizes its prana, this will register in concrete, measurable ways: higher rates of employee engagement and improved performance, reduced absenteeism and healthcare costs, and overall stronger workplace culture and better business outcomes, just to name a few.

In order to ensure the organization's prana is flowing, I work with companies to conduct a "corporate wellness assessment" (CWA). The Prananaz CWA uncovers pain points and obstacles that the business and its people face, delivering a hands-on assessment of physical and social environments within and around the workplace that influences employees' prana, mindsets, and behaviors.

We look at a company as if it were a person, holistically analyzing its overall well-being. Companies receive "culture of wellness" and "employee engagement" scores. If these are low, we design and implement tailored wellness solutions to increase the score. Activities like fun group challenges, gamification, and experiential workshops bring mindful wellness into the heart of a company's day-to-day culture.

In the same way, I tailor solutions for individual clients. For my client Jessica (see "Build a Healthy Lifestyle, Habit by Habit," pages 58–60), her travel schedule as an executive with a global Fortune 500 company made it difficult to exercise regularly or feel in control of her life. When exhaustion and depleted energy became her norm, I helped her implement incremental improvements to her routines and habits, and I encouraged her to do mindful self-check-ins throughout the day, specifically focused on her energy level. By logging in her responses, she was able to see the connections between her energy level and her habits, and she discovered her energy sweet spot. I helped empower her to unblock and optimize her prana.

You, too, can find your energy sweet spot when action and awareness come together like they did with Jessica (see this chapter's Action Steps). What is most important is that we find our way from point A (our current location) to point B (where we want to be). Our prana flows when we remove blockages: limiting beliefs, fear, anxiety, stress, and burnout. Find your path of least resistance and begin effortlessly flowing.

Unblocking Prana

The first time I learned about prana was in a yoga class, when a teacher taught pranayama, the practice of controlling your breath. I soon became obsessed with the concept of prana, and it has helped me to both understand and take control of my own life.

By being aware of your breath, you can monitor how well your prana is flowing, and at any time, you can use breathing exercises to unblock prana or improve its flow. In this chapter's Action Steps, I provide two time-tested breathing exercises you can use.

- Prana is breath.
- Prana is energy.
- Prana is life force.
- Without prana, you are dead.

As long as you are alive, you always have prana. The quality of your prana depends on how you choose to live your life. Mindful and healthy choices result in free-flowing prana. Living on autopilot constricts and contorts your prana.

When you are ready to take empowered action, improvement occurs. You must personally commit to taking action and making a change. You have to do this for yourself, not because someone else wants you to take action.

The most challenging clients are those who come to me at the request of their superior or spouse. It is challenging to create change when it is not a self-actualized need or desire. The benefits reaped depend entirely on the effort that is put in. If you are not ready to take action, you will only continue down the path of resistance. You must be willing to create change mindfully and of your own accord.

Like any teacher or coach, I cannot wave a magic wand and have someone reach their destination. I can help foster mindfulness and provide guidance only when someone is ready, willing, able, and motivated to change.

Obstructed prana will hinder you from fulfilling your desires and from being your authentic Self. Cultivating free-flowing prana and putting yourself on the path of least resistance enables you to become unstoppable!

You will be able to show up as your best Self, with focused energy for all the roles you play in life, whether as a leader, parent, partner, friend, or colleague.

When prana flows at its best, you feel great vitality, and positive changes manifest. This attracts other people who are living parallel lives. Free-flowing prana promotes a higher awareness and consciousness, both for you and for those around you.

Manage Entrepreneurial Energy

Many ambitious entrepreneurs come to me seeking mindfulness, resilience, clarity, and overall well-being. They work excessive hours, do not prioritize their own well-being, and often manifest illness, developing disorders such as adrenal fatigue (whose symptoms include fatigue, body aches, nervousness, sleep disturbances, and digestive problems).

One of my clients, Michael, chose to start working with me after he had a wake-up call. He was burning the candle at both ends by working sixteen-hour days for months; he was not eating or sleeping well; and he had no time for friends, family, or the gym. Michael was experiencing chronic back pain and frequent headaches. One day he hit his limit and passed out in the middle of a meeting with investors. He had to be rushed to the hospital due to adrenal fatigue. There was no doubt that he was on the path to burnout. His prana, his vital life force, was obstructed by his habits of overworking without recovery time. I helped him reassess his priorities, shift his mindset, and create better habits. As a result, all areas of his life skyrocketed, and he was able to promote himself to the CEO of his well-being.

When you are working with depleted energy, you are not engaged in what you are doing. You are easily distracted and end up making poor choices. Consequently, your performance becomes subpar. You are more irritable and tired, and your business suffers. You do not wake up with the energy needed to tackle the day or to make tough decisions. In Michael's case, he was "busy," but he was not an effective leader. Before working together with me, he had prioritized doing well over being well and ended up with neither.

When clients ask me how they can manage stress by better managing their time, or say they just wish they had more hours in a day, I tell them that time management is less about time or people management and more about energy management.

Time, like prana, is a commodity. We can optimize our time by managing and optimizing our energy to achieve our goals. What time of day do you have the most energy? Being self-aware of your energy levels at different points throughout the day can help you optimize how you spend your time.

For example, I know I am not a crack-of-dawn morning person like my husband. It takes a little time for me to start my day. When possible, I refrain from scheduling meetings first thing in the morning, and I prefer to schedule my fitness classes during lunch, so that I can show up energized and fully engaged.

Clients come to me with the entrepreneurial stresses many of us know too well: lack of capital, loss of company direction and focus, rapid growth, loss of control, fear of the unknown, lack of sleep and self-care, and living in constant stress and uncertainty. I help my clients create a roadmap to move away from what they do not want and move toward what they want, both professionally and personally.

Opening up their prana gives them the energy, the drive, and the creativity to be their best Self. As their best Self, they will be more aware of their stresses and can take steps to mitigate them by doing things like practicing the Seven A's and making better choices to adopt a healthy lifestyle.

The key for anyone to remain forward-thinking, mindful, and energized is to recognize when their prana is blocked, and then remove the obstacles, so this vital life force can flow freely once again.

Model Effective Executive Energy

We need the ultimate wealth, our well-being, to create impact and be effective leaders. Without energy and flowing prana, we will be unable to achieve our goals, and the demands and pressure of work and life will accumulate and weigh heavily upon us. This leaves us feeling depleted and out of control. The solution is not drinking copious amounts of caffeine for an energy boost. We need genuine focus that does not come from energy drinks or coffee.

During my sessions with CEO clients, I have noticed that they share a prominent trait — the ability to stay laser-focused. Some of these clients strive to be more focused, while other clients are laser-focused to the extreme. While being laser-focused is a powerful ability and is vital to running a successful business, being excessively laser-focused can be detrimental to health and well-being.

Many people believe that working long hours without a break leads to successful outcomes. They might not recognize that this behavior can be counterproductive when self-care is compromised. As people sacrifice play and recovery time and neglect their connection with friends and family, they move into a vicious cycle, one that defined my earlier career. They often turn to processed comfort foods for a false sense of energy and convenience and skip the gym in an effort to gain more time, but their increasingly compromised well-being undermines their laser focus and productivity. They unwittingly take a route that leads toward burnout and away from success.

I often see leaders who run around all day with back-to-back meetings. They have loads of energy and a great deal of activity but zero focus. Without focus, how can they lead a company to excel and fulfill its vision? Their work is not as effective or meaningful as it could be.

Be wary of entering a spiral of hyper energy without focus and activity without creativity and clarity. This eventually leads to boredom, disengagement, demotion, or possibly losing one's job.

The kind of flow you seek fosters a mindful focus, not mania. It attends to physical health and well-being, allocates adequate time for play and recovery, and includes breaks to allow yourself to reboot. Flow works with your body's natural rhythms.

Part of being an excellent leader is modeling healthy, mindful behavior. A culture of wellness will not take root in a company if the leader's choices run counter to it. Conversely, if you commit fully to cultivating free-flowing prana, that investment will pay off exponentially, both for you and your company. Flowing prana has ripple effects that influence others in positive ways. When a company's prana flows, this drives employee engagement and better business outcomes.

The key to activating your prana flow state lies at the intersection of action and awareness, and aligning these comes from cultivating what I call the *Three C's*: clarity, concentration, and confidence (see this chapter's Business Hacks).

Prana Flow State: The Heart of Prananaz

When I went back to school to study holistic health, it became clear that the power of holistic approaches was not simply about any one problem. These approaches work because they address the whole system. When people say they want to reduce stress or they cannot sleep, the problem is not just about that one issue; it involves an entire underlying picture. The larger map links the whole of their lives: career, finances, relationships, physical activity, diet, self-awareness, environment, and overall lifestyle and well-being.

When I started my business, Prananaz — which delivers tailored, high-touch, high-tech corporate wellness programs — I was fully engaged and excited. I was living with high-quality and free-flowing prana. Despite working long hours, I was able to avoid falling into bad habits. To my surprise, work seemed effortless. I was and still am able to tap into a prana flow state regularly.

When I replaced my old fears with a new sense of confidence, my friends often remarked with astonishment that I was doing twice as much as they could do in a single day. They noticed that I now had loads of energy, and creative ideas flowed through me.

I no longer spent the night tossing and turning and worrying about the future. My prana was now unobstructed by fear and anxiety. My efforts seemed to flow with ease, like a river. I was managing my prana above all else, which enabled me to be my best Self and the best leader for others.

Without the energy I gained from my flowing prana, maintaining this lifestyle would have worn me out or landed me in a productivity trap. My eustress would have converted into chronic stress, and I could have quickly accrued sleep debt and bad habits.

Making time for mindfulness and opening your prana does not take away from your day. It adds to it. Like the tree that falls into the river and partially blocks the flow of water, the daily stresses of everyday life and obstacles cause blockages in your prana.

Be aware; being tired or irritable is just one sign that you need to unblock your prana. Always ask yourself: *What is blocking my flow?* Overwork and lack of self-care — existing on chocolate, coffee, and fifteen-hour days — are likely culprits. Even when we are passionate about our work, we are only human. We cannot sustain peak performance without attending to our well-being. Attempting to do so comes with a price we cannot afford, which is burnout and, at its most extreme, karoshi, or death by overwork.

Mindfully put yourself on the path of least resistance by working and living with free-flowing prana. This helps you make the leap from merely surviving — which is possible despite obstructed prana — to thriving, which requires unobstructed prana. Fluid prana cultivates engagement, vitality, joy, and success.

Pause. Breathe. Choose.

Engagement is a choice.

Prana flow state is a choice.

Choose to live your life fully energized and engaged by making healthier, mindful choices, and you will *do well* and *be well* at the same time.

You can tap into your prana flow state and achieve peak performance and your highest potential. You will be unstoppable!

Take a breath. Take another conscious breath. How do you feel?

What will you do now?

BUSINESS HACKS

Tap Into Your Prana Flow State through the Three C's

The key to activating your prana flow state lies at the intersection of action and awareness. Cultivate prana flow state through the Three C's:

1. **Clarity:** Have clear, well-defined goals to understand what actions need to be taken for success. Visualize and write down the best outcomes and revisit them regularly throughout the day. Meditate, and sleep seven to nine hours daily. Play often. Eat whole, clean, nutrient-dense foods.

2. **Concentration:** Commit to embody complete concentration and engagement in your intended action. To avoid procrastination, use a timer to help you get past the biggest mental hurdle, which is getting started. Set the timer for anywhere between twenty-five and forty-five minutes depending on your task and preference. When the timer goes off, take a two- to five-minute break (if you want) and set the timer again. Repeat accordingly. Block out all distractions (prioritize and delegate beforehand) and stay present. Focus.

3. **Confidence:** In a prana flow state, we are too immersed in the present moment and task at hand to be concerned with protecting our ego, which releases inhibitions and makes us feel like we can achieve anything. You become unstoppable when you choose to listen to your Inner Coach, not your Inner Critic, and when you reframe every challenge as an opportunity for improvement, strengthening your opportunity mindset. Visualize the best version of your Self and write it down. Ingrain this in your mind and heart through repetition while simultaneously taking small steps toward becoming that version of yourself.

Be Laser-Focused Like Steve Jobs

Write down ten career-related things you want to achieve in the next year. Steve Jobs would say, "This is how I do it. I take a sheet of paper, and

I say, 'If my company can only do one thing next year, what is it?' Literally, we shut everything else down."

Steve applied this strategy at his executive retreats. On the last day of the retreat, he would stand in front of his team with a whiteboard and take suggestions for what Apple should do next. Then he would narrow the list down to the ten best suggestions, only to disregard those that were not among the top three. Try a similar approach with your team.

1. Know your goals.
2. Narrow your strategies.
3. Focus your energy.

Conduct a Corporate Wellness Assessment

In order to cultivate a culture of wellness at your organization that is impactful, hire a corporate wellness consultant who can work with HR to conduct a corporate wellness assessment (CWA). This is an effective first step in evaluating the current state of your workforce and learning about your employees' needs and interests.

The findings of a CWA will provide all the necessary information to design and implement a tailored corporate wellness solution based on your vision and goals, as well as the specific needs and interests of your workforce. You can use this as a tool to identify how to transform your culture of wellness from where you are to where you want to be, and more importantly, how to take impactful action and create a strong workplace culture with happy and healthy employees. Finally, a CWA will provide a baseline by which to measure progress. The CWA is the key difference between an effective employee well-being program that engages employees and improves their well-being and one that falls flat.

Discover Your Energy Sweet Spot

In order to optimize your energy, productivity, and achievements, discover your energy sweet spot. You may already have a sense of this, but for one or several days, track yourself to confirm it. Throughout the day, take a brief pause and conduct a mindful self-check-in (see "Mindful Self-Check-Ins: Be Present to Stress," pages 96–98). Ask yourself: *How am I feeling? Am I tired, energized, sluggish? What made me feel this way? Was it something I ate, my sleep cycle, a meeting, a conversation, my activity level?* On a scale of 0 to 10 (10 being the highest), rate your energy level. Create a habit to measure your energy. Wearable devices can also monitor and track your activity. Log your answers with the time of day and review them at the end of each day to discover patterns.

Pinpoint the time of day you have the most energy. Are you a morning person? Do you hit a wall at 3 PM? When you identify the specific time of day you are most energized and productive, tackle your most important projects, or your least desirable tasks, at that time. Knock them out to avoid procrastination.

Learn how to increase and manage your energy instead of wasting it by trying to manage only your time. To keep laser-like focus, work smarter, not harder.

Breathwork: Ujjayi Pranayama

Pranayama is Sanskrit for "breath control." The quality of your breath, whether it is fast, slow, shallow, or typical, indicates the quality of your prana (your emotional, mental, and physical state). When you are scared or nervous, your breath will be shallow or quick. When you are calm, your breath will be slow, deep, and in sync. Become aware of the quality and cadence of your breath.

There are many different types of breathing exercises, but here I provide two that I practice regularly. Employ these approaches to your breath and start reaping the benefits immediately.

Ujjayi (pronounced *ooh-JAI-yee*) is translated as "victorious breath," and commonly referred to as the "oceanic breath." It has been used for thousands of years to enhance hatha yoga practice, and it will simultaneously relax and energize your mind and body. The sound that Ujjayi makes helps us to synchronize our breath with our movements during yoga, making the entire yoga practice more rhythmic and dynamic.

Ujjayi has a balancing effect on the entire cardiorespiratory system. This type of breathing releases feelings of irritation and frustration and helps calm the mind and body. A simple practice can yield powerful benefits. Ujjayi breathing does the following:

- Boosts energy
- Encourages free-flowing prana
- Increases the oxygen in the blood
- Builds internal body heat
- Relieves tension
- Regulates blood pressure
- Detoxifies mind and body
- Increases feelings of presence and self-awareness, and has meditative qualities

The best times to use Ujjayi breath are the following:

- When you are agitated or nervous: Since the Ujjayi breath is especially useful for settling agitation and stress and calming the mind, use it whenever you find yourself becoming aggravated or worried.
- When you are practicing hatha yoga: Try focusing on Ujjayi breathing while practicing yoga to help you stay focused and grounded as you flow from one posture to the next.
- When you are exercising: Ujjayi is also useful when you are doing aerobic exercises, such as running or cycling. In fact, some Olympic-level athletes have improved their respiratory efficiency by introducing Ujjayi into their training routines.

HOW TO PRACTICE UJJAYI BREATH

1. Sit in a comfortable position, either upright in a chair with your feet planted on the floor or seated with legs crossed beneath you.
2. Start with your mouth open to experience the feeling and sound of the Ujjayi breath first, and then proceed with your mouth closed.

3. Open your mouth, and take a deep slow inhale, starting first to fill your lower belly. The same breath rises to the lower rib cage and finally moves into the upper chest and throat.

4. Exhale deeply and slowly. Begin to slightly constrict the passage of air in your throat. Imagine that you are fogging up a pair of glasses, making a distinct, breathy "haaah" sound.

5. When you are comfortable with the exhale, begin to apply the same constriction ("haaah") of the throat to the inhales. When you can control your throat on both the inhale and the exhale, close your mouth, and breathe the same way through your nose.

6. Continue applying the same contraction to your throat that you did when your mouth was open. The breath will still make a loud "haaah" sound from the constriction of your throat. (Some people compare the sound of the Ujjayi breath to Darth Vader from *Star Wars*.)

Breathwork: Kapalabhati Pranayama

Kapalabhati breathing is an advanced yogic technique known as "skull-shining breath." The word *kapalabhati* comes from two Sanskrit words: *kapala*, which translates to "skull," and *bhati*, which means "light." However, it is more commonly known as the "breath of fire," providing energy and warmth. This breath purifies, rejuvenates, and invigorates the mind and body. When you practice this kind of breathing, visualize your skull filling with a bright light; this is how its name came about. I like to imagine myself as a dragon blowing fire.

This cleansing breath can help you release stress and toxins from the mind and body. It consists of a series of forceful exhalations followed by passive inhalations.

Most people who practice Kapalabhati regularly do it because it gives them a boost of energy and a surge of heat. However, Kapalabhati breathing provides the following myriad of benefits:

- Energizes and clears your mind
- Focuses attention
- Cleanses the lungs and respiratory system
- Strengthens the diaphragm and abdominal muscles

- Releases toxins
- Increases oxygen to the cells, purifying blood in the process
- Improves digestion
- Warms the body

The best times to use Kapalabhati breathing are the following:

- In the morning: For an exhilarating wake-up call or as an alternative to meditation, try it first thing in the morning for an energy boost.
- When you are cold: Kapalabhati, the breath of fire, creates internal heat, so if your body is cold, a few rounds can warm you right up, even on a frigid day.
- Midafternoon: If you experience a midafternoon slump, try a few rounds of Kapalabhati to energize your mind and body. It will help you power through the rest of your day.

That said, there is never a bad time to focus on your breath. Even one mindful breath can clear an obstructed path for life force and vitality.

HOW TO PRACTICE KAPALABHATI BREATH

It is important to remember that your inhalation should be gentle and passive, while your exhalation should be an active, forceful, and powerful movement. Start this practice at a slow pace, and with time, build up speed with your breath and extend the duration, if you feel comfortable doing so. See also the cautions below.

1. Sit in a comfortable position, either upright in a chair with your feet planted on the floor or seated with your legs crossed beneath you. Rest your hands on your lower belly.
2. Take a deep, cleansing breath, in through your nose and out through your mouth.
3. Inhale deeply through your nose, filling your belly with air.
4. In a quick, forceful motion, expel all the air from your lungs as you pull your navel in toward your spine. The primary movement should be from your diaphragm.
5. Allow the next inhalation to happen naturally, with no effort, as you release the belly, and then exhale forcefully again.

6. Try this for fifteen to thirty seconds at first (or less time, if you get too dizzy), and increase the amount of time gradually.

7. At the end of your practice, allow your breathing to return to normal.

8. Sit quietly with your eyes closed for a minute or two, breathe normally, and observe the sensations in your body.

CAUTIONS FOR PRACTICING KAPALABHATI BREATH

Do not practice Kapalabhati if you are pregnant, menstruating, have high blood pressure, acid gastric issues, abdominal pain, heart disease, if you have suffered from a stroke, or if you have epilepsy. Instead, practice using long, deep breathing.

If you feel dizzy or anxious while practicing Kapalabhati, slow down or stop entirely and revert to regular breathing. If you suffer from vertigo, use caution in practicing this breathing exercise.

KEY TAKEAWAYS

- *Prana* is the Sanskrit word for breath and life force. It is the universal principle of vital energy and defines our lives and well-being and is the very essence that keeps us alive and thriving.
- Employee engagement and cash flow are to a business what prana is to our body. Employees are the most significant contributors to a company's success. Employees are the life force and energy of a company; they are the company's prana. A business cannot exist without them. When they show up to work feeling energized and engaged, they are experiencing free-flowing prana. They are able to perform at the top of their game, creating a better workplace culture, and therefore driving better business results.
- Tapping into the prana flow state is when you effortlessly achieve peak performance and access your highest potential. The key to activating your prana flow state lies at the intersection of action and awareness.
- As long as you are alive, you always have prana. The quality of your prana depends on how you choose to live your life. Mindful and healthy choices result in free-flowing prana. Living on autopilot constricts and contorts your prana. Prana, at its best, is when you feel great vitality. Positive changes in your life manifest when you are living with flowing prana, and you become unstoppable.
- Stress management is less about time or people management and more about energy management. We can optimize our time by managing and optimizing our energy to achieve our goals. Discover your energy sweet spot with mindful self-check-ins.
- Part of being an excellent leader is modeling healthy, mindful behavior to cultivate a culture of wellness. Your free-flowing prana will have ripple effects throughout your company.

CHAPTER TWELVE

---- • ----

PURPOSE, OUR DRIVE FOR MEANING

---- • ----

THE THREE P's

Pain

Prana

PURPOSE

Do you know who you are? Do you want to live the way you do right now? How do you want to be remembered?

At some point in life, we must answer these questions. Whatever you have accomplished, pause, breathe, and choose to evaluate or reevaluate what you are doing here on this earth.

What is your purpose? Has your purpose changed?

Who are you? Has your sense of self changed?

Are you making the impact you want? Are you making the world a better place?

What if we brought our mind and heart together as one? What would that look like?

To promote your Self to the CEO of your well-being, you must address the Three P's: treating pain like a teacher, cultivating free-flowing prana, and identifying your life's purpose. Passion is what starts the engine, and purpose is what drives the vehicle. In other words, you need the engine of passion, and the drive for meaning, to accelerate toward being your best Self.

A Meaningful Life: Maslow's Hierarchy of Needs

Human beings have a spectrum of needs that range from the tangible to the intangible. One way to look at these needs is through Abraham Maslow's psychological theory of the hierarchy of needs. At the bottom are physiological needs, which represent the most basic necessities for survival: food, water, and shelter. These are the needs we tend to first. Next is safety and security: employment and health. Only after that do we attempt to address our social needs: love and a sense of belonging. This is followed by the most complex needs: esteem and self-actualization. We can easily lose sight of these last two needs at the top because it seems we do not require them to survive, but we do require them to thrive and innovate.

MASLOW'S HIERARCHY OF NEEDS

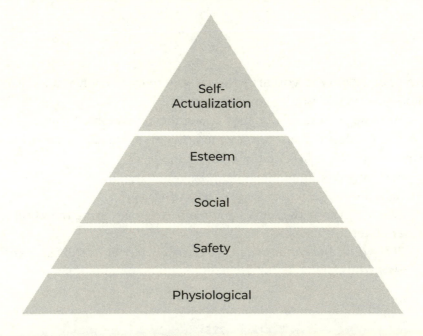

Everyone works to attain the most basic and fundamental physiological needs at the bottom of the pyramid. These are the measurable needs, such as putting a roof over your head and food on the table. However, in order to truly live your best life, you must strive to reach the top of the pyramid and find your purpose. You must find a way to live your life with intention, passion, and meaning.

This applies not just to each person individually but to companies as well. What is your company culture like? What kind of morale is in the air? What aspirations dominate people's motivations?

Is your company a place where employees only seek to fulfill the basic needs of survival, those at the bottom of Maslow's pyramid? Do people work only for a paycheck, so they can afford food and a roof over their head, but otherwise work on autopilot or feel unable to satisfy higher needs — like a sense of belonging, self-esteem, and self-realization?

Or in your company, do employees reach for those higher achievements? Do they work fully engaged and with intention, confident that they are contributing to the company, are supporting and supported by others, and fulfilling their goals? In an optimized company like this, everyone's prana would be open and flowing. Each employee would show up as their best Self, with energy and intention, to do their utmost in work that they enjoy.

A company has a strong culture of purpose when the employees' personal purpose and their professional purpose are in alignment with the organization's purpose. When that happens, people show up to work, not with a job or career mindset, but with a purpose mindset. The increased energy of purposeful companies is evident in higher employee engagement and in higher rates of investment in expansion and innovation.

Purpose, Intention, and Inspiration

It goes without saying that purpose relates to one's beliefs and values, and it can mean many different things. In order to live a more meaningful and conscious life, it is important to understand that purpose is not about personal ego or fear and cannot be assigned by another. Purpose to some may mean a higher instruction from God or a spiritual calling.

Beyond any religious connotations, I see our purpose as being human and humane — being good and doing good in a self-actualized way. Purpose is what fulfills us and helps others: a source of joy and healing that keeps us grounded and motivated as we navigate the physical world. It is our life's message or mission: what we wish to drive in the world.

Purpose is the choice to engage with all you have got, rather than struggle against everything you are not. Follow the path of least resistance. Focus on the strengths that bring you joy and bring value to others.

For you, perhaps purpose and happiness come from the ability to create opportunity for people or from using your strong skills to fulfill an unmet need. This is purpose. We do not have to cure cancer to live a meaningful life. Having a purpose is something we all aspire to, regardless of how big or small that purpose may seem to others.

It is imperative to remember that there are two different types of purpose. On a macro level, there is our life purpose, the reason we exist. On a micro level, there is the purpose of taking action with intention and ambition on a daily basis. We can infuse purpose in everything we do, even seemingly mundane chores like cleaning. A clean home creates an attractive and healthy environment in which to live, and a clean office is both of those as well as more efficient. A clean hospital saves lives.

You do not have to be an iconic leader like Steve Jobs to share your conviction and passion, lead a meaningful life, or run an impactful business. If you are contributing to the world in a way that makes you and others happy, and that gives you a higher purpose, you are on the right path.

A Stanford study found that the most satisfied people are those who have a sense of meaning in their lives, and that meaning is directly related to being a giver and working toward a higher purpose. A related survey found that employees who find meaning in their work not only report higher levels of job satisfaction and engagement, but they are three times as likely to stay with their organization.

The bottom line is, what do *you* want?

This simple yet profound question is what I first ask my clients. They tend to say things like *more money*, *success*, *partnership*, or *a vacation*. The truth is, that is not really what they want. The underlying wish always boils down to one or a combination of these five desired outcomes (in no particular order):

- To be happy
- To feel a sense of belonging
- To be loved

- To live a life of truth and authenticity
- To be safe

Money will not help you realize your unknown deep desires. If you are not living your best life, with prana, passion, and purpose, then at best, money can bring comfort.

When I ask someone what their purpose is, or if they have found meaning in their life that is greater than their basic needs, what I am asking is this:

When you are on your deathbed, will you be able to say that you are happy with the way you have lived your life?

Think of passion as a flame that can be lit over and over again, as long as you have the solid (wood) foundation of purpose.

People change, life takes unexpected turns, and flames die out but passion can be relit with purpose. When this occurs, you will never lack meaning.

Meaning, fulfillment, passion, and intention, these all give you purpose in your life. In the big picture, and on any given day, you must seek to get in touch (and stay in touch) with what provides you with these needs.

Purpose Drives Change and Evolution

With mindfulness as the solid ground beneath us, we can use the tools and strategies of the Seven A's to change our relationship to stress, increase resilience, and live a healthy, connected life. We can use daily, mindful choices as building blocks to evolve toward our best Self.

In other words, mindful choices and healthy habits help us move up Maslow's pyramid toward our highest aspiration: a purposeful life. Purpose also helps those mindful choices and healthy habits take root as lasting change.

Mirroring Maslow's hierarchy of needs is another pyramid by Robert Dilts (inspired by Gregory Bateson) called *the logical levels of change*. This visualizes six levels of personal and organizational change and transformation.

Changing something on a lower level of this hierarchy, such as the context of your environment, would not necessarily impact the levels above it. However, making a change at an upper level trickles down and reinforces all the other levels of change. For example, my client Alex used

LOGICAL LEVELS OF CHANGE

Purpose
Reason for being

Identity
Sense of self

Values and beliefs
What is important and true

Skills and capabilities
Methods, approaches, and strategies

Behavior
Actions

Environment
Contexts

to bounce from job to job because he did not get along with any of his bosses. He believed that he just had bad luck with each respective boss. Changing his environment in order to work with someone else was not the solution since the same issues kept repeating themselves. Then he dabbled in the third level and learned a new skill in conflict resolution and communication. His new skill improved his communication and relationship marginally in the short term. However, when we started working together, we went deeper into his beliefs and identity and uncovered his blind spot: He was the common denominator in each of these situations, and blaming his bosses was a limiting belief that was preventing him from taking responsibility for his undesired outcomes and finding effective solutions. Once he changed his beliefs related to his sense of self and identity, this change at the upper level of the hierarchy supported all the levels below it and proved to be a lasting change.

We seek to evolve toward a purposeful life and to lead a purposeful organization. That purpose, in turn, promotes future change and evolution. Our reality consists of each level, and I use this model with my clients as a general roadmap for the process of sustainable change and to design action plans for both organizations and individuals. This framework offers insight into how belief, action, and behavior reinforce one another. The logical levels of change help identify what promotes or limits our effectiveness as leaders and organizations.

Snooze Button

I worked in pharmaceutical sales over a decade ago, and in the beginning, I loved it. It was a challenging new endeavor and the reason for my determination to succeed. I was able to exercise my brain every day, and I mastered this new job rather quickly.

However, it was not long before my day-to-day life at the company grew dull. I woke up every morning and drove in my company car from doctor's office to doctor's office, hospital to hospital, to meet with eight doctors per day. I waited in waiting rooms to see doctors in between patients, and I had scheduled lunch meetings several times a week. This was my routine.

Every morning, the worst possible sound in the world was the blaring beeping of my alarm clock. It would jar me awake, and my gut response was, *No! I'm still tired.* Hit the snooze button. Roll over.

I would rack my brain for what I could give up in my morning routine just to sleep for a few more minutes. Most of the time, I opted to skip breakfast.

That snooze button was a huge trigger for me. I wanted to be able to jump out of bed at the first sound of my alarm. Why was I not able to do that? Instead, I woke up tired, regardless of how many hours I slept.

Before that, at Yahoo!, I had also found myself hitting the snooze button. Even though, since then, I had improved my diet and adopted a healthier lifestyle, here I was again, unable to meet the day with the kind of energy and vigor I desired. This made me wonder what I had to do to not feel this bad in the morning. What would make me leap out of bed, even without an alarm, feeling naturally energized?

The answer, of course, was that an upgraded lifestyle was not enough.

Being healthier was not enough. I needed what is at the top of both pyramids, life purpose. I had an unfulfilled need for a life of real meaning.

It took me some time to fully realize this, and then more time to explore what it was that I was missing. But eventually, that was how I ended up on a silent monk's mat in a cave deep in the jungles of India, where I connected the dots on my map and found my higher purpose.

Design and Pursue a Life of Purpose

What will you do? How do you find your passion so that you live life with purpose, with meaning, and create the legacy you want to leave behind? Trust your heart. Be open to the universe's signs and pursue your true passion. Be upset, feel disappointed, or be discouraged; just never quit seeking your purpose.

As I say, sometimes we require a shock to the system to dislodge us when we are cruising through life on autopilot. Sometimes a catalyst appears unexpectedly and turns our life upside down. Sometimes we engineer our own catalyst and set it in motion. And sometimes it is a combination of both.

I engineered my own catalyst by making a conscious choice to journey to India. I knew my true Self craved a higher purpose and that it involved wellness, but I sought additional clarity and validation. I also knew that my yoga and meditation practice had brought me to that place, so I took that one sure thing and ran with it to the other side of the world.

I took a big chance. I moved outside of my comfort zone. This led to moments of terror and doubt, but also to moments of transcendence and confirmation. I found what I was looking for. "When the student is ready, the teacher appears." A swami shared these wise words with me after the life-altering encounter with the silent monk. That adage held true for me: I had readied myself by deepening my practice of yoga and meditation, and then by creating my own catalyst.

This led to my encounter with the silent monk, and the memory of that day will stay with me forever. My experience in India, and my time on the monk's mat in the middle of the jungle, confirmed that I was on the right path. Everything became crystal clear to me. I was present to the signs from the universe and understood that what I was doing was both right and meaningful. Developing a deeper connection with my Self also gave me the courage to change my life. It gave birth to the realization that, since I was not happy, I could quit my job and pursue my passion.

I could, and I did.

I quit the day after I returned, with no time to waste.

However, to find passion and purpose, it is not necessary to do something as drastic as traveling to India. Not everyone has that luxury. Not everyone can quit their current job. But anyone can find purpose in everyday life; in fact, a purposeful life is something that is built day by day. It is an ongoing matter of awakening your heart and your mind through mindfulness practices and strengthening the connection between the two.

At Stanford University, one of the most popular classes is called Designing Your Life. A central tenet of the course is to teach students how to think like a designer in order to discover the career and life they want. The creators of the class say to look to *flow* and *energy* as clues that you are on the right path.

One example of this is Marie Curie. Flow and energy led to her purpose. She would eventually become one of the most accomplished scientists in history, winning two Nobel Prizes. Yet she had no grand epiphany. Her purpose "quietly crept up on her" over years of tinkering in the lab. She simply devoted herself to work that gave her "deep fulfillment through meaning, flow, and freedom," and over time, her purpose crystallized.

In my experience, to do this, first we must tap into our heart by quieting our mind in order to hear our true desires speak. Next, guided by our intuition, we take explorative action to pinpoint what makes us happy. This involves experimentation, trying things out, and diving deeper into what inspires us and provides meaning and connection. To find your true passion, rather than thinking and overthinking, take a leap of faith. You do not need to have an epiphany to find your purpose. You just need to keep exploring. Think of your purpose as a work in progress. Through intention and persistence, you can build and pursue a life of purpose.

This may involve getting outside of your comfort zone, as it did for me, but ultimately, once you have found clarity and validated your true passion, the courage to pursue that passion often follows. That is when you become a Mindful MAP Maker; you shape a path based on your passion and build a purpose-filled life (which I discuss in chapter 13). This map frees you to be the person you are meant to be, your authentic Self. It empowers you to share your passion and gift with the world, and in doing so, to make the world a better place.

I decided to start my own company, Prananaz. I thought, *If I can handle six weeks in India alone, I can handle starting a company in the United States — the land of opportunity.* This was not easy at first. In fact, it was challenging and difficult most of the time, and fear crept in. Sometimes it is easy to question yourself when doors close and obstacles arise, and some people regard difficulties as signs that they should not be pursuing their passions and dreams. Some give up or decide to settle for less; they choose the familiar, the comfortable, and the less meaningful, rather than risk following their heart and intuition.

When these fears and doubts came up for me, I realized that the greatest regret in my life would not be the possibility of failing; it would be not trying at all. Actual failure, for me, would be *not* taking the leap. This was something I was not willing to risk. I refused to allow fear to get the best of me. My intuition told me I was making the right decision, despite the warnings and criticism of some friends and family, who expressed sentiments like not even knowing me anymore. This is another sign that you have found your true passion, when a fire within drives you forward despite doubts and difficulties. I did not want to sacrifice the possibility of experiencing joy, truth, and my authentic Self. Quitting Prananaz was never an option.

I knew, for me, this was about thriving, not just surviving.

What made me happy was helping people live their best life.

Steve Jobs said, "Have the courage to follow your heart and intuition," and also, "Make a dent in the universe." That was precisely my goal, and I hope it will be yours as well. This sense of purpose will lead you to the life that you truly desire. To find your passion is to discover your highest potential for energy, creativity, intention, clarity, and inspiration.

Remember, discovering your life's purpose and true passion will not arrive all at once in an epiphany; it will emerge over time. And it cannot be figured out by thinking. It will arrive through your heart; you will find it in whatever naturally brings you joy. Explore your authentic desires. Listen to the universe. Notice what makes you jump out of bed in the morning, without an alarm. Do whatever brings you the most joy.

Pause. Breathe. Choose to explore your current situation. Embrace curiosity.

Practice mindfulness daily to tap into greater clarity and creativity.

Apply the Seven A's to manage stress, build resilience, and make healthy and mindful choices a habit.

Realize your full potential by optimizing the Three P's. Regard pain as your greatest teacher. Cultivate free-flowing prana to give you vital energy. And pursue your passions to identify your purpose, or what gives your life meaning.

Live with intention on a daily, moment-to-moment basis. Be mindful of what you are doing, thinking, feeling, saying, smelling, and seeing. Even when we are unsure of our life's purpose, this is how we make life meaningful every day. Do not wait for certainty or a lightbulb moment. Make your life meaningful by making the necessary changes to live with purpose all the time, rather than live on autopilot.

If you lead with your heart and provide value, you will make an impact in this world.

You will find your meaning, and you will carry out your purpose.

Always ask yourself:

What would my purpose, career, and relationships look like if I connected my mind with my heart?

How can I lead differently from my heart?

How can I choose to make a positive impact?

Pause.

Breathe.

Choose to lead with your heart and intuition.

BUSINESS HACKS

Practice the Power of Daily Intention

Tune in to all your senses, and ask, *What is my purpose or intention in this moment?*

The phone rings, or an email or text comes in. Ask: *What is my purpose or intention in this moment? Will this distract me and take me away from my prana flow state?*

Think of a typical workday meeting. You may have an agenda, but do you have an intention? Go beyond what you want to cover in a meeting and pinpoint your larger intent, both for yourself and for the participants.

Here are some simple ways to practice this:

- Before getting out of bed, intend to have an exploratory day or a productive day.
- Before you enter your workplace, intend to learn something new or be helpful.
- Before a meeting, intend to listen more or lead more.

In phone calls, meetings, and company parties, you can always put an intention behind your actions, making them more meaningful and powerful. Follow that intention to see how it aligns with your purpose and life's messages.

Share Purposeful Company Stories

A culture of purpose starts from the top and permeates throughout the entire organization. As a leader, take the time to gather teams and colleagues and encourage them to share their own stories about how your mutual purpose drives their work. Ensure that all leaders encourage their teams to do the same.

Talk about the client engagements you are most proud of or projects you have completed, both in small and large ways, to illustrate what advancing your purpose looks like. This can be a great way to start weekly meetings on a high note.

It is also worth creating programs to recognize individuals and teams that bring your organization's purpose to life.

Write a Life Mission Statement

A mission statement defines the essence of the purpose of a company. It states what a company stands for and why it exists in the first place. It serves as the North Star, keeping everyone informed of the direction the company is headed.

Take a good look at the mission statements of some of the world's most well-known companies. Apple's original mission statement was: "To make a contribution to the world by making tools for the mind that advance humankind." It focused on the *why* rather than the *what*.

Your life mission statement should encompass your purpose, whether that is caring for others or changing the world. Richard Branson's personal mission statement is: "Have fun in your journey through life and learn from your mistakes."

Do not worry if you do not know your personal mission statement yet. All it takes is a little brainstorming. Answer these questions for some inspiration:

- What are my core desired feelings? (How do I want to feel every day?)
- What are my core values?
- What makes me lose track of time?
- What are my strengths? What am I good at?
- What value do I bring? To whom?
- How can I serve? (Choose what inspires and energizes you.)
- What is my desired outcome, personally and/or professionally?
- How do I want to be remembered?

Always include the *why*. Dig deeper than what is shown or heard on the surface. Listen to your heart and intuition.

Get Outside of Your Comfort Zone

Do your best to move outside of your comfort zone (the place you live inside yourself without fear). Choose a frequency and duration that is attainable yet challenging. For example, start by choosing to do one or two things outside of your comfort zone per day or per week. Ask yourself:

What would I do that would energize me if I knew I couldn't fail?
What kind of legacy do I want to leave?

Your legacy does not have to be the size of Steve Jobs's legacy. Your name does not have to be written in history books. Your legacy is whatever you want it to be. It just needs to be a vocation that makes you happy.

Perhaps your legacy will be to leave your kids with the wisdom you have gained over the years. They will be your legacy. Maybe it will be to make your partner proud and to remain deeply connected with them. Or perhaps your goal is for your company to make the "Best Places to Work" list year after year by taking care of your employees while maintaining customer loyalty. That will be your legacy.

Most things we want are outside of our comfort zone. We must break free from the familiar and venture into the unfamiliar so that we can be more comfortable with being uncomfortable. This is where the magic happens and we can *make a little dent in the universe*.

Learn to trust your intuition. Practice being open and aware of the signs and making the connections.

KEY TAKEAWAYS

- At the bottom of Maslow's hierarchy of needs are our survival needs, followed by safety and security, then love and a sense of belonging. Self-esteem and self-actualization are at the peak of the pyramid, and they are the needs most often ignored. While we can survive without them, they are crucial if we are to thrive, innovate, and pursue our purpose.

- Your purpose is about being human and humane — being good and doing good in a self-actualized way. Purpose is what fulfills us and helps others: a source of joy and healing that keeps us grounded and motivated as we navigate the physical world. It is our life's message or mission: what we wish to drive in the world.

- There are two types of purpose. On a macro level, there is our life purpose, the reason we exist. On a micro level, there is the purpose of taking action with intention and ambition on a daily basis.

- Everyone wants one or a combination of these five desired outcomes: to be happy, to feel a sense of belonging, to be loved, to live a life of truth and authenticity, and to be safe.

- The six logical levels of change help identify what promotes or limits our effectiveness as leaders and as organizations. Sustainable change and evolution occur at the highest level of the pyramid, which is named as "Purpose," and trickles down and reinforces all the other levels of change.

- Your heart will lead you to your life's passion and purpose. Tap into your heart by quieting your mind so you can hear your true desires, and then take explorative action.

- To find your passion is to discover your highest potential for energy, creativity, intention, clarity, and inspiration. Step out of your comfort zone and expand your horizons. Give yourself the opportunity to find what it is that makes your heart happy and the world a better place.

CHAPTER THIRTEEN

MINDFUL
MAP MAKING

A map can function in several ways. It reflects a vision of the world around us and helps us chart a path through that world. It tells us where we have been, where we are going, and where we might go. It is a tool for planning our life's journey.

A map is a story. How we make (and constantly remake) our map is how we shape (and reshape) our story.

We are all mapmakers. However, one of our highest aspirations should be to become a Mindful MAP Maker so that we can take charge of our experiences and be the CEO of our well-being.

Everything in the book leads to this final stage of the process where everything comes together. Part I discusses mindfulness, the Big M, which is the foundation of a life well lived. Mindfulness is imperative for anyone seeking to live a healthy and happy, self-actualized, and successful life. This is especially crucial today, when so many forces push and pull us to be distracted and disconnected, to live on autopilot. By awakening your heart and mind, and strengthening the connection between them, you can both *be well* and *do well*.

This involves developing a regular, consistent mindfulness practice, which cultivates the focus and self-awareness you need to make mindful choices about how to live your best life. Mindfulness is the solid ground beneath your feet, even as your mindfulness journey will always be a work in progress, evolving and deepening.

Part II introduces the Seven A's, which are interconnected, complementary tools and strategies for making healthy choices, for upgrading both your behavior and your mindset, and for living a more connected life. One main objective of the Seven A's is managing stress, which is omnipresent in our lives. Not all stress is bad, but when stress goes unmanaged and unchecked, it can spiral into chronic stress, which undermines our health and effectiveness and can become deadly. Sometimes stress even prevents us from taking a proper breath.

The *Pause. Breathe. Choose.* Method and the ACE Method are ways you can recognize, manage, and move beyond stress. They help you to pause, be present, and make mindful choices, so that you take charge of stress rather than let stress be in charge of you.

Managing stress is essential, but not enough. The Seven A's also help us to build resilience, an inner reserve that protects us from the destructive effects of stress, as well as to embrace stressors as opportunities for growth and to cultivate all our connections, which include Self, others, the world, and the universe. Both mindfulness and the Seven A's are building blocks you can use on a daily, even moment-to-moment basis to stay on track and construct a healthy life.

Then, part III discusses the Three P's: pain, prana, and purpose. By regarding pain as your greatest teacher, you learn what you love and care about most deeply. This attitude embraces two truths: that how you respond to pain defines who you are, and that facing pain is how you grow, evolve, and find your purpose. The vehicle that takes you from pain to purpose is prana. When this vital inner energy flows freely, and activates your prana flow state, it helps you make mindful, healthy choices. Prana is the fuel that allows you to attain and sustain peak performance in your professional and personal life.

The goal of all these tools, practices, and choices is to identify and then live your life's purpose, which in turn gives your life passion and meaning.

This final chapter connects the dots of the three parts of this book that make up the MAP Method and describes how to take empowered, aligned action to live a purpose-filled, meaningful life by becoming a Mindful MAP Maker.

The MAP Method

MAP is a useful acronym to remember my method for a holistic approach to living your best life, and the MAP Method uses the metaphor of a map to chart that purposeful life. The acronym stands for:

- **M** — Master mindfulness (the Big M)
- **A** — Apply better choices to manage stress and build resilience (the Seven A's)
- **P** — Promote your Self to the CEO of your well-being (the Three P's)

Mindfulness is the foundation for my coaching practice, for my corporate programs, for this book, and for my life. Practicing mindfulness can empower you in any situation. It enables you to act with intention and consequently make wiser and healthier choices. You pause and breathe to step out of autopilot and into awareness.

Applying better choices to create healthy habits, manage stress, and build resilience requires a commitment to a holistic, healthy lifestyle. The strategies of the Seven A's enable you to be agile and resilient in a stressful world, and to forge the connections essential to living a fulfilled life.

Promoting your Self to be the CEO of your well-being is the ultimate goal, as shown in the MAP Method pyramid. The Three P's enable you to evolve and reach your highest potential.

THE MAP METHOD PYRAMID

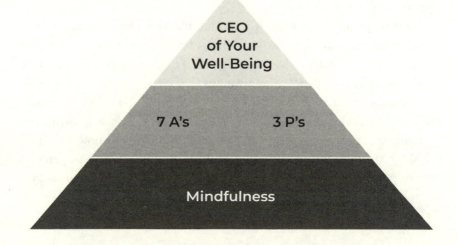

The MAP Method is a holistic framework and method to help you navigate your own mindful journey (your MAP) of authentic self-discovery, better choices, and purposeful growth. Becoming a Mindful MAP Maker means putting everything together into a coherent narrative. We all have a set of personal and professional experiences from the past (deep within our familial roots) that have shaped who we are today. We also have a set of aspirations, dreams, and visions for the future. Both of these shape our life's map.

As we go through life, we construct representations of our experiences and leave a trail we can look back on as a unique blueprint that has defined, and continues to define, our personal realities. The trail, the dots, and the footsteps, as we wander and pause, eventually form the landscape that is our life.

We are ultimately a fusion of our experiences; the pictures, sounds, feelings, smells, and even tastes of our past combine to make us who we are in the present. Those representations are narratives. Human beings are storytellers and stories are a vessel for meaning: a way to communicate a perception of our Self, others, the world, and the universe. We are all meaning makers.

I use the metaphor of mapmaking because these narratives not only shape our understanding of our past but also guide us in navigating the future. The maps we construct as we connect the dots of our past with our plans for the future are stories of who we are and who we are becoming.

The Mindful MAP Maker is empowered to respond proactively to unexpected change, to the inevitable curveballs life throws at us. The Mindful MAP Maker responds instead of reacts and sees change as an opportunity, not as an obstacle.

Our maps are tools that we must adjust and refine along the way. Because our maps are a narrative, we must revise the stories we tell about ourselves (see this chapter's Action Steps). We are all a work in progress, and so must be our stories and our maps.

Perhaps this is what distinguishes those who thrive from those who merely survive. Our maps are like a living organism, always growing and evolving, constantly engaged in the present, the here and now. As Mindful MAP Makers, our lives will be shaped by how we choose to perceive and respond to our experiences. Our personal realities, no matter how many stops and detours we take, become meaningful when we choose to reframe them, deal with them, and accept them as the stepping-stones that create who we are right now and who we hope to become.

Becoming a Mindful MAP Maker means reflecting consciously about the past and intentionally charting a path forward. It is about taking empowered and aligned action to shape the story of your life in the way that best serves your purpose.

Write Your Story, Map Your Life

People differ over what might be the single most distinguishing characteristic of our species, *Homo sapiens*. Some say it is the size of our brains, that we walk upright, or our opposable thumbs.

Jonathan Gottschall suggests that what truly makes us human is the fact that we tell stories. He calls us a "storytelling animal" (in his book *The Storytelling Animal*). It is not just that we compulsively tell stories every day and dream them every night. "We live our lives inside stories," he says. In other words, in a sense, we *are* stories.

We are all storytellers, all mapmakers. The question is: Is that process a mindful and intentional one?

Psychologist Dan P. McAdams suggests a simple way to look at our psychological evolution. From a very early age, we are actors who experiment with different behavioral traits, different roles. We never stop becoming actors, but in our teen years, we become agents as well, making more intentional decisions about the person we want to be.

In our developing years, there is not always a lot of rhyme or reason to our choices. We have not yet developed a coherent narrative about our lives. As we do so in adulthood, we now become authors, actively shaping the story of our lives.

This is what being a Mindful MAP Maker means: to mindfully shape your story, both the story of how you came to be the person you are today and the story of who you want to become tomorrow. That is my challenge to you.

People are not always mindful or intentional about shaping their stories. For instance, the tendency of our monkey mind is to run through the same stories over and over, like an endless looping film reel. When our minds are anxious and distracted, our stories are invariably about past regrets and worries about the future. Distraction and rumination are counterproductive to shaping helpful stories, since they mire us in negativity and block our prana.

When I work with a client to hit the reset button and upgrade to a more positive mindset, I am essentially helping them become a mindful, positive storyteller instead of a negative, mindless one. This is why gratitude journals and starting a conversation with "What's new and good?" are powerful tools.

Hitting the reset button and reframing potentially stressful situations as welcome challenges are both about revising our story. They help us tell the stories of our days in ways that energize us rather than deplete us and hold us back. They help us feed our Inner Coach (who tells a positive story) and starve our Inner Critic (who tells a negative story).

Being a Mindful MAP Maker is about both present-moment awareness and seeing the bigger picture. We can shape our ongoing present by pausing and breathing and staying attuned to the moment, to ourselves, and to those around us. We can shape our future through the better choices we make to live a healthy and happy, engaged, and purposeful life.

We shape our past as well. Throughout this book, I discuss how a mindset change or upgrade often precedes other changes. We form our identity by how we choose to perceive our experiences, how we integrate them into our MAP and narrative, and by the meanings we attach to those experiences. How we tell the stories of our past reflects who we are in the present. That story, in turn, sets the tone for how we approach the future. As we grow and evolve, our stories must grow and evolve as well. Otherwise, they become old and stagnant, reflecting an outdated version of ourselves, while holding us back from being our best Self.

We may see the past as fixed, as set in stone, when in fact, it is fluid, a work in progress. With age, new experiences, and insights, these old stories can and should be revised. This is an essential part of being a Mindful MAP Maker.

Our stories and maps must evolve with us. Revising and remaking them allows us to continue growing.

Revise your stories. Change your map.

Connect the Dots

Some people know at an early age what their life purpose is. It is possible, for example, for a five-year-old who dreams of being a doctor to eventually actualize that dream and love their job.

When I look back on my trail so far, when I look at my map and the journey I took from the beginning of my life all the way to becoming the CEO of my well-being, I do not see a straight, direct, or tidy line. My map is messy. It veers, loops, and detours.

Many people have a messy map, full of exploration and experimentation. For certain periods, life can seem to be a smooth flight across endless blue skies, and you may think you have the future laid out — that is, until a crash landing shatters your map, and your plan is reduced to shambles.

The truth is that our directions are ever-changing, so we must be flexible and do our best to recalibrate. I choose to look at all of these dots on my map as the meaningful experiences that led me to where I am today, intentionally or not. If I were to wish that my personal blueprint looked different, that would be equivalent to wanting to be someone else.

I embrace the dots on my map because they define who I am. I was just two years old when my parents came to the United States from Iran on a "vacation" that uprooted and resettled us permanently. Even while my parents held on to the culture and traditions of Iran, my childhood home was Palo Alto, California.

I was a toddler and do not recall our move, but the first two dots on my journey, Iran and California, hold great significance. Without that first trek, I would not be the person I am today. Because of the Iranian Revolution, I would have had a very different education in Iran, living in a restrictive culture that does not promote world exploration or, for women, even being alone in public. Since then, the country has changed, but at that time, I would likely not have discovered my passion and purpose, or career. Instead I would have been married with kids by my early twenties. My map would have been drastically different.

I choose to look mindfully at these dots and connect them to see how they have shaped who I am and how they have helped me grow.

My travels and exploration of the world started when I was young. My father is in the travel business, and throughout my childhood and teens, my family spent most summers in Europe, since we have relatives in France and Germany. I appreciated the broader perspective these experiences gave me and felt like a citizen of the world.

While attending college at UC Santa Cruz, instead of partying with other students on campus, I explored the nightlife of San Francisco, my favorite city at the time. I did not want to leave San Francisco after graduating, and I was set on finding a job that would enable me to connect with eclectic people and live in the city.

At the age of twenty-one, I was fortuitously offered an interview at Apple, but as I describe, I was initially reticent. My heart was set on living and working in San Francisco. However, when Steve Jobs made me an offer, my sentiment changed. Knowing it was a great opportunity, I accepted. I compromised by living closer to Cupertino, at my parents' home in Atherton. That way, I would not be wasting money on an apartment in the suburbs, nor would I be commuting every day from San Francisco. I looked at this dot on my map as temporary, a great exploration of my opportunities.

Of course, I did not earn a psychology degree in order to become Steve Jobs's executive assistant. However, looking back now, I can clearly see how veering a little (or a lot) from our intended path can often open our future in ways we might not expect.

After I left Apple, I took a month to travel around Italy, exploring my independence, traveling off the beaten path, and experiencing new things. During this time, I received many job offers with high pay and good benefits. It turned out that working for Steve Jobs as the first stop on my professional map opened doors to lots of opportunities.

Itching to try something new, I turned those offers down and instead chose to work at a small technology startup to expand my experience in the high-level corporate world.

After working with the startup, I wanted to open my own yoga studio and wellness center. I completed an intense yoga teacher training program. However, my then-boyfriend suggested I work in sales. I was insulted. *Sales?* All it made me think of were stereotypical scam-artist, sleazy salesmen, but my boyfriend convinced me otherwise, and so I applied for a junior sales position at Yahoo!.

Imagine my shock when I was offered the executive sales position, even though I had interviewed for the junior position. I put my yoga studio idea on hold, took the Yahoo! job, and this led to my pharmaceutical sales position at AstraZeneca, which turned out to be my last corporate job.

As I describe throughout, that job initiated the most significant turning point in my life, the one that led me to India, to going back to school for holistic health, to the founding of my company Prananaz, and to this book. I have committed to a meaningful and purposeful future, but I cannot know what detours will arise. What I do know is that I will continue to connect the dots, define my meaning and purpose, and revise my story.

Your MAP Is Always a Work in Progress

Even when we are fortunate enough to identify our life purpose, to know what gives our life meaning and passion, and to develop a clear vision of how to get from point A to point B, expect life to throw you curveballs every now and then. These disruptions and detours force us to revisit and recalibrate our maps, sometimes in small ways, sometimes in more fundamental ways.

This means, to be a Mindful MAP Maker, we have to be agile, aware, and ready for transitions, which figure prominently in almost everyone's journey, as they have in mine. Even when obstacles do not lead us to revise our life purpose, they can force us to rethink and adjust our plans, our path, and our map.

Many of my clients are challenged by transitions. When my client Rob (see "Break the Cycle," pages 92–94) first came to me, he was experiencing what he considered a midlife crisis. He could no longer recognize himself in the mirror, due to sleepless nights, bad habits, loneliness, chronic stress, and disconnection. His perspective and priorities were changing. He wanted to make space in his life for a relationship and for kids. He no longer wanted to feel lonely and continuously stressed out. Yet he remained committed to the tech startup he had founded. Being an entrepreneur remained his life purpose.

Rob was in the middle of a transition, but he did not want everything to change. I worked with Rob to mitigate his personal stress, develop healthier habits, and improve the communication and culture within his company. By mindfully turning a personal crisis into an opportunity to learn and grow, Rob was able to dramatically reduce his stress levels while growing and improving his company. His map gained a detour, but his professional destination remained the same.

You, too, will encounter personal as well as professional transitions. In some cases, that change may be forced upon you. You may be let go from a job or relocated. Your company could be acquired by another. Or you might initiate a transition yourself, as Rob did and as I did. You might decide that your current position or profession no longer inspires you or fits your life purpose. Either way, in our fluid and ever-changing world, most people end up reinventing themselves several times throughout a career.

As you navigate through change and revise your map, I encourage you to apply the following tools and principles that define a Mindful MAP Maker. This encapsulates what I present in this book:

- Use the *Pause. Breathe. Choose.* Method to help you step back, become present, and make better choices.
- Remember that the ultimate wealth is well-being. Instill a culture of wellness in your life and within your company.
- Adopt a mindfulness practice that works for you and make a habit of regular mindful self-check-ins throughout the day.
- Strengthen the connection between your head and your heart.
- Upgrade your mindset and listen to your Inner Coach, not your Inner Critic.
- Replace judgment with curiosity.
- Realize there is no such thing as "failure," only feedback to evolve.
- Upgrade your behavior. Small, consistent changes ripple throughout your life and ultimately generate big results.
- Manage stress and build your resilience reserve, so that life's challenges are opportunities you shape, not obstacles that dictate your path.
- Choose to focus on what you can control because that is where energy flows.
- Use mindfulness, healthy choices, and a positive mindset to unblock and free your vital energy, your prana.
- Be fully present to the pain of challenging situations and allow that pain to be your teacher and perceive it as an opportunity to evolve. Uncover the lesson and the upside from your pain.
- Attend to your connections, starting with Self, and expanding outward to family, friends, colleagues, community, the world, and the universe.
- Allocate time for play and recovery. We must reboot and

recharge for greater clarity, creativity, energy, and joy.

- Embody a culture of learning, professionally and personally, as the CEO of your well-being. This will help you anticipate change and respond to it with nimbleness and agility.
- Lead with your heart. Be intention driven and purposeful to achieve your full potential.

Be a Mindful MAP Maker

My journey toward mindfulness has been long, winding, and brimming with excitement and adventure. I have traveled the world and braved every obstacle that has been set before me. I have risen to every challenge and often triumphed. I have met and spent time with extraordinary people from all walks of life along the way.

In hindsight, I am grateful that I was adamant, right out of college, to experience different positions within different companies, which prepared me for what I was meant to be doing all along. At the time, I never thought that the CEOs and leaders around me would be future clients.

When I look at my map mindfully, I can see how everything, from being accidentally uprooted from Iran to publishing this book, has been necessary to becoming the person I am truly meant to be: an entrepreneur who is making a dent in the universe by changing lives and companies. Without mindfully connecting all of these dots on my map, would I have found my true passion and purpose? Would I have become the successful CEO I am today?

My passion has become my profession.

I have found my purpose.

I am the CEO of my well-being.

This is what I want for you as well.

Many of my clients tend to be ambitious overachievers and hardworking perfectionists. They often burn the candle at both ends and are in danger of burning out, or have already burned out, or have had a wake-up call. Sometimes, they have already begun to make more mindful, healthy choices, but they do not have a comprehensive approach to wellness and have yet to achieve their full potential. This may describe you as well.

Regardless of where each of us is on the spectrum of wellness, all of our paths have much in common. We all share common fears of failure, pain, loneliness, rejection, disappointment, ridicule, and death. We all struggle with a world that can, at times, deaden and distract us. A world that can disconnect our head from our heart. A world that can push us toward the unhealthy choices that come from living on autopilot.

We struggle with regret and the fear of the unknown. We wonder about our impact and legacy.

Living a fulfilled and engaged life is not easy. Like yoga, like mindfulness, it is an ongoing practice you must commit to. It is a choice to take empowered and aligned action to create the map you desire. I promise the investment you make in becoming the CEO of your well-being is one of the best returns on investment possible.

Choose to live your best life.

Do not settle for anything less.

If you have not found your purpose, continue to explore until you find it. Live every day with intention. Never stop.

You will experience obstacles, challenges, and pain along the way. If you allow it to, that pain will block your prana. Do not let it hinder you. Use it to evolve.

Enable your prana to flow freely. Apply everything you have learned about living mindfully. Free your Self from the noise and chaos so that you can listen to your intuition.

Awaken your mind.

Awaken your heart.

Connect your mind with your heart.

Be mindful of the signs.

Have the courage to lead with your heart and intuition.

You have the ability to make this world a better and more meaningful place to live. It is a matter of accessing and allowing yourself to be your true Self.

Enjoy the journey.

No matter where you are starting, you *can* be the CEO of your well-being. Just take the first step.

Pause.

Breathe.

Choose.

BUSINESS HACKS

Connect the Dots in Business

Connecting the dots in your job, workplace, or business means having the intuition and perspective to know that individual events, whether they be accomplishments or setbacks, occur in the context of a larger plan that can be looked back on later with appreciation and understanding. Stay innovative by connecting the dots from your past to pinpoint opportunities in the present and future. Strive daily to notice how many dots you are connecting.

Another advocate of connecting the dots is Richard Branson, whose mantra is ABCD, or "Always be connecting the dots." To me, this means the following:

- Connect diverse people to gain a broad range of talents, experience, and perspectives.
- Connect customers with business to receive feedback, increase engagement, and gain insight.
- Connect customer pain points to improve or create products and services.
- Connect ideas from different places, across geographies and sectors, to think outside the box and create unique concepts.
- Connect business with new business models to be innovative and more profitable.
- Connect media channels and market networks to amplify impact and reach.
- Connect customers with one another to cultivate a sense of community.

Your skill lies in being able to see the bigger picture and having the imagination to make unlikely and uncommon connections to create better products, methods, teams, projects, and more. Your ideas will be unique to you and your situation in ways no one else could ever imagine.

Always be connecting.

Create a Career or Business Roadmap to Success

Like a GPS, a roadmap can help you get from your current location to your desired destination, whether in your career or your business. In order to avoid delays, detours, and accidents as much as possible, be strategic and pragmatic in your approach. The first step is to have a crystal-clear long-term vision that aligns with your core values and purpose. Dream big and focus on success.

Use your vision to guide you in creating a roadmap. Ask these questions:

- What are my business or career objectives?
- What do I want?
- Why do I want it?
- What are my strategies to achieve my objectives?
- What are the potential roadblocks and how can I mitigate or overcome them?
- What is my big-picture action plan?
- What are the critical milestones?
- How can I break these milestones down into small steps?
- What is the first step I can take now?

In your business, make sure to share your roadmap with your team to ensure everyone is on the same page and has a clear understanding of your current state and your desired end state. Identify strategies and action steps, and then prioritize and delegate accordingly.

Finally, keep in mind that the terrain of the business world is in constant flux. Anticipate change by reading about trends and new developments in your industry and in business in general. Take time to pull back and consider the big picture and the long view.

ACTION STEPS

Connect the Dots on Your Map

Mindful MAP Makers know they can learn from their past and all the experiences that have contributed to who they are today. They do not forget or gloss over the road they have traveled.

Take time to review your entire life so far and see it as a series of experiences that generate a larger picture of yourself, one that is created from your internal map, or from your perceptions of the world. Our internal map starts at a micro level and is composed of countless sense memories of images, sounds, feelings, smells, and tastes, as well as significant life events. Then the map moves outward, and reflects how you choose to perceive, respond to, and create meaning from those experiences. This creates a larger picture that is your mindful vision of your life, your place in the world.

How have you used all of your experiences to make decisions about your reality? What are all the stops you have made? What kind of path have you followed?

Do your best to connect the dots. Acknowledge the importance of every little dot and how it has contributed to the person you are and what you are doing today. Know that your reality is structured around your map thus far, which has shaped your perceptions and experience.

Revise Your Narrative to Change Your Map

When you feel lost, unhappy, or dissatisfied, when you look at your situation and realize you do not know where you are going, revise your map. In order to change your current experience, you must move away from what you do not want and toward what you do want. This often requires revising the stories you tell about your life, the ones based on perspectives that no longer serve you.

Human beings are storytellers because stories are vehicles for meaning. In other words, it is not what happens to us that is most crucial, but the meaning we ascribe to those events and experiences. We are storytellers, and we are meaning makers. These stories become our beliefs, and if our beliefs are causing pain, then it is time to update those beliefs by revising our old stories.

Pain is our greatest teacher, and it often indicates the parts of our story that need revision. Where are your pain points? How can you use prana to move away from that pain and toward your purpose?

Perhaps you are in the middle of delays and detours, or maybe you have even crash-landed, yet you are still here, and you can create a new path moving forward. Acknowledge how your stories have led to where you are today. Identify any heavy baggage that no longer serves you. Be grateful and willing to let go of it. There is no need to hold on to heavy baggage from your past or from younger versions of yourself.

Choose to release the baggage. *We have to let go of something to upgrade to the next level of our evolution.*

- MAP is a useful acronym for my holistic approach to living your best life. It stands for *master mindfulness* (the Big M), *apply better choices to manage stress and build resilience* (the Seven A's), and *promote your Self to the CEO of your well-being* (the Three P's). The MAP Method is a framework to help you navigate your own mindful journey of authentic self-discovery, better choices, and purposeful growth.

- Our MAP is also our story. Like a metaphor of an actual map, it is a tool to help us shape our life's journey into a coherent narrative. We are all mapmakers. We all have a set of experiences that have shaped who we are today. We also have a set of aspirations, dreams, and visions for the future. However, one of our highest aspirations is to become a *Mindful* MAP Maker so that we can take charge of our experiences and be the CEO of our well-being.

- The Mindful MAP Maker is empowered and responds proactively to the inevitable curveballs life throws at us. The Mindful MAP Maker responds instead of reacts and sees change as an opportunity and not as an obstacle.

- Our stories and beliefs are shaped by how we choose to perceive and respond to our experiences. Our personal realities, no matter how many stops and detours we take, are ultimately given meaning by how we choose to frame our experience.

- Our stories and maps are works in progress. With age, new experiences, and new insights, our stories can and should be revised. Mindful MAP Makers are flexible and revise their stories in order to change their experience of life, their map.

- Being a Mindful MAP Maker means reflecting consciously about the past and intentionally charting a path forward. It is about taking empowered and aligned action to shape the story of your life in the way that best serves your purpose.

· THE MAP METHOD SUMMARY ·

M — MASTER mindfulness (the Big M)

A — APPLY better choices to manage stress
and build resilience (the Seven A's)

> ADOPT a healthy lifestyle
>
> ALLOCATE play and recovery time
>
> AVOID unnecessary stress
>
> ALTER the situation
>
> ADAPT to the stressor
>
> ACCEPT what you cannot change
>
> ATTEND to connection with Self, others,
> world, and universe

P — PROMOTE your Self to the CEO
of your well-being (the Three P's)

> PAIN, our greatest teacher for growth
>
> PRANA, our energy to be fully engaged
> at work and in life
>
> PURPOSE, our drive for meaning

ACKNOWLEDGMENTS

I am profoundly grateful to have discovered and pursued my passion and purpose and to be able to interact with so many fascinating people who enrich my days — and who choose to be the CEO of their well-being. Thank you to my clients and all the people who have been a part of my journey thus far.

I would especially like to thank Steve Jobs for hiring me and inspiring me to write this book. Kent Gustavson and Don Ramer for helping me embark on a writer's path and for encouraging me to start writing. Rita Rosenkranz, my ever-present and savvy literary agent, for taking on a first-time author. Georgia Hughes, editorial director, and Jeff Campbell, editor, along with the rest of the publishing team at New World Library, thank you for your genuine enthusiasm and continuous support.

To my beta readers — Elena Pons, Osanna Avanesova, Rich Macary, MaryAnn Godwin, and Beth Sandri — thank you for your valuable time and feedback.

Thank you to Jessica Robinson, Gary Su, Matthew Cowan, Laura Garnett, and Alex Jamieson for being generous connectors. Mozhan Marno and Naida Bongo for creative design input. Scott Doyle and Heather Hummel for additional edits.

My deep gratitude and appreciation for my loving and supportive husband, Chris Lavery, and my parents, Nasrin Tavakolian Beheshti and Cyrus Beheshti, for their unwavering belief in me and in my work.

And to all of you who are on the path of self-discovery, better choices, and purposeful growth, thank you for reading this book and taking aligned action.

ENDNOTES

Chapter 2: Mindfulness in Action

p. 37　*A Harvard Business Review article argues rightly that we should focus*: Tony Schwartz and Catherine McCarthy, "Manage Your Energy, Not Your Time," *Harvard Business Review*, October 2007, https://hbr.org/2007/10/manage-your-energy -not-your-time.

p. 39　*Other reviews document reduced symptoms in a range of health conditions*: Patrick K. Hyland, R. Andrew Lee, and Maura J. Mills, "Mindfulness at Work: A New Approach to Improving Individual and Organizational Performance," *Industrial and Organizational Psychology* 8, no. 4 (December 2015): 576–602, https://pdfs .semanticscholar.org/3097/6a1ad823574c0deaa447aa78bb0306e1ce08.pdf.

p. 39　*New research suggests that mindfulness might be able to reverse the effects*: Ivana Buric et al., "What Is the Molecular Signature of Mind–Body Interventions? A Systematic Review of Gene Expression Changes Induced by Meditation and Related Practices," *Frontiers in Immunology* 8, no. 670 (2017), doi: 10.3389 /fimmu.2017.00670.

p. 39　*Those who perceive themselves to be under a great deal of stress*: Abiola Keller et al., "Does the Perception That Stress Affects Health Matter?" *Health Psychology* (September 2012): 677–84, https://www.ncbi.nlm.nih.gov/pmc/articles/PMC3374921.

p. 40　*Several studies suggest mindfulness intervention may be more effective*: Stacy Lu, "Mindfulness Holds Promise for Treating Depression," *American Psychological Association*, 46, no. 3 (March 2015), https://www.apa.org/monitor/2015/03/cover -mindfulness.

p. 40　*A study led by Massachusetts General Hospital was the first*: Massachusetts General Hospital, "Mindfulness Meditation Training Changes Brain Structure in Eight Weeks," *ScienceDaily*, January 21, 2011, http://www.sciencedaily.com/releases /2011/01/110121144007.htm.

p. 40　*Mindfulness can literally reshape and rewire the brain*: Christopher Bergland, "How Do Neuroplasticity and Neurogenesis Rewire Your Brain?" *Psychology Today*,

February 6, 2017, https://www.psychologytoday.com/blog/the-athletes-way/201702/how-do-neuroplasticity-and-neurogenesis-rewire-your-brain.

p. 40   *Programs in the workplace have been demonstrated to help employees*: Ute Hülsheger et al., "Benefits of Mindfulness at Work: The Role of Mindfulness in Emotion Regulation, Emotional Exhaustion, and Job Satisfaction," *Journal of Applied Psychology* 98, no. 2 (2013): 310–25, https://pubmed.ncbi.nlm.nih.gov/23276118.

p. 40   *A paper published in the journal* Progress in Brain Research: Matt Richtel, "The Latest in Military Strategy: Mindfulness," *New York Times*, April 5, 2019, https://www.nytimes.com/2019/04/05/health/military-mindfulness-training.html.

p. 40   *Research shows that meditation builds resilience, boosts emotional*: Emma Seppälä, "How Meditation Benefits CEOs," *Harvard Business Review*, December 14, 2015.

p. 41   *As two significant reviews of the literature point out*: Darren J. Good et al., "Contemplating Mindfulness at Work: An Integrative Review," *Journal of Management* (2015): 1–29, https://pdfs.semanticscholar.org/c1d0/16228416d185dda7102ae516e56ddd9d8287.pdf; Hyland, Lee, and Mills, "Mindfulness at Work."

Part II: Apply Better Choices to Manage Stress and Build Resilience: The Seven A's

p. 49   *Our current patterns of thought and behavior are not permanent*: Charles Duhigg, *The Power of Habit: Why We Do What We Do in Life and Business* (New York: Random House, 2014).

Chapter 3: Adopt a Healthy Lifestyle

p. 52   *Karoshi remains such an epidemic that antikaroshi*: Zaria Gorvett, "Can You Work Yourself to Death?" *BBC News*, September 13, 2016, http://www.bbc.com/capital/story/20160912-is-there-such-thing-as-death-from-overwork.

p. 52   *The National Defense Council for Victims of Karoshi says*: Gorvett, "Can You Work Yourself to Death?"

p. 52   *The title of a 2017* New York Times *article summed up*: Makiko Inoue and Megan Specia, "Young Worker Clocked 159 Hours of Overtime in a Month. Then She Died," *New York Times*, October 5, 2017, https://www.nytimes.com/2017/10/05/world/asia/japan-death-overwork.html.

p. 52   *Many Americans forgo using all of the vacation days*: Patti Neighmond, "Overworked Americans Aren't Taking the Vacation They've Earned," NPR, July 12, 2016, https://www.npr.org/sections/health-shots/2016/07/12/485606970/overworked-americans-arent-taking-the-vacation-theyve-earned.

p. 52   *Every year, forty million people die prematurely from noncommunicable*: World Health Organization, "Global Action Plan for the Prevention and Control of Noncommunicable Diseases: 2013–2020," 2013, http://www.who.int/nmh/events/ncd_action_plan/en.

p. 53   *"The leading cause of death is personal decision-making"*: Ralph L. Keeney, "Personal Decisions Are the Leading Cause of Death," *Operations Research* 56, no. 6 (2008): 1335–47, https://pubsonline.informs.org/doi/abs/10.1287/opre.1080.0588.

p. 53   *In Austin, Texas, Jonas Koffler was an ambitious recent college*: Jonas Koffler, "What I Learned From a Stroke at 26: Make Time to Untangle," *New York Times*, September 24, 2016.

p. 53   *In 2013, twenty-one-year-old Moritz Erhardt was found dead*: Oliver Joy, "Intern's Death Puts Spotlight on Banks' Working Culture," CNN, August 22, 2013, https://www.cnn.com/2013/08/21/business/intern-hours-bank-of-america-erhardt /index.html.

p. 53   *Here are a few more shocking statistics*: The details in this list come from the following: Jennifer Yang, "Wednesday Is Peak Suicide Day, Study Finds," *Globe and Mail*, July 8, 2009, https://beta.theglobeandmail.com/life/wednesday-is-peak -suicide-day-study-finds/article582562; and Salleh Mohd Razali, "Life Event, Stress, and Illness," *Malaysian Journal of Medical Sciences* 15, no. 4, (October 2008): 9–18, https://www.ncbi.nlm.nih.gov/pmc/articles/PMC3341916.

p. 54   *In fact, a growing body of evidence shows that we would be better off*: Tony Schwartz and Catherine McCarthy, "Manage Your Energy, Not Your Time," *Harvard Business Review*, October 2007, https://hbr.org/2007/10/manage-your-energy-not-your-time.

p. 54   *A recent Harvard Medical School study of senior leaders found*: Leslie Kwoh, "When the CEO Burns Out," *Wall Street Journal*, May 7, 2013, https://www.wsj.com/articles /SB10001424127887323687604578469124008524696.

p. 58   *I recommend using the Fogg Method, which was*: "Fogg Method: Three Steps to Changing Behavior," BJ Fogg, http://www.foggmethod.com, accessed 2015.

p. 59   *In his book* The Power of Habit, *Charles Duhigg writes about*: Steven Benna, "Eight Keystone Habits That Can Transform Your Life," *Business Insider*, August 6, 2015, http://www.businessinsider.com/keystone-habits-that-transform-your-life-2015-8.

p. 61   *A growing body of evidence finds that "sitting is the new smoking"*: James Vlahos, "Is Sitting a Lethal Activity?" *New York Times*, April 14, 2011, http://www.nytimes .com/2011/04/17/magazine/mag-17sitting-t.html.

p. 62   *A new French law bans work emails after hours to prevent burnout*: David Z. Morris, "New French Law Bars Work Email After Hours," *Fortune*, January 1, 2017, http://fortune.com/2017/01/01/french-right-to-disconnect-law.

p. 62   *Harvard Business School professor Leslie A. Perlow has extensively*: Leslie A. Perlow, *Sleeping with Your Smartphone: How to Break the 24/7 Habit and Change the Way You Work* (Boston: Harvard Business Review Press, 2012).

p. 64   *"Eat food, not too much, mostly plants"*: This quote about how to eat healthily is from my class notes, January 29, 2012, with Michael Pollan.

p. 64   *Treat treats as treats or follow the "No S" diet*: Reinhard Engels and Ben Kallen, *The No S Diet* (New York: Penguin/Perigee, 2008).

p. 65   *Regular physical activity helps you live longer*: James McKinney et al., "The Health Benefits of Physical Activity and Cardiorespiratory Fitness," *BC Medical Journal* 58, no. 3 (April 2016): 131–37, http://www.bcmj.org/articles/health-benefits-physical -activity-and-cardiorespiratory-fitness.

p. 66   *Studies show that humming can help protect against sinus infections*: Anahad O'Connor, "The Claim: Humming Can Ease Sinus Problems," *New York Times*, December 20, 2010, http://www.nytimes.com/2010/12/21/health/21really.html.

Chapter 4: Allocate Play and Recovery Time

p. 72   *One study found that after participants were awake*: A.M. Williamson and Anne-Marie Feyer, "Moderate Sleep Deprivation Produces Impairments in Cognitive and Motor Performance Equivalent to Legally Prescribed Levels of Alcohol Intoxication," *Occupational and Environmental Medicine* 57, no. 10 (October 1, 2000), http://oem.bmj.com/content/57/10/649.short.

p. 72   *Researchers for the* Harvard Business Review *found a link between*: For the studies in this paragraph, see the following: Nick van Dam and Els van der Helm, "There's a Proven Link Between Effective Leadership and Getting Enough Sleep," *Harvard Business Review*, February 16, 2016, https://hbr.org/2016/02/theres-a-proven-link-between-effective-leadership-and-getting-enough-sleep; Mark R. Rosekind et al., "The Cost of Poor Sleep: Workplace Productivity Loss and Associated Costs," *Journal of Occupational and Environmental Medicine* 52, no. 1 (2010), 91–98; and Jennifer Turgiss and Stephanie Allen, "Asleep on the Job: The Causes and Consequences of Employees' Disrupted Sleep and How Employers Can Help," *Virgin Pulse*, https://www.yumpu.com/en/document/view/25016839/asleep-on-the-job-report-from-virgin-pulse, accessed August 27, 2020.

p. 73   *According to Dr. Walker, restorative sleep can improve your*: Personal notes while working with Dr. Matthew Walker at the Center for Human Sleep Science at University of California, Berkeley, June 2014.

p. 73   *Now we know the REM state is so important*: Chip Brown, "The Stubborn Scientist Who Unraveled a Mystery of the Night," *Smithsonian*, October 2003, https://www.smithsonianmag.com/science-nature/the-stubborn-scientist-who-unraveled-a-mystery-of-the-night-91514538.

p. 73   *These same researchers found that our sleep cycles are part*: Srini Pillay, *Tinker Dabble Doodle Try: Unlock the Power of the Unfocused Mind* (New York: Ballantine Books, 2017).

p. 73   *"Idleness is not just a vacation"*: Tim Kreider, "The 'Busy' Trap," *New York Times*, June 30, 2012, https://opinionator.blogs.nytimes.com/2012/06/30/the-busy-trap.

p. 74   *Scientists used to dismiss DMN as a "doing mostly nothing" state*: Ferris Jabr, "Why Your Brain Needs More Downtime," *Scientific American*, October 15, 2013, https://www.scientificamerican.com/article/mental-downtime.

p. 77   *Employees who say they have supportive superiors are 1.3 times*: Tony Schwartz and Christine Porath, "Why You Hate Work," *New York Times*, May 30, 2014, https://www.nytimes.com/2014/06/01/opinion/sunday/why-you-hate-work.html.

p. 77   *The concept of the "learning organization" was introduced*: Peter Senge, *The Fifth Discipline: The Art & Practice of the Learning Organization* (New York: Doubleday, 2006).

p. 77   *"When people are too busy or overstressed by deadlines"*: David A. Garvin, Amy C. Edmonson, and Francesca Gino, "Is Yours a Learning Organization?"

Harvard Business Review, March 2008 , https://hbr.org/2008/03/is-yours-a-learning
-organization.

p. 78 *According to a* Virgin Pulse *survey, new employees are thirty*: "What Employees Love
About Work," *Virgin Pulse* survey report, 2015, http://community.virginpulse.com
/laborlove_web.

p. 78 *"If the person who works at your company is 100% proud"*: Eric Schurenberg,
"Richard Branson: Why Customers Come Second at Virgin," *Inc.*, no date, accessed
August 27, 2020, https://www.inc.com/eric-schurenberg/sir-richard-branson-put
-your-staff-first-customers-second-and-shareholders-third.html.

p. 79 *reading can reduce stress levels by 68 percent*: "Reading 'Can Help Reduce Stress,'"
Telegraph, March 30, 2009, http://www.telegraph.co.uk/news/health/news/5070874
/Reading-can-help-reduce-stress.html.

p. 80 *Research finds that walking meetings increase creative thinking*: Marily Oppezzo and
Daniel L. Schwartz, "Give Your Ideas Some Legs: The Positive Effect of Walking
on Creative Thinking," *Journal of Experimental Psychology: Learning, Memory, and
Cognition* 40, no. 4 (2014): 1142–52.

Chapter 5: Avoid Unnecessary Stress

p. 87 *Research shows that chronic stress can contribute to the development*: A. Baum and
D. Posluszny, "Health Psychology: Mapping Biobehavioral Contributions to
Health and Illness," *Annual Review of Psychology* 50 (1999): 137–63.

p. 87 *Instead, chronic stress puts our life at risk by manifesting*: Neil Schneiderman, Gail
Ironson, and Scott Siegel, "Stress and Health: Psychological, Behavioral, and Bio-
logical Determinants," *Annual Review of Clinical Psychology* (2005), https://www
.ncbi.nlm.nih.gov/pmc/articles/PMC2568977.

p. 91 *Financial stress is the number-one stressor in the United States*: American Psychological Association, "American Psychological Association Survey Shows Money Stress
Weighing on Americans' Health Nationwide," February 4, 2015, http://www.apa.org
/news/press/releases/2015/02/money-stress.aspx.

p. 92 *According to the American Psychological Association, stress*: David Krantz, Beverly
Thorn, and Janice Kiecolt-Glaser, "How Stress Affects Your Health," American Psychological Association, https://www.apa.org/topics/stress-facts.pdf, accessed August
27, 2020.

p. 93 *Studies show that a positive mindset toward a challenging*: Margaret E. Kemeny,
"The Psychobiology of Stress," *Current Directions in Psychological Science* 12, no. 4
(August 2003), http://journals.sagepub.com/doi/abs/10.1111/1467-8721.01246.

p. 93 *People who feel this way have what psychologists call an external*: Richard B. Joelson,
"Locus of Control," *Psychology Today*, August 2, 2017, https://www.psychologytoday
.com/blog/moments-matter/201708/locus-control.

p. 94 *In 1998, researchers looked at thirty thousand US adults*: Abiola Keller et al., "Does the
Perception That Stress Affects Health Matter?" *Health Psychology* (September 2012):
677–84, https://www.ncbi.nlm.nih.gov/pmc/articles/PMC3374921.

p. 95 *Body chemistry helps explain this initially surprising disparity*: Alia Crum et
al., "The Benefits of a Stress-Is-Enhancing Mindset in Both Challenging and

Threatening Contexts," December 2015, https://mbl.stanford.edu/sites/default/files
/crum_et_al_stress_mindset_in_challenge_and_threat_12.6.15_ur.pdf.

p. 95   *Neuroscientist Ian Robertson studies stress and has found*: Quote by Ian Robertson
in Zlata Rodionova, "Why a Moderate Amount of Stress Is Good for You, According to a Cognitive Neuroscientist," *Independent*, June 13, 2016, https://ianrobertson
.org/moderate-amount-stress-good-according-cognitive-neuroscientist.

p. 96   *If you label it as "excitement" as opposed to "anxiety," this reframing*: Alison Wood
Brooks, "Get Excited: Reappraising Pre-Performance Anxiety as Excitement,"
Journal of Experimental Psychology 143, no. 3 (2014).

p. 96   *However, Dr. Alia Crum, a researcher at Columbia Business School*: Sue Shellenbarger,
"Turn Bad Stress Into Good," *Wall Street Journal*, May 7, 2013, https://www.wsj.com
/articles/SB10001424127887324766604578461221992471926.

p. 97   *This was demonstrated by a University of Rochester program*: Michael Krasner et
al., "Association of an Educational Program in Mindful Communication with
Burnout, Empathy, and Attitudes Among Primary Care Physicians," *Journal of the
American Medical Association*, September 23, 2009, https://jamanetwork.com
/journals/jama/fullarticle/184621.

p. 97   *The psychological framework for these mindful self-check-ins*: Dave Asprey, "Brendon
Burchard: Confidence, Drive, and Power," *Bulletproof* podcast #190.

p. 100   *According to the* Journal of Consumer Research, *this is*: Vanessa Patrick and Henrik
Hagtvedt, "'I Don't' versus 'I Can't': When Empowered Refusal Motivates Goal-
Directed Behavior," *Journal of Consumer Research* 39, no. 2 (August 2012): 371–81.

Chapter 6: Alter the Situation

p. 114   *Research in fields from airline safety to hospital emergency rooms*: Atul Gawande,
The Checklist Manifesto: How to Get Things Right (New York: Metropolitan Books,
2010).

p. 114   *This is especially important in a changing economy*: Boris Groysberg and Michael
Slind, "Leadership Is a Conversation," *Harvard Business Review* 90, no. 6 (June 2012).

p. 124   *Research indicates that working in ninety-minute intervals*: Drake Baer, "Why You
Need to Unplug Every 90 Minutes," *Fast Company*, June 19, 2013, https://www
.fastcompany.com/3013188/why-you-need-to-unplug-every-90-minutes.

p. 126   *studies have shown that watching animal videos can be used*: Jessica Gall Myrick,
"Emotion Regulation, Procrastination, and Watching Cat Videos Online: Who
Watches Internet Cats, Why, and to What Effect?" *Computers in Human Behavior*
52 (November 2015): 168–76.

Chapter 7: Adapt to the Stressor

p. 130   *"I can't believe this is happening"*: *60 Minutes*, "Flight 1549: A Routine Takeoff Turns
Ugly," *CBS News*, February 8, 2009, https://www.cbsnews.com/news/flight-1549-a
-routine-takeoff-turns-ugly.

p. 134   *"Long-established organizations are really being rocked to their core"*: Alyson Shon-
         tell, "11 Ways to Completely Reinvent Yourself," *Business Insider*, March 16, 2011,
         https://www.businessinsider.com/fast-company-practically-radical-bill-taylor-10
         -secrets-to-a-successful-pivot-2011-3.

p. 139   *Researchers have discovered that a daily gratitude practice*: Robert Emmons, "Why
         Gratitude Is Good," *Greater Good Magazine* (UC Berkeley), November 16, 2010,
         https://greatergood.berkeley.edu/article/item/why_gratitude_is_good.

p. 140   *Studies show optimism helps people cope with disease and recover*: Harvard Health
         Publishing, Harvard Medical School, "Optimism and Your Health," May 2008,
         https://www.health.harvard.edu/heart-health/optimism-and-your-health.

Chapter 8: Accept What You Cannot Change

p. 148   *Psychologists find that we are more vulnerable to stress and anxiety*: Shirley S. Wang,
         "Worrying About the Future, Ruminating on the Past: How Thoughts Affect Men-
         tal Health," *Wall Street Journal*, August 10, 2015, https://www.wsj.com/articles
         /worrying-about-the-future-ruminating-on-the-pasthow-thoughts-affect-mental
         -health-1439223597.

p. 150   *An ongoing mindfulness practice will increase*: Tom Ireland, "What Does Mindful-
         ness Meditation Do to Your Brain?," *Scientific American*, June 12, 2014, https://blogs
         .scientificamerican.com/guest-blog/what-does-mindfulness-meditation-do-to-your
         -brain.

p. 150   *"Where focus goes, energy flows"*: Tony Robbins, "Where Focus Goes, Energy Flows:
         Create a Vision for Your Business and Your Life," accessed November 4, 2020,
         https://www.tonyrobbins.com/career-business/where-focus-goes-energy-flows.

p. 153   *"started with what incredible benefits can we give"*: Steve Jobs quote in "Steve Jobs
         1997 — Customer Experience First," YouTube, posted August 28, 2014, https://www
         .youtube.com/watch?v=916Ye9XmIjI.

p. 154   *Yet studies have found connections between forgiveness and our personal*: Everett L.
         Worthington Jr., "The New Science of Forgiveness," *Greater Good Magazine* (UC
         Berkeley), September 1, 2004, https://greatergood.berkeley.edu/article/item
         /the_new_science_of_forgiveness.

Chapter 9: Attend to Connection with Self, Others, World, and Universe

p. 159   *In fact, studies have found that boredom*: Clive Thompson, "How Being Bored Out
         of Your Mind Makes You More Creative," *Wired*, January 25, 2017, https://www
         .wired.com/2017/01/clive-thompson-7.

p. 164   *Research indicates that improved relationships in the workplace*: Tom Rath and Jim
         Harter, "Your Friends and Your Social Well-Being," *Gallup News*, August 19, 2010,
         http://news.gallup.com/businessjournal/127043/friends-social-wellbeing.aspx.

p. 165   *"When oxytocin is released"*: Kelly McGonigal, *The Upside of Stress* (New York: Random House, 2015), 52.

p. 165   *He sums up the study's biggest lessons in a popular TED Talk*: Robert J. Waldinger, "What Makes a Good Life? Lessons from the Longest Study on Happiness," TEDx Talk, November 2015, https://www.ted.com/talks/robert_waldinger_what_makes_a _good_life_lessons_from_the_longest_study_on_happiness.

p. 166   *"When the study began, nobody cared about empathy"*: Liz Mineo, "Good Genes Are Nice, But Joy Is Better," *Harvard Gazette*, April 11, 2017, https://news.harvard.edu /gazette/story/2017/04/over-nearly-80-years-harvard-study-has-been-showing-how-to -live-a-healthy-and-happy-life.

p. 175   *A LinkedIn study found that 46 percent of business*: Kaytie Zimmerman, "Can Having a Best Friend at Work Make You More Productive?" *Forbes*, December 5, 2016, https://www.forbes.com/sites/kaytiezimmerman/2016/12/05/can-having-a -best-friend-at-work-make-you-more-productive/#20db778243bb.

p. 175   *"reducing isolation at work is good for business"*: Vivek Murthy, "Work and the Loneliness Epidemic," *Harvard Business Review*, September 2017, https://hbr.org /cover-story/2017/09/work-and-the-loneliness-epidemic.

p. 176   *Research shows that acts of generosity or charity result*: Ashley Whillans, "Want to Do Something Good for Your Health? Try Being Generous," *Washington Post*, January 1, 2016, https://www.washingtonpost.com/posteverything/wp/2016/01/01 /want-to-do-something-good-for-your-health-try-being-generous.

p. 178   *Vulnerability opens up connection*: Adam Grant, "How Vulnerability Can Help You Connect with an Audience," *Knowledge @ Wharton*, October 20, 2017, http://knowledge.wharton.upenn.edu/article/how-vulnerability-can-help-you-connect -with-an-audience.

Chapter 10: Pain, Our Greatest Teacher for Growth

p. 188   *Even the most painful experiences can be our greatest teachers*: Psychology professor Carol Dweck developed the concept of the growth mindset versus the fixed mind-set to describe the underlying beliefs people have about learning and intelligence. The terms were popularized in her book *Mindset: The New Psychology of Success* (New York: Random House, 2006).

p. 190   *"I didn't see it then, but it turned out that getting fired"*: Steve Jobs, "You've Got to Find What You Love," Stanford commencement address, *Stanford News*, June 12, 2005, https://news.stanford.edu/2005/06/14/jobs-061505.

p. 193   *Survivors of traumatic events often report positive changes*: Birgit Kleim and Anke Ehlers, "Evidence for a Curvilinear Relationship between Posttraumatic Growth and Posttrauma Depression and PTSD in Assault Survivors," *Journal of Traumatic Stress* 22, no. 1 (February 22, 2009), https://www.ncbi.nlm.nih.gov/pmc/articles /PMC2877993.

p. 194   *Psychologists have found that traumatic events often lead to increased*: P. Frazier

et al., "The Relation between Trauma Exposure and Prosocial Behavior,"
Psychological Trauma: Theory, Research, Practice, and Policy 5, no. 3 (2013): 286–94,
http://dx.doi.org/10.1037/a0027255.

p. 196 *"turn your wounds into wisdom"*: Oprah Winfrey, commencement address, Wellesley
College (May 30, 1997), https://www.wellesley.edu/events/commencement/archives
/1997commencement/commencementaddress.

Chapter 11: Prana, Our Energy to Be Fully Engaged at Work and in Life

p. 207 *A growing body of research demonstrates the health benefits of yoga*: Pallav Sengupta,
"Health Impacts of Yoga and Pranayama: A State-of-the-Art Review," *International
Journal of Preventive Medicine* 3, no. 7 (July 2012), https://www.ncbi.nlm.nih.gov
/pmc/articles/PMC3415184.

Chapter 12: Purpose, Our Drive for Meaning

p. 227 *The increased energy of purposeful companies is evident in higher employee*: Dan
Pontefract, *The Purpose Effect: Building Meaning in Yourself, Your Role, and Your
Organization* (Boise, ID: Elevate, 2016); and Punit Renjen, "About Us: Culture of
Purpose," Deloitte, 2013, https://www2.deloitte.com/us/en/pages/about-deloitte
/articles/culture-of-purpose.html.

p. 228 *A Stanford study found that the most satisfied people are those*: Clifton Parker, "Stanford Research: The Meaningful Life Is a Road Worth Traveling," *Stanford News*,
January 1, 2014, https://news.stanford.edu/news/2014/january/meaningful-happy
-life-010114.html.

p. 233 *The creators of the class say to look to* flow *and* energy *as clues*: Ainsley Harris,
"Stanford's Most Popular Class Isn't Computer Science — It's Something Much
More Important," *Fast Company*, March 26, 2015, https://www.fastcompany
.com/3044043/stanfords-most-popular-class-isnt-computer-science-its-something
-much-m.

p. 233 *Her purpose "quietly crept up on her" over years*: Roman Krznaric, *How to Find
Fulfilling Work* (New York: Picador, 2013).

p. 237 *Apple's original mission statement was: "To make a contribution"*: Jim Schleckser,
"Apple's Boring Mission Statement and What We Can Learn From It," *Inc.*, August
16, 2016, https://www.inc.com/jim-schleckser/apple-s-boring-mission-statement-and
-what-we-can-learn-from-it.html.

p. 237 *"Have fun in your journey through life and learn from your mistakes"*: "Sir
Richard Branson: On a Mission to Mentor," *Motivated* magazine, May 4, 2011,
http://motivatedonline.com/sir-richard-branson-on-a-mission-to-mentor.

INDEX

abandonment, 186

abdominal pain, 223

abuse, 186

acceptance, 150, 155

accept what cannot be changed, 6; Action Steps, 154–56; author's experience, 146–48; Business Hacks, 152–53; control and, 143–44, 146–48, 152, 157; defined, 48, 144, 157; forgiveness and, 145, 154–55, 157; greater fulfillment through, 160; Key Takeaways, 157; MAP Method and, 258; perspective and, 127; pivoting and, 150–51, 152–53, 157; resetting for, 148–50, 156, 157

accidents, 53

ACE Method: benefits of, 98; case study, 94; components of, 88, 98; goal of, 88; *Pause. Breathe. Choose.* Method applied within, 96; stress management using, 85, 88–89, 107, 206, 242

aches/pains, 90

achievement, overfocus on, 1

acquisitions, corporate, 133–34, 164

action: compartmentalization of, 17; control of, 152; empowered, 93, 98; explorative, 23–24, 33, 45, 233; mindfulness and, 13; negativity vs., 97–98; prana flow state and, 224

Action Steps: for accepting the unchangeable, 154–56; for altering the situation, 125–27; benefits of, 208; for connection, 177–79; for healthy lifestyle, 64–67; how to use, 6; for Mindful MAP Making, 255–56; mindfulness, 31–32, 45; for pain, 199–201; for play/recovery, 81–82; for prana, 219–23; for purpose, 237–38; for stress avoidance, 101–6; for stressor adaptability, 139–40

adaptability, 130, 134

adapt to the stressor, 6; Action Steps, 139–40; author's experience, 129–30, 132–33, 148; Business Hacks, 137–38; defined, 48; during disasters, 129–31, 141; flexibility and, 129–30; greater fulfillment through, 160; Key Takeaways, 141; MAP Method and, 258; mindset shift for, 130–31, 133; perspective and, 127; proactivity for, 131–32; resilience and, 133–36, 141; SAP for, 133; Seven A's and, 131; unsuccessful attempts at, 144

addictions, 89

adopt a healthy lifestyle, 6; Action Steps, 64–67; author's experience, 55–57, 148, 231; breaking bad habits for, 56–60, 68; Business Hacks, 61–63; as choice, 110; defined, 48; dietary changes for, 55–57,

ABOUT THE AUTHOR

Naz Beheshti is a CEO, executive wellness coach, corporate wellness consultant, speaker, writer, change agent, wellness warrior, nature and animal lover, and world explorer. She began her career as the executive assistant to Steve Jobs, the cofounder and CEO of Apple. Jobs, her first mentor, remains a wellspring of inspiration.

In 2012, Naz founded Prananaz, Inc., a corporate wellness company that provides tailored, high-touch, high-tech programs improving leadership effectiveness, employee well-being and engagement, company culture, and business results. Some of her clients include Nike, JPMorgan Chase, UCSF, and Columbia University. Prananaz delivers programs, workshops, keynotes, coaching, consulting, and training to teams and companies of all sizes.

Naz's diverse experience includes a decade in the high-stress environments of tech startups, Fortune 500s, and pharmaceutical companies (Apple, Yahoo!, AstraZeneca). She also cofounded Rise2Shine, a nonprofit school committed to helping alleviate the suffering of young children in Haiti.

Naz is a regular *Forbes* contributor with over a hundred published articles on mindful leadership and corporate wellness and has written for *Entrepreneur* and Thrive Global. She holds a BA in psychology from the University of California, Santa Cruz. She is a certified Holistic Health Coach, certified Transformational Coach, certified Advanced NLP (neurolinguistic programming) Practitioner, certified yoga instructor and lifelong practitioner, and trained Transcendental Meditation practitioner.

Naz lives in New York City with her husband, where they enjoy spending time with eclectic friends and taking fitness classes. Her global company is based in New York City and San Francisco.

For more information, please visit www.prananaz.com and www.naz beheshti.com.

ABOUT PRANANAZ

Our mission: Changing lives and helping companies excel. We help teams build better habits for sustainable change that ripples through company culture, driving employee engagement and better results.

We ignite prana, breath and life force. Prana is the universal principle of vital energy, the essence that keeps us alive and thriving. Employees are the life force and energy of a company. Employee engagement and well-being are a company's prana.

Prananaz combines high-touch and high-tech wellness solutions to deliver comprehensive and holistic programs that improve leadership effectiveness, employee well-being, and business outcomes. Our proprietary corporate wellness assessment helps us tailor a program that fits a company's specific needs and goals and provides a baseline by which to measure success. Our holistic approach is rooted in neuroscience, mindfulness, and positive psychology.

Prananaz is based in New York City and San Francisco and works with clients worldwide. Some of our clients include Nike, JPMorgan Chase, UCSF, Columbia University, General Assembly, and Omega Institute. For more information, visit www.prananaz.com.